THE CHARLES SCHWAB

GUIDE TO FINANCES
After Fifty

THE CHARLES SCHWAB

GUIDE TO FINANCES
After Fifty

Answers to Your Most Important Money Questions

CARRIE SCHWAB-POMERANTZ

with Joanne Cuthbertson

CROWN
BUSINESS
NEW YORK

Copyright © 2014 by The Charles Schwab Corporation

All rights reserved.
Published in the United States by Crown Business, an imprint of the Crown Publishing Group, a division of Random House LLC, a Penguin Random House Company, New York.
www.crownpublishing.com

CROWN BUSINESS is a trademark and CROWN and the Rising Sun colophon are registered trademarks of Random House LLC.

Crown Business books are available at special discounts for bulk purchases for sales promotions or corporate use. Special editions, including personalized covers, excerpts of existing books, or books with corporate logos, can be created in large quantities for special needs. For more information, contact Premium Sales at (212) 572-2232 or e-mail specialmarkets@randomhouse.com.

Library of Congress Cataloging-in-Publication data is available upon request.

ISBN 978-0-8041-3736-2
Ebook ISBN 978-0-8041-3737-9

Printed in the United States of America

Jacket design by Madelene Lees
Jacket photography by Jack Huynh/Orange Photography

10 9 8 7 6 5 4 3 2 1

First Edition

To Chuck,
who I am proud to call Dad.
Your passion and energy inspire me every day.

Contents

Foreword by Charles R. Schwab

I founded Schwab when I was in my late thirties. At that point in my life I was ambitious, optimistic, and determined to make my mark on the business world. I wasn't thinking about leaving a legacy or even securing my future. But as a young entrepreneur I did recognize a bad situation—and an opportunity to right a wrong.

That wrong was Wall Street. Before the Securities and Exchange Commission deregulated commissions in 1975, a stock trade could cost hundreds or even thousands of dollars. Brokers were simply salesmen; they could have been peddling vacuum cleaners or aluminum siding. They just wanted to make their hefty commissions. Individual investors didn't stand a chance against the sales pitches, fees, and conflicted advice.

Thankfully, the investing world has changed dramatically. A long series of reforms and technological advances has helped give individual investors more control. You can research investments from your home computer and buy and sell stocks, bonds, and funds with the click of a mouse, paying few or no fees. You can participate in the growth of the American economy along with the big guys.

But there's a hitch. Along with this power has come responsibility—largely mandated by government policy that has incentivized employers to move away from fixed pensions and toward IRAs and 401(k)s. In addition, although I believe that Social Security will be around for a very long time, it isn't—and was never intended to be—a ticket to a comfortable life. Plus, thanks to advances in medicine and more knowledge about healthy lifestyles, we're living decades longer than previous generations. Taken together, this adds up to a sizable challenge for every adult. Put bluntly, it means you need more money. We're living in a world of taking care of yourself.

Forty-plus years after founding Schwab, with the perspective that can only come from decades of experience, I have a new wish: In the face of our new realities, I would like every American to feel confident and knowledgeable as they take control of their own financial future. I would like every adult to face this challenge head-on, knowing that they will succeed.

I feel privileged to work on behalf of millions of Americans who are doing just this. In our early years, Schwab clients were strictly independents, or "do-it-yourselfers." Today, some like to be independent while others prefer working closely with an advisor. Regardless, we are gratified that the majority not only are involved with their financial lives, but also feel a sense of optimism as they look to the future.

As you look ahead, I hope you share this sense of optimism. Yes, the financial world is complicated. And yes, we face ongoing challenges as technology, government policy, and the regulatory environment continue to evolve. But I remain confident that you can succeed. You can read books like this one, ask tough questions, and demand straight answers. You *can* secure your financial future.

Charles R. Schwab
Founder and Chairman

Introduction

When I first started to work on this book, I and everyone else at Schwab referred to it as the "retirement" book. That was our shorthand for talking about life in the later part of our lives. But the label never felt right. As I think about my colleagues, my friends, my family, and our clients, some "retire" in the traditional sense of the word. But the majority of us continue to work in some capacity, whether or not we get a paycheck. We're active, involved, and full of things we want to do for ourselves and for others.

I don't know about you, but when I turned 50 I had a bit of a heart-to-heart with myself. "Okay, Carrie, you're 50, you're really an adult, and you've learned a lot. Now, with less than half of your life to go, what do you want to accomplish? What impact can you have?"

That's the real reason I'm writing this book. I want everyone to be able to accomplish whatever it is that makes them feel whole, or complete. I want every person to be able to reach into their own bank of talents and use them to the best of their ability.

Of course this often takes money—and hopefully that's where this book can help. I've never been a fan of money for money's sake. It's what financial security allows you to *do* that's valuable. Nobody ever told us that getting older would be easy. But they also didn't tell us that getting older, despite the aches and pains and tough times, would be cool. That we would feel smart, and capable, and ready to use our brains and our hearts to do good things.

I grew up in the company that my father founded, and I share his passion for helping all Americans become financially secure. In addition to spending decades working with clients, I've overseen national financial education programs and served on the President's Advisory Council on Financial Capability. For the last ten years, I've also been answering readers' personal finance questions in my weekly syndicated column, "Ask Carrie." This book is the result of that experience, combined with the best thinking and advice from my colleagues in the Schwab Center for Financial Research. Together, we're attempting to answer the most common questions about money and life after 50.

Yes, we fifty-plusers are an enormous and diverse group, and "retirement" means something different to each one of us. But we face common issues around planning, saving, investing, insurance, Social Security, paying for health care, estate planning, and caring for our loved ones. This book is my attempt to address them all.

Before you get started, I'd like to point out **My Top Ten Recommendations for Every Age,** which start on page 1. These few pages are Personal Finance 101—required steps for every financially independent adult.

One parting thought: In my opinion, the financial world has become unnecessarily and disturbingly complex, particularly when it comes to preparing for and living in retirement. There are too many types of accounts, and too many products, policies, and regulations. Too many decisions, period. To try to simplify, I have organized this book into easy-to-find, bite-sized pieces. Some of you may want to read every word. But if not, you can dip in and out to get the answer to your current question. I have done my best to avoid financial jargon, providing straightforward, honest explanations and guidance in plain English. Hopefully this will help you make the best decisions for this important time in your life.

Carrie Schwab Pomerantz

Carrie Schwab-Pomerantz

My Top Ten Recommendations for Every Age

Your financial life begins long before age 50, whether it's with your first savings account or your first job. So before we get into the questions that particularly concern finances after 50, I'd like to share some financial steps that I believe are essential at every age—whether you're 25, 50, or 75. Think of them as exercises you can do to make sure you're in the best financial shape for whatever the next phase of your life brings. I suggest you review them one by one, and keep them handy for future reference. And please share them with anyone—at any age—who wants to be financially fit.

1. Figure Out Your Net Worth

This simply means writing down and adding up what you own (your assets) and then subtracting what you owe (your liabilities). Are you in the plus or the minus? Knowing your net worth will help you decide next steps for saving, debt reduction, and budgeting. It also gives you a way to measure future progress. If your net worth is in the plus, great. If it's in the minus, read on. Many of the questions in this book will help you take positive action.

SET UP A PERSONAL NET WORTH STATEMENT IN THREE EASY STEPS

Setting up a net worth statement is as easy as creating a simple checklist and doing some basic math.

1. **List your assets** (what you own), estimate the value of each, and add up the total. Include items such as:
   o   Money in your bank accounts
   o   Value of your investment accounts
   o   Value of your car
   o   Value of your home
   o   Business interests
   o   Personal property, such as jewelry, art, furniture
   o   Cash value of any insurance policies

2. **List your liabilities** (what you owe), and add up the outstanding balances. Include items such as:
   o   Mortgage
   o   Car loan
   o   Credit card balance
   o   Student loans

3. **Subtract your liabilities from your assets** to determine your personal net worth.

2. Track Your Spending and Make a Budget

Now that you have the big picture, let's get into the details. Are you on top of monthly expenses? Write down your essential expenses such as your mortgage, food, transportation, utilities, and loan payments. (Include savings in this list!) Then write down nonessentials—restaurants, entertainment, even clothes. Be sure to factor in big-ticket items that come periodically, such as insurance premiums and real estate taxes. Does your income easily cover all this? If it doesn't, it's time to prioritize.

SMART MOVE: Track your spending for thirty days. Does reality match your projections? If you need to cut back, **Question 2** has some practical suggestions.

3. Reduce Your Debt

Should you get out of all debt? Not necessarily. Some debt, like a mortgage, can actually work in your favor. But how much debt is too much? An industry rule of thumb is that no more than 28 percent of your pretax income should go toward home debt; no more than 36 percent should go toward all debt (home, car, credit cards, etc.). If possible, it's wise to stay well below those limits. For more on debt reduction, see **Question 13**.

➔ **SMART MOVE:** To efficiently pay down credit card debt, focus on the highest interest rate balances first.

GOOD DEBT VS. BAD DEBT

Not all debt is equal. Some types of debt can be used as a financial tool to provide opportunities; other types can derail your carefully laid plans. The key is to know the difference.

- **Debt that can work for you**—To work for you, debt should ideally be low-cost and have potential tax advantages. For instance, with **mortgages and home equity lines of credit**, you're borrowing to own a potentially appreciating asset, and it may be tax-deductible. You can deduct the interest on mortgage debt of up to $1.1 million on your primary and/or secondary residence, whether the loan is to purchase the home or make major improvements. (Up to $100,000 of this can be home equity debt such as a home equity line of credit, which can be used for any purpose; be sure to check with your tax advisor.) Likewise **student loans** have comparatively low rates, and interest can be tax-deductible, depending on your income. The benefit is enhanced career opportunities and increased earning potential.

- **Debt that can work against you**—Generally speaking, debt that's high-cost and isn't tax-deductible is bad for you. Think **credit cards and auto loans.** This type of debt usually carries the highest interest rates. It's the most costly over time. And it means you're borrowing to own something that depreciates, so you're immediately losing value—like when you drive a new car off the lot!

4. Create an Emergency Fund

What if the unexpected happens—you lose your job or have a medical emergency? Will you have the cash you need? Best to build an emergency fund that covers at least three months of essential living expenses so you don't derail your financial plans. Keep these funds in a checking or savings account, or a money market fund where they're easily accessible. If you have enough equity in your home and have good credit, you might also consider opening a home equity line of credit (HELOC). You don't pay any interest until you use it, and if you do, interest payments may be tax-deductible. It's a smart way to cover yourself "just in case."

5. Determine If Your Retirement Savings Are on Track

The earlier you start, the less you'll have to save each year. If you're 50 and haven't started to save for retirement, you're going to have to sock away a large percentage of your income every year for many years. But if you're 30 or 40, you can save a smaller percentage. Even if you've been saving regularly, you might be surprised by just how much you'll need—especially when you factor in health-care costs. To see if you're on track, see **Question 1**. If you're confused about which retirement account is best for you, see **Question 4**.

AT A GLANCE: HOW MUCH SHOULD YOU BE SAVING?

Age you start saving	% salary you need to save
20s	10–15%
30s	15–25%
40s	25–40%
50s	40% or more

The benefit of these guidelines is that once you start to save, the percentage won't change as you get older. The person who starts to put away

12 percent for retirement when she's 25 will never have to save more than 12 percent of her income. And unfortunately, if you wait too long to start saving, you're just setting yourself up for failure. You may not be in a position to save enough, so you'll have to adjust your expectations. Starting early is a huge advantage.

SAVING FUNDAMENTALS: WHAT SHOULD YOU SAVE FOR FIRST?

One of the hardest things about saving is figuring out where your money should go first. The Schwab Center for Financial Research has developed these eight Savings Fundamentals to help you prioritize and make the most of your savings dollars.

1. Contribute enough to your company retirement plan to take full advantage of your employer match
2. Pay down high-interest consumer debt
3. Build an emergency fund
4. Maximize retirement savings
5. Save for a child's education
6. Save for a home
7. Pay down other debt
8. Keep investing

To make it easier on yourself, follow the first four fundamentals in order. Complete the final four according to your personal priorities and situation. But above all, save, save, save!

6. Automate Your Finances

Do you have your monthly bills on auto-pay? How about your savings? Don't stop with the automatic contributions to your 401(k). Set up automatic monthly payments to your IRA and savings or brokerage accounts as well. You can even take it a step further by directing your savings automatically into a mutual fund or exchange-traded fund.

7. Check In with Your Portfolio

When was the last time you took a close look at your portfolio? Market ups and downs can have a real effect on the percentage of stocks and bonds you own—even when you don't do a thing. Without overdoing it, it's smart to pay attention. If your investments don't reflect your current goals and feelings about risk, it's time to rejigger (in investment language, this is known as changing your *asset allocation*, or *rebalancing*). For ideas on how to invest, see **Question 5**, pages 71–73.

> ☎ **TALK TO AN EXPERT:** Think of a financial advisor like a personal trainer. If you know you'll need someone to help you get your finances in shape, an organization such as the National Association of Personal Financial Advisors (napfa.org) can help you find a reputable advisor in your area. Also, see **Question 6**, pages 77–81, for tips on choosing a financial advisor.

8. Review Your Insurance

We all need health insurance, and many of us also need car insurance as well as either homeowner's or renter's insurance. For some of us, a supplemental umbrella policy, disability insurance, life insurance, and professional liability coverage provide necessary and important coverage. Long-term care insurance? Possibly. After that, tread very carefully. Mortgage insurance, life insurance for a child, pet insurance, travel insurance, wedding insurance, and a host of other specialized policies are often a waste of money. See **Questions 7, 16, 17,** and **27** for more.

DECIDE IF YOU NEED LONG-TERM CARE INSURANCE (LTCI)

Whether you'll need long-term care—and therefore LTCI—depends a lot on your own health and family history. But according to the U.S. Department of Health and Human Services, 70 percent of people turning 65 can expect to use some form of long-term care during their lives. About 20 percent will need it for longer than five years. What if you're one of the 20 percent? What would you do? If you have family to care for you, that might minimize your need for LTCI. If you have considerable assets, you might be able to pay for care out of pocket. Someone with a low net worth might qualify for long-term care provided under Medicaid. However, if none of the above fits you, see **Question 7**, page 83, for more help.

➡️ **SMART MOVE:** Don't wait too long to explore long-term care insurance. It's generally most cost-effective to purchase a policy between the ages of 50 and 65, provided that you're in good health.

9. Create or Update Your Estate Plan

If you don't have a will, make this a priority, especially if you have children who would need a guardian. Also check that the beneficiaries on your retirement accounts and insurance policies are up-to-date. Make sure you have an advance health-care directive and assign powers of attorney for both finances and health care. Consider a revocable living trust as a way of avoiding probate. To get started, see **Question 38**, page 303. **Note:** Estate planning is not a do-it-yourself activity. Even if your situation is pretty straightforward, it's best to consult with an estate planning attorney.

10. Organize Your Records

A simple financial organization system will help you keep everything else on track. First, take a look at your record keeping. Do you know where all of your important documents and statements are? Could you streamline by keeping some records electronically? Next, make a list of all your accounts and where they're located. Consider consolidating to make things simpler. Also make a list of your advisors, with names and contact information. Finally, put important dates on your calendar, that is, estimated taxes, property taxes, and any required minimum distributions from retirement accounts. For more, see **Question 11**, page 114.

➲ **SMART MOVE:** Keep **My Top Ten Financial Recommendations** as a handy checklist and refer to them periodically to stay on track and measure your progress.

Important Disclosure

Rebalancing and asset allocation cannot ensure a profit, do not protect against losses, and do not guarantee that an investor's goal will be met.

PART I

When Retirement Is at Least Ten Years Out

As we start to contemplate retirement, partial retirement, intermittent retirement, or whatever arrangement we choose, perhaps the biggest challenge is being able to picture our future selves. It's hard to look into the future and imagine how we will feel and how we will want to live our lives. And some of the answers are unknowable. How long will we live? Will we be healthy? Will we want or be able to work? Will we want to live in the same house and will we have the same interests?

Answering these types of questions with complete accuracy isn't possible. And some people may think that it's a waste of time. But the more we think about these issues, the more likely we are to prepare financially. And that gives us more choices down the road.

As you go through this process, it's essential to keep the lines of communication open—with your spouse or partner and other family members, with your closest friends, and perhaps with financial and other professional advisors. Talking about things makes it real. It is also the best way I know of to evaluate your choices from different angles and make smart decisions.

This section identifies the core financial issues that you should consider as you plan for retirement that is approximately a decade out: How much should I be saving? Which retirement accounts make the most sense? How should I invest? What should I expect from a financial advisor? By understanding your choices and doing some calculations now, you are laying the foundation for a rewarding and secure future.

Q1.

I'm saving for retirement— but how much is enough?

When you hear various projections about how much money it takes to retire comfortably—$1 million, $2 million, maybe more—it can take your breath away. And it can be downright discouraging. But before you throw your hands up in despair, realize that, like so much in financial planning, how much is enough for *you* depends on a lot of personal factors. For instance, will you live a quiet life in a small town or do you plan to travel the world? Will you really call it quits and retire completely or will you keep your hand in with a little part-time work?

> **FACT:** According to the Employee Benefit Research Institute, in 2013 the percentage of workers confident of having enough money for a comfortable retirement was at a record low. While more than half expressed some level of confidence, 28 percent were not at all confident, and 21 percent were not too confident. And only 46 percent reported they and/or their spouse had tried to calculate how much money they will need to have saved by the time they retire so that they can live comfortably in retirement.

While you may not have precise answers now, with a little imagination and a bit of forward thinking you can get a good sense of how much you'll need. You'll want to determine three things:

- What you expect to spend each year
- How much money you'll need in your portfolio to support that spending
- How much more you have to save to get there

Start by Projecting What You're Likely to Spend

Will you spend less in retirement? The same? Opinions differ. Many people believe that their expenses will decline dramatically once they're retired, and in previous generations that may have been true. But today, people are living longer, they're healthy, and they want to continue to lead busy, active lives. That takes money.

When we look at national statistics, retired households spend about 80 percent of what working households spend. Most of that goes to home-related and health costs. Statistics also show that spending tends to decline with age, especially as we get into our eighties or nineties. That makes sense and, in general, would seem to imply that you'll need less money in retirement than you live on today. Of course, this may also be because you simply don't have the money to spend more.

Regardless, when you contemplate your own retirement, it's best to get specific. Do a sample budget. List projected nondiscretionary expenses—the *must-haves*—such as housing, everyday living, health care, insurance, and taxes. Then add in projected discretionary expenses—the *nice-to-haves*—such as travel and nights on the town. How does it add up compared to your current expenses?

On the positive side, you'll no longer be contributing to your retirement account or paying payroll taxes. You won't have the same professional expenses. If your income declines, so will your income taxes. On the other hand, health-care costs will likely increase. So may travel and entertainment, especially in the early years.

Granted, I'm pretty conservative, but to be on the safe side, I think it's wise to assume you'll want to spend just about the same amount of money in retirement as you're spending now. But you're the best judge. If you're planning to stay in the same home, your housing expenses won't change.

If you're planning to scale back, you may have substantial savings. If you're unsure about a particular item, for now I'd err on the high side.

LIVING EXPENSES IN RETIREMENT

What May Go Up	What May Go Down
Health care	Work-related expenses
Entertainment and activities	Payroll taxes
Travel	Savings
Property taxes	Mortgage

Then Calculate How Much You Will Need in Savings by the Time You Retire

Once you have an idea of how much you expect to spend, it's time to figure out what this will mean in terms of savings. First add up all the income you can rely on from all sources *except* your portfolio: Social Security, a pension, a trust, or real estate. Your savings will have to make up the difference between the total of this income and the amount you want to spend.

> *Example:* You and your spouse currently spend $110,000 per year and want to retire in ten years with the same standard of living. You anticipate receiving a $20,000 annual pension from past employment. You also expect to get $30,000 a year from Social Security and $20,000 in rental income. The total so far is $70,000. To get to the $110,000 you want, you'll have to withdraw about $40,000 each year from your portfolio.

> ⊙ **SMART MOVE:** Get an estimate of your Social Security benefits at socialsecurity.gov.

In this example, to come up with $40,000 a year, you'd need a portfolio of about $1 million. Why so much? That figure is based on the "4 percent guideline," a handy estimate that says you can withdraw 4 percent of your portfolio's value in your first year of retirement, increase that amount every year for inflation, and have a 90 percent level of confidence that you won't run out of money for thirty years. It also assumes that you'll have anywhere from 20 to 60 percent of your money invested in a mix of stocks. See **Question 5** for more information on how to invest.

Another way to look at it is that your portfolio should be roughly 25 times larger than your first year's withdrawal: $40,000 × 25 equals $1 million. If that sounds like a lot, it is. For many people, it's unattainable. Of course, depending on your own scenario, you may need less. But whatever your own number, now's the time to take action. If you, like so many others, are in the position of having to catch up on savings, see the suggestions in **Question 2**. If you know you'll need to cut back on expenses, take a look at **Question 24**.

HOW BIG DOES YOUR PORTFOLIO NEED TO BE? HERE'S A SAMPLE SCENARIO FOR A COUPLE.	
Total first-year spending goal (including taxes)	$110,000
Minus Social Security	($30,000)
Minus annual pension	($20,000)
Minus rental income	($20,000)
First-year withdrawal	$40,000
	x 25
Retirement portfolio target	$1,000,000

➡ **SMART MOVE:** To feel confident that your money will last throughout your retirement, aim for a portfolio roughly 25 times larger than your first year's withdrawal.

Finally, Figure Out How Much You Need to Save Each Year Before You Retire

Start with your savings now. Take a look at all of your accounts, and add them up. Then use a compound interest calculator to get a preliminary sense of how much more you need to save to get to your goal.

Example: Continuing our example from above, let's assume that you've saved $500,000 and want to retire in ten years with a $1 million portfolio. Using a compound interest calculator, you'll see that to meet your goal you'll need to save an additional $15,000 every year and make an average return of 5 percent.

Of course this is just one scenario. If you have fewer than ten years until retirement, you'll have to save more. If you expect to earn a higher average annual rate of return, you can save less.

☎ **TALK TO AN EXPERT:** At some point I highly recommend that you do a more precise calculation. For example, this estimate doesn't take into account the impact of inflation. A million dollars today won't have as much value as a million dollars next year, and certainly not in ten years. A retirement calculator like the one on schwab.com will let you play with the numbers and test out different scenarios. That's a great way to start planning on your own. I also highly recommend that you work with a financial advisor to get a more accurate picture. He or she can talk to you about your expectations and priorities, crunch numbers for different scenarios, and help you craft a personalized plan. I talk more about working with a financial advisor in **Question 6.**

⦿ **FACT:** According to a study by the Employee Benefit Research Institute in 2013, workers often guess at how much they will need to accumulate (45 percent), rather than doing a systematic, retirement needs calculation. Eighteen percent indicated they did their own estimate and another 18 percent asked a financial advisor, while 8 percent used an online calculator and another 8 percent read or heard how much was needed.

MAKING THE 4 PERCENT GUIDELINE WORK FOR YOU

The 4 percent guideline is a great rule of thumb to get a feel for your savings goal. If you do just this one calculation, you're way ahead of most Americans when it comes to retirement planning. However, when you apply this guideline to your own situation, it's good to look deeper and remain flexible. Here are some things to consider:

- **How dependent are you on that 4 percent for fixed expenses like housing, food, and medical care?** If you can cover most of these nondiscretionary expenses by other income streams such as a pension or Social Security, it's prudent to withdraw less from your portfolio (or at least not adjust for inflation), especially when the stock market has a down year. Conversely, if the stock market is doing well, you can think about taking a little more.

- **Do you have the potential or desire to earn some money from part-time work during your retirement?** If so, consider taking less from your portfolio, giving yourself that much more protection for the future.

- **Could your retirement last longer than thirty years?** If you're healthy and longevity runs in your family, think about withdrawing less. Conversely, if you're fairly certain that you won't need your income for thirty years, you can think about increasing the amount.

- **What's your risk tolerance?** The 4 percent guideline is designed to provide you with a 90 percent certainty that you won't outlive your money. If you're comfortable with a lower confidence level, say 80 percent, you can withdraw more—say 5 percent. But if you want to increase your confidence, you should withdraw less than 4 percent.

- **How active do you want to be?** Many retirees find that their lifestyle is much more costly in the early part of their retirement while they're traveling and pursuing other interests. If you're confident that you'll spend less as you age, you can budget accordingly.

Next Steps

- Review your Social Security benefits at socialsecurity.gov. See **Questions 30–34.**
- If you haven't been saving enough and need to do some catching up, see **Question 2.**

Q2.

I'm 50 and haven't started to save for retirement. What can I do?

For many of us, it isn't until about age 45 or 50 that the impending reality of retirement hits home. So the first thing to realize is that you're not alone. More than half the respondents to the *2013 Retirement Confidence Survey* of workers age 25 and older, conducted by the Employee Benefit Research Institute (EBRI), said they had less than $25,000 in total savings; 28 percent had less than $1,000. And more than a third of those age 55 or older who were surveyed said they aren't currently saving for retirement. Of course, knowing that there are a lot of people in the same boat doesn't make your situation any brighter. I'm hoping, though, that it will motivate you to get ahead of the pack.

There are a number of actions you can take to make up for lost time. Unfortunately, none of them is too thrilling. In fact, much of it gets back to the old-fashioned advice of spending less and saving more. The good news is, it works. Here's a practical to-do list to help you get on the right track.

Create a Budget

By this I mean a realistic budget. Take a long, hard look at what you earn and what you spend. And don't try to fool yourself. This is the time for complete honesty. Here's a simple approach:

- Divide your expenses into two categories, *nondiscretionary* (the must-haves) and *discretionary* (the extras), and put dollar amounts next to each item. This will give you a picture of where you *think* your money is going.
- Track your spending for thirty days, comparing your projections with what you actually spend. This will give you a picture of where your money is *actually* going.

With your spending pattern in front of you, adjust your budget so that you can direct as much as possible to savings. Where can you cut back? Could you eat out less? Postpone buying a new car? Even small economies like negotiating lower rates with your phone and cable providers can add up—and give you a few extra dollars each month.

If you need help staying on track, an online budget tool, such as the spending tracker on schwabmoneywise.com, will make it easier to see precisely where your money is going and where you can make changes.

> ⊙ **SMART MOVE:** Change your thinking. Make savings a part of your non-discretionary expenses. In fact, when you create your budget, put this at the top of the must-haves list.

CASH FLOW: DO YOU KNOW WHERE YOU STAND?

It's easy to say "create a budget." Actually doing it is a bigger challenge. The best way I know is to start with a big picture of your annual cash flow. The formula is simple enough: Subtract your expenses from your income to see if you're in the red or the black. Based on those numbers, you can make some changes. But the devil is in the details, so here's a step-by-step guide that you can follow:

1. **List your expenses**
   - Nondiscretionary: mortgage or rent, groceries, transportation, insurance premiums, and taxes. Be sure to include debt payments such as credit cards and auto loans. Don't forget things like education expenses and out-of-pocket medical care costs. Make retirement savings a line item here, too!
   - Discretionary: restaurants, entertainment, travel, even clothing

2. List your sources of income
- Regular wages, bonuses, gifts, income from rental property, interest or investment income, government checks, or any other source

3. Put real numbers next to your line items

4. Do the math
- Add up your income and expenses
- Subtract your expenses from your income

Coming up short? It's time to prioritize. Ending up with a little extra? Put that toward your retirement savings!

Contribute to Your 401(k) and/or an IRA

As I mention in **Question 4**, retirement accounts offer savers significant tax advantages, the primary one being that your money can compound tax-deferred, leading to potentially faster growth. This advantage is most powerful when you contribute to retirement accounts regularly. And of course, time is a factor—meaning the earlier you start, the better. For anyone over 50, there's no time like the present.

If you have a retirement plan at work, I'd start there. Another interesting insight from the retirement survey I mentioned earlier is that workers who contribute to an employer-sponsored retirement plan are considerably more likely to have saved at least $50,000 more than those who don't contribute. So to anyone who has access to a plan like a 401(k), 403(b), or 457(b), I say what are you waiting for? It's one of the easiest ways to save because your contributions come directly out of your paycheck. And, except for a Roth 401(k), the contributions are made with before-tax dollars, so you'll be decreasing your taxable income at the same time that you're saving. (While Roth contributions are made with after-tax dollars, withdrawals are tax-free.)

Plus, if your employer provides a company match, that can mean extra money in your pocket. Contribute at least enough to get the match, more if you can. The maximum annual contribution for 2013 is $17,500.

Employees 50 and older can make an additional catch-up contribution of $5,500. If you can do it, now's the time!

To save even more, you could also contribute to a traditional IRA or Roth IRA, if you're eligible, and make catch-up contributions once you're 50. If you don't have a 401(k) or similar employer-sponsored plan, an IRA is a must. **Question 4** gives you the inside story on these accounts and how they can work together.

CATCH-UP CONTRIBUTIONS REALLY DO WORK

You're about to turn 50 and you haven't saved a thing. You wake up on your birthday morning and finally see the light. You're a born-again saver.

Scenario 1: Every year starting at age 50 you contribute the maximum to both your 401(k) and IRA—at the standard 2013 rate of $17,500 plus $5,500 ($23,000 in all). Assuming a 6% annual return, by the time you retire at age 65 you'll have about $570,000.

Scenario 2: You're really serious about saving, and decide to take advantage of your fifty-or-over status by making full catch-up contributions to both your 401(k) and your IRA. This allows you to contribute $23,000 to your 401(k) and $6,500 to your IRA, for a total contribution of $29,500 each year. Again assuming a 6% annual return, at age 65 you'll have about $730,000.

The fine print: This example assumes a hypothetical 6% return, year in, year out. Your return will vary, of course, depending on your portfolio and market conditions. It also assumes that you continue to contribute at the 2013 rates. In reality, you'll be able to increase your contributions as the rates rise, adding to your savings.

⊃ **SMART MOVE:** If you're self-employed or own your own business, check into a SEP-IRA or an Individual 401(k). See **Question 15** on how these accounts could help you maximize your savings.

SMART WAYS TO SAVE MORE

- Make savings a line item on your budget
- Always contribute enough to your 401(k) to capture a match; ideally save the max allowed by the IRS
- Set up automatic payments into your IRAs and savings accounts
- Earmark salary increases and bonuses for retirement
- If you're 50+
  - Contribute an extra $1,000 per tax year to your IRA
  - Contribute an extra $5,500 per year to your 401(k)

➤ **SMART MOVE:** Don't stop with retirement accounts. If you can save even more, put that extra money in a savings account or taxable brokerage account.

Get Out of Debt

If you're carrying nondeductible consumer debt like credit card balances, try to eliminate those quickly. Let's say you're being charged 15 percent interest and paying only the minimum. Think about it. Those interest charges are actually increasing your debt. Paying down those cards is like giving yourself that extra 15 percent—money you can then add to your savings. You also may be able to consolidate balances on credit cards and other loans into lower-cost forms of debt.

On the other hand, mortgage debt can offer some tax benefits as long as you have a low-interest, low-risk mortgage. See **My Top Ten Recommendations,** page 3, for more on the difference between "good" debt and "bad" debt.

Develop an Investment Plan You Can Stick With

Once you've accumulated some savings, put it to work by investing it. Think about two things: 1) how much time you have to keep your money growing; 2) how much risk you're comfortable taking. The ideal is to come up with a combination of stocks, bonds, and cash that has the potential for growth *and* that you can live with—and stick with—whether the market is going up or going down. But here's a note of caution: Don't think you have to be overly aggressive with your investments just because you're starting late. You also want to protect what you save, so balance is the key. For ideas on how to invest, see **Question 5.**

Don't Wait Any Longer!

As you can see, there's a lot you can do to catch up. But at the end of the day, it comes down to old-fashioned financial discipline. And the clock is ticking, so get started right away!

RETHINK RETIREMENT—OR HOW TO PLAY CATCH-UP

There's no formula for the perfect retirement. Maybe you don't want to retire at all. But whatever retirement means to you, how you approach it will determine how far your money will go. So think creatively. You could:

- **Spend less in retirement.** The Schwab Center for Financial Research suggests that you plan for as much income in retirement as when you were working (less what you were saving for retirement, of course). However, if you've paid off your mortgage and eliminated debt, you might be able to get by with less.

- **Postpone retirement.** This would allow you to build a bigger retirement portfolio and shorten the time you'll rely on savings. You can also increase your potential Social Security benefit 8 percent a year by waiting past your full retirement age to receive payments (up to age 70).

- **Work part-time.** Many retirees are including some type of work in their retirement plans for extra income as well as social interaction and a sense of purpose.

- **Tap into your home equity.** If you own your home, a reverse mortgage (see **Question 26**) is an option, albeit with caveats. Or you could scale down to a smaller home and add the difference to your retirement nest egg.

Next Steps

- Need to open an IRA? See **Question 4** on your choices.
- Get your savings working. **Question 5** has ideas on how to invest before retirement.
- If you need to focus on reducing your debt, **Question 13** offers advice on how to do it.
- Trying to get a handle on how much you need to save? Go to **Question 1.**

Q3.

How can I save for my kids' college without derailing my retirement?

Saving for college is no easy task in the face of all the other costs of raising children. Once you've paid all the bills and put something aside for college, it can seem like there's no money left for you, let alone anything extra to add to your retirement account. But here's where you have to take a step back. Can you really afford to think of your retirement as an *extra*?

While I know it goes against the grain of being a parent, when it comes to retirement, you have to put yourself first. It's kind of like the airline emergency instructions to position your own oxygen mask before you help your child. In other words, you won't be of much use to your child or anyone else if you don't take care of yourself. Now this doesn't mean you have to completely sacrifice one savings goal for the other. It just means that you have to stay true to your retirement savings plan while looking realistically at all the choices you have for handling college costs.

A national Sallie Mae study, *How America Pays for College 2013*, found that the typical family covered just 27 percent of their kids' college costs through savings and income in 2012–13. So how did they cover the rest? That's the challenge. But with a little research and planning, you can do it.

⊃ **SMART MOVE:** Prioritize your savings. Review "Saving Fundamentals" on page 5. Notice that saving for college is number 5—after contributing to your 401(k), creating an emergency fund, getting out of debt, and *saving even more* for retirement.

Be Tax-Smart About Saving for College

Hopefully you're taking full advantage of your employer's retirement plan as well as saving more if you can in a traditional or Roth IRA. Just as these are tax-smart ways to save for retirement, there are tax-smart ways to save for college. Here are the two main choices:

- **529 plans**—A 529 plan is a state-sponsored, tax-advantaged way for parents, relatives, and friends to save and invest for a child's college education. Most states offer at least one 529 plan, but you don't have to live in a state to participate in that state's 529 plan. While plans differ in terms of costs, features, and investment selections, and some plans provide tax benefits to in-state residents, the federal tax benefits are the same:
  - Tax-free growth—All earnings are free from federal income tax, so your investment has the potential to grow at an even faster pace than it would in a taxable account.
  - Tax-free withdrawals—You pay no federal taxes on withdrawals as long as they're used for qualified education expenses (for example, tuition, fees, books, room and board).
  - Special gift tax exclusion—You can contribute a lump sum of up to $70,000 ($140,000 per couple) and make five years of contributions for each beneficiary in a single year without incurring the gift tax (based on 2013 annual per-individual limit of $14,000). Once you've done this, though, any additional gifts to that individual in the next five years would be subject to the gift tax.
  - High contribution limits—Although they vary by state plan, there are generally much higher contribution limits for 529 plans than for other education savings options.

➡ **SMART MOVE:** A 529 plan is a great way for grandparents to contribute to their grandchild's college fund.

- An added benefit of a 529 plan is that you control the account. The funds can be used for qualified education expenses, but they never become the direct property of the beneficiary. Plus you can change the beneficiary to any eligible family member of the current beneficiary at any time.

➡ **SMART MOVE:** Before you choose a 529 plan, check to see if your home state's plan offers a state income tax deduction on contributions for state residents.

- **Education Savings Accounts**—ESAs, also known as Coverdell Education Savings Accounts, offer tax-free growth and tax-free withdrawals like a 529 plan. But unlike a 529 plan, withdrawals can be used for qualified elementary and secondary education expenses as well as for college costs. However, an ESA isn't for everyone. There are qualifications and restrictions you need to consider:
  - Only couples with adjusted gross incomes of less than $220,000 are eligible to open and contribute to ESAs (less than $110,000 for individuals).
  - Contributions are limited to a maximum of $2,000 per year until the beneficiary's 18th birthday. That maximum assumes a modified adjusted gross income less than $95,000 (less than $190,000 for married couples filing jointly) and is gradually reduced above that level.
  - The account must be liquidated at age 30; however, the designated beneficiary may roll over the full balance to a different Coverdell ESA for another family member, thus potentially avoiding taxes and penalties.

➡ **SMART MOVE:** Want to be a super-saver? Contribute to both a 529 plan *and* an ESA.

For the record, you can also save for a child's education in a custodial account, but there are minimal tax advantages. Also, the money becomes the property of the child as soon as he or she reaches 18, 21, or 25, depending on the state. (Do you really want to fund that trip to Tahiti or that new car?) In my opinion, a 529 plan offers the best in tax advantages, control, and flexibility. See the following chart for a more detailed comparison of 529s and ESAs.

AT A GLANCE: COMPARE 529 PLANS AND COVERDELL EDUCATION SAVINGS ACCOUNTS

	529 Plan	Coverdell Education Savings Account
Description	A state-sponsored tax-deferred college investment program that can be set up by anyone—parent, relative, or friend	An ESA set up and managed by a parent or guardian for the benefit of a minor
Earnings	Tax-deferred	Tax-deferred
Amount that can be contributed gift-tax-free	Up to $70,000 ($140,000 per couple) per beneficiary in a single year if the contributor elects to recognize that gift over five years for tax purposes and makes no additional gifts to that beneficiary over the next five years	N/A
Withdrawals	Federal-tax-free when used for qualified postsecondary education expenses	Federal-tax-free when used for qualified elementary, secondary, and postsecondary education expenses
Contribution limits	Lifetime limit per beneficiary that varies by state, generally upward of $200,000 per beneficiary	$2,000 per year, subject to adjusted gross income limitations (phase-out: $190,000–$220,000, married filing jointly; $95,000–$110,000, single)

AT A GLANCE: COMPARE 529 PLANS AND COVERDELL EDUCATION
SAVINGS ACCOUNTS (*continued*)

	529 Plan	Coverdell Education Savings Account
Penalty for nonqualified use	Earnings taxed as ordinary income and may be subject to a 10% federal penalty	Earnings taxed as ordinary income and may be subject to a 10% federal penalty
Investment choices	Choice of investment portfolios that are chosen by state's plan administrator	Investment choices up to parent or guardian
Impact on financial aid	Counted as assets of parent or account owner; minimal impact on financial aid	Counted as assets of parent or account owner; minimal impact on financial aid
Beneficiaries	No age limit on beneficiaries; can change beneficiary at any time	Beneficiary must be under 18; all assets must be distributed or transferred to an eligible beneficiary by child's 30th birthday

Note: Data are for 2013.

⊙ **SMART MOVE:** Once you have a child in college, be sure to talk to your tax advisor about available college tax credits and deductions.

Research—and Apply for—All Financial Aid

A lot of parents make the mistake of thinking their kids won't qualify for financial aid—and make the even bigger mistake of not applying for it. But whether it's through private scholarships or government grants and loans, there's a considerable amount of financial help out there—and not all of it is asset based.

According to the College Board, in 2011–12, full-time undergraduate students received an average of $13,218 per student in financial aid from a combination of federal loans and other sources. That's pretty encouraging.

Equally encouraging is the fact that the U.S. Department of Education has made the **Free Application for Federal Student Aid (FAFSA)** process more streamlined and easier to navigate. Consider, too, that in FAFSA calculations, only 5.64 percent of parents' assets are considered available for college expenses. There's also an asset protection allowance (which increases as the parents age), so a certain percentage of assets won't be counted. Retirement accounts and the value of your primary residence are also excluded.

Another factor that increases eligibility for aid is how many kids you have in college at the same time. If you have more than one child in college, this can work in your favor in terms of financial aid. So don't hesitate to factor financial aid into your college saving equation.

⬤ **SMART MOVE:** As your kids approach college age, be sure to check out sites like finaid.org or collegeboard.org for more information on planning and paying for college.

Take Advantage of Student Loans

There's a lot written about the burden of student debt these days, and there's no denying that paying back student loans can be an albatross for many years if not managed wisely. But today, student loans are a fact of life and a viable way to pay for an education. According to a report by the Joint Economic Committee of the U.S. Congress, two-thirds of the class of 2012 had student loans on graduation, with an average balance of just over $27,000.

I'm not suggesting that you have to saddle your kids with debt. But if what you can save for college comes up short, you could finance a certain percentage of college costs through student loans (ideally federal) and help your kids pay them back over time.

Get the Kids to Help

There's nothing that says you have to do all the saving yourself. Get your kids involved early on. Encourage them to get a summer job and put a percentage of their earnings toward college. Once they're in school, suggest the possibility of working part-time during the school year.

It's not unusual for kids to contribute toward their education. According to a 2013 study by Sallie Mae, students pay about 11 percent of college costs from their own savings and income, and the U.S. Census Bureau reports that in 2011 the majority of undergraduates—72 percent—worked during the year.

You could also suggest that a portion of any monetary gifts go toward a college account. Speaking of gifts, when grandparents or other relatives want to buy something for your kids, suggest a contribution toward their education. It all adds up!

AT A GLANCE: HOW THE TYPICAL FAMILY PAYS FOR COLLEGE

Parent savings and income	27%
Parent borrowing	9%
Student savings and income	11%
Student borrowing	18%
Grants and scholarships	30%
Relatives and friends	5%

Source: *How America Pays for College 2013*, Sallie Mae's National Study of College Students and Parents.

DON'T USE RETIREMENT ACCOUNTS FOR COLLEGE SAVINGS

A 2013 study by Sallie Mae, *How America Saves for College*, revealed some disturbing trends. In a survey looking into the types of accounts the typical family uses to save for college, 17 percent listed retirement accounts! To me this just doesn't make sense.

First, if you withdraw money from your 401(k) to pay for your child's educational expenses before you're 59½, you will have to pay a 10 percent penalty on that money—on top of income taxes. You're not hit with the penalty if you withdraw educational money from your IRA, but you will have to pay taxes. In other words, those withdrawals for college costs are going to add to your tax bill! A 529 account makes much more tax sense because any earnings grow tax-free *and* withdrawals are tax-free when used for qualified education expenses.

But perhaps even more important, if you raid your retirement savings to pay for college, you're selling yourself short. Remember, you can't borrow money to fund your retirement, but most students are eligible for some form of financial aid. Make sure you're maxing out your retirement accounts first (and don't touch that money), then prioritize your other savings goals and contribute appropriately. (See the "Saving Fundamentals," page 5.)

When your kids have graduated and are on their own, they'll be doubly grateful that you've not only helped them through college, but have taken care of yourself as well.

Next Steps

- See **Question 1** for help in determining if you're saving enough for retirement.
- Need to jump-start your retirement savings? **Question 2** has some tips.
- If you're thinking about borrowing from your 401(k) to cover college costs, **Question 8** will show you why this probably isn't a good idea.

Q4.

There are so many different types of retirement accounts. What do I really need?

Few people get pensions these days, and as a result, most of us are responsible for our own retirement savings. Saving can be difficult enough, but things can get really confusing when you consider the whole array of different retirement accounts—in my opinion, far too many! Unfortunately, all of this choice can be overwhelming, and even counterproductive, preventing people from acting at all. But act we must—and the sooner the better.

To help you take action, I'll provide an overview of the most common employer-sponsored and individual retirement accounts, pointing out key features and things to think about along the way. If you work for yourself or own a small business, see **Question 15**.

First, Decide If You Want to Pay Taxes Now or Later

Regardless of the retirement account you ultimately select, the most important benefit will be a smaller tax bill, allowing you to direct more of your money to savings. This type of "tax-advantaged" account comes in one of two flavors: "tax-deferred" or "tax-free." What's the difference?

- **Tax-deferred accounts, like a traditional 401(k) or an IRA, give you tax benefits up front.** In a nutshell, with a tax-deferred account your contribution will be deducted from your taxable income. Any earnings grow tax-free and you won't pay income taxes until you withdraw your money—preferably in retirement—at which time it will be taxed as ordinary income. *If your tax bracket is lower when it's time to withdraw, this can work to your advantage.* (Note, though, that traditional IRAs may not be deductible; see the box on page 42 for more.)
- **Tax-free accounts, like a Roth 401(k) or Roth IRA, give you a tax break down the road.** With a tax-free account there is no upfront tax deduction, but any earnings grow tax-free and withdrawals after age 59½ are tax-free, provided you've held the account for a minimum of five years. *If your income tax bracket is the same or higher at that point, you benefit.*

It's important to take some time to think about which of your options will work best for you. While it's impossible to predict exactly what your tax bracket will be when you retire, you probably have some idea about your future income. If you expect your income to be less when you begin to make withdrawals, a traditional, tax-deferred IRA might make the most sense. If you expect your income to be much higher, a tax-free Roth might make the most sense. For this reason, a Roth account can be a good choice for younger investors who haven't yet hit their peak earnings years; when you're older, the choice can be trickier.

Take Advantage of Your Company Plan

If your employer offers a retirement plan—whether tax-deferred or tax-free—that can be a great place to start. Not only will you get tax benefits, but you'll also have the advantage of an automatic payroll deduction. Sweetening the deal, many employers match a portion of your contribution—in effect giving you free money. Here are a couple of examples:

Example: Jen, who is 50 years old, wants to contribute just enough to her 401(k) to capture the maximum employer match. She earns $100,000, and her company matches 50% of her contribution up to a maximum of 6% of her salary. Jen directs 6% of her salary ($6,000) to her 401(k). Her employer contributes another $3,000, for a total contribution of $9,000.

▶ **SMART MOVE:** Always contribute enough to your 401(k) to capture the maximum employer match. Otherwise, you're just walking away from free money.

Example: Terry, who is 50 years old, wants to contribute the maximum to her 401(k). She earns an annual salary of $100,000 and her company matches 50% of her contribution up to a maximum of 6% of her salary. Terry defers 17.5% of her salary ($17,500) plus a catch-up contribution of $5,500. Her employer contributes another $3,000, for a total contribution of $26,000.

🔍 **FACT:** At Schwab Retirement Plan Services, Inc., participants who used third-party, professional 401(k) advice tended to increase their savings rate, were better diversified, and stayed the course in their investing decisions.

▶ **SMART MOVE:** If you are 50 or older, you can often contribute extra money to your retirement plan. In 2013, this extra "catch-up" contribution is $5,500 for a 401(k) or 403(b), $1,000 for a traditional or Roth IRA.

Review Your Choices

Although companies have some room for determining plan features (for example, one company's 401(k) may allow you to borrow money from the plan and another's may not; one organization's 403(b) may match your contribution and another's may not), the basic rules for all tax-advantaged accounts are set by the Internal Revenue Service. As you probably know, IRS rules leave little room for interpretation. Ignorance does not bring bliss.

As you review your choices, here are some things to think about:

- Is the plan tax-deferred or tax-free? Some employers now offer a Roth 401(k) or Roth 403(b), which are simply tax-free versions of the traditional plans.
- Does your company provide a match? A match is not required by law, but many companies offer it as an extra benefit.
- Does the plan offer a wide range of investment choices?
- Does the plan provide flexibility in changing investments?
- Can you continue to contribute to the plan at any age and even if you're not working?
- Can you borrow money from the plan? Although I never recommend taking money from your retirement savings, a loan is preferable to an early withdrawal. Personally, I like the idea that my money is pretty much locked in. Sometimes, though, a loan can come in handy, provided you know you can pay it back on time. See **Question 8** for more on 401(k) loans.
- Will you get hit with a penalty if you need to make a withdrawal? The magic age for most retirement plans is 59½. Withdraw money before that and you will likely be hit with a 10 percent penalty. However, if you have a Roth IRA you can withdraw your contributions (but not your earnings) at any time without paying taxes or a penalty. When it comes to withdrawing your earnings, you have to be 59½—plus you must have held the account for a minimum of five years.
- Are you required to start making withdrawals at a certain point? All plans except a Roth IRA have an annual required minimum distribution (RMD) starting at age 70½. For more on RMDs see **Question 23**, pages 200–201.

⊃ **SMART MOVE:** If your 401(k) plan offers personalized advice, take advantage of it! Often this advice is free (or available at a very low cost) and can be very worthwhile, especially if you're not a financial expert.

Following is a quick look at the major players, both tax-deferred and tax-free. I've grouped them by employment because to a large extent your work will determine your choices.

AT A GLANCE: MAJOR TYPES OF COMPANY RETIREMENT PLANS

For-Profit Companies

	401(k)	Roth 401(k)
Tax Treatment	Tax-Deferred	Tax-Free
2013 Contribution limit	$17,500 plus $5,500 catch-up if you are 50 or older	$17,500 plus $5,500 catch-up if you are 50 or older
Employer match	Yes, depending on plan	Yes, depending on plan
Loan	Yes, depending on plan	Yes, depending on plan
Withdrawal	Ordinary income tax rate; 10% penalty if you are under 59½, with exceptions	Contributions always tax-free; 10% penalty on earnings if under 59½ and haven't held account for 5 years
Required minimum distribution	Yes, unless you are still employed	Yes, unless you are still employed or rolled into a Roth IRA
Special feature	Can be rolled over to an IRA when you leave your job	Unlike a Roth IRA, no income restrictions. Can be rolled over to a Roth IRA when you leave your job

➡ **SMART MOVE:** Short on cash? Think twice before you take out a loan on your 401(k); see **Question 8** for details.

WHAT HAPPENS TO MY MONEY IF MY COMPANY GOES BANKRUPT?

If your company declares bankruptcy, your retirement plan assets are protected under federal law—the Employee Retirement Income Security Act of 1974 (ERISA). The law covers all "qualified" retirement plans, which include:

- Defined-contribution plans: 401(k), 403(b), 457(b), and equivalent self-employment plans

- Defined-benefit plans, or pensions

ERISA requires retirement plan assets to be kept separate from a company's business assets, so your retirement funds are secure from your company's creditors. In addition, defined-benefit pension plans might be insured by the federal government's Pension Benefit Guaranty Corporation (PBGC). See **Question 19** for more on the PBGC.

Also realize that if your plan is terminated, your company owes you all of the benefits you have earned up to that point.

See the Department of Labor's website for more on how bankruptcy can affect your retirement benefits.

⚠ **CAUTION:** With a private 457(b), your money is not separately protected from the organization's finances.

➡ **SMART MOVE:** If you participate in a 403(b), are age 50 or older, and have worked for the same employer for at least 15 years, you may be able to make up to an additional $3,000 catch-up contribution (on top of the $5,500 catch-up). Ask your employer.

Nonprofit Organizations

	403(b)	Roth 403(b)	Private 457(b)
Tax Treatment	Tax-Deferred	Tax-Free	Tax-Deferred
2013 Contribution limit	$17,500 plus $5,500 catch-up if you are 50 or older	$17,500 plus $5,500 catch-up if you are 50 or older	$17,500 plus $5,500 catch-up if you are 50 or older
Employer match	Yes, depending on plan	Yes, depending on plan	Uncommon
Loan	Yes, depending on plan	Yes, depending on plan	No
Withdrawal	Ordinary income tax rate; 10% penalty if you are under 59½, with exceptions	Contributions always tax-free; 10% penalty on earnings if under 59½ and haven't held account for 5 years	10% penalty if under 59½
Required minimum distribution	Yes, unless you are still employed	Yes, unless you are still employed	Yes
Special feature	Extra $3,000 contribution for 15-year employees	Extra $3,000 contribution for 15-year employees. Unlike a Roth IRA, no income restrictions; can be rolled over to a Roth IRA when you leave your job	Additional catch-up allows employees in final three years to double contributions to make up for previous years. Only available to highly compensated employees

SMART MOVE: If you have a 401(k), 403(b), or SIMPLE IRA *as well as* a 457(b), you can contribute the maximum to both.

State or Local Government

	Public 457(b)
Tax-Treatment	**Tax-Deferred**
2013 Contribution limit	$17,500 plus $5,500 catch-up if you are 50 or older
Employer match	Uncommon
Loan	No
Withdrawal	No
Required minimum distribution	Yes
Special feature	Additional catch-up allows employees in final three years to double contributions to make up for previous years

EXCEPTIONS TO THE 10 PERCENT EARLY WITHDRAWAL PENALTY

The IRS discourages you from withdrawing money from your retirement accounts before you reach the age of 59½ by slapping on a 10 percent penalty. However, in some cases they concede that it makes sense to take a distribution without a penalty:

- You become disabled

- You die and a payment is made to your beneficiary or estate

- If you make a series of "substantially equal periodic payments" (also known as 72(t) distributions), made at least annually for your life, or life expectancy, or the joint life expectancies of you and your beneficiary

- You pay for medical expenses that exceed 7.5 percent of your adjusted gross income (AGI)

- You leave your job after reaching age 55 (called "separation of service")

- In keeping with a divorce decree or separation agreement (a "qualified domestic relations order" or QDRO)

- You pay for higher education expenses (IRA only)

- Up to $10,000 for a first-time home purchase (IRA only)

- You're unemployed and you pay for health insurance (IRA only)

Also see **Question 8** for IRS rules regarding a "hardship distribution."

Consider Opening an IRA

If your employer doesn't offer a retirement plan, you can still invest for your retirement in either a traditional IRA or a Roth IRA. To qualify, you simply need to have what the IRS calls "earned income," which includes:

- Wages, salaries, and tips
- Union strike benefits
- Long-term disability benefits received prior to minimum retirement age
- Net earnings from self-employment

Revenue that's not considered earned income includes interest and dividends from investments, pensions, Social Security benefits, unemployment benefits, alimony, and child support.

As I discussed at the beginning of this question, a traditional IRA generally gives you a tax deduction up front but withdrawals are taxed at ordinary income tax rates. With a Roth IRA there's no up-front tax break, but earnings can be withdrawn tax-free.

The maximum IRA contribution for 2013 for either type of IRA is $5,500 (or $6,500 if you are 50 or older). If your taxable income is less than that, you can contribute only up to the dollar amount of your earned income for the year.

However, there are income limitations on who can contribute to a Roth IRA. If you're married filing jointly, and your income is less than $178,000, you can contribute up to the full amount (phased out if your income is between $178,000 and $188,000); for single filers this phase-out happens between $112,000 and $127,000. Earn more and you're not eligible for a Roth; your only choice is a traditional IRA.

AT A GLANCE: TRADITIONAL IRA VS. ROTH IRA

	IRA	Roth IRA
Tax Treatment	**Tax-Deferred**	**Tax-Free**
Good for	Anyone who believes their tax bracket will be lower in retirement	Anyone who believes their tax bracket will be higher in retirement
2013 Contribution limit	$5,500 plus $1,000 catch-up if you are 50 or older	$5,500 plus $1,000 catch-up if you are 50 or older
Loan	No	No
Withdrawal	Ordinary income tax rate; 10% penalty if you are under 59½, with exceptions	Contributions always tax-free; 10% penalty on earnings if under 59½ and haven't held account for 5 years
Required minimum distribution	Yes	No
Special feature	Can only contribute up to the year in which you turn 70½	In 2013, eligibility phased out between $178,000 and $188,000 for married filing jointly; between $112,000 and $127,000 for singles; $10,000 for married filing separately; no age limit for contributions

⮞ **SMART MOVE:** For many reasons, it can make sense to have more than one retirement account. Even if you have an employer-sponsored plan, consider opening an IRA to boost your savings. If you're self-employed or own a small business, don't be content with an IRA. See **Question 15** for more on small business plans that let you save more.

CAN YOU CONTRIBUTE TO AN IRA IF YOU DON'T HAVE A JOB?

In a word, yes. The spousal exception allows a working spouse to make a contribution on behalf of a nonworking spouse. If you're married filing jointly, you can contribute the maximum into two separate IRAs, one for each spouse—even if one of you doesn't have earned income—provided the working spouse has income equal to both contributions.

BEHIND THE SCENES: IS YOUR CONTRIBUTION TO A TAX-DEFERRED IRA DEDUCTIBLE?

The deductibility of your IRA contribution depends on two things: your income and whether your company (or your spouse's company) offers a retirement plan. There are three possible scenarios:

1. If you (and your spouse, if you are married) are *not* what the IRS calls an "active participant" in a qualified workplace retirement plan, like a 401(k), a 403(b), or a traditional pension plan, then you *can* deduct annual contributions of up to $6,500.

2. If you *are* an active participant in a company-sponsored plan, your IRA contribution is deductible only if your income is below certain thresholds: $59,000–$69,000 for single taxpayers; $95,000–$115,000 for married filing jointly; and less than $10,000 for married filing separately. Deductibility is phased out between these numbers.

3. If you are not an active participant, but your spouse is, you can contribute and deduct the full $6,500 provided your income is below $178,000. Deductibility is phased out between $178,000 and $188,000.

Note: If you contribute to a workplace retirement plan, you are an "active participant." Even if you don't participate through payroll deduction, you might be an active participant according to IRS rules. For example, if your company has a traditional pension plan, you are probably an active participant if you're *eligible* to participate—even if no contributions are being made. Check with your human resources department if you're unsure.

SMART MOVE: A Roth IRA is a great way to pass on money to your heirs, who will be able to withdraw money income-tax-free.

The Bottom Line: Putting It All Together

If all this information has left you with glazed eyes, I understand—and sympathize. Although I like to believe that all these plans and rules were designed with good intentions, unraveling the details for each is overwhelming.

I certainly don't want to add to the confusion, but the truth is that sometimes having more than one type of retirement account can work to your advantage. To help you find the best combination, the Schwab Center for Financial Research has come up with the following guidelines:

1. **Start with your company plan.** If your company plan offers a matching contribution, that's probably the best place to start. Contribute enough to capture the maximum match.

2. **Then think about an IRA.** If you're eligible to make a deductible contribution to a traditional IRA (see **Behind the Scenes** on page 42 for details), consider putting your next $5,500 (or $6,500 if you are 50 or older) there. You're still getting a deduction as you would with a 401(k), but you'll likely have more investment choices. If you're not eligible to make a deductible contribution to a traditional IRA but you're eligible for a Roth IRA (see income requirements above), consider putting your next $5,500 (or $6,500 if you are 50 or older) in a Roth. Your contribu-

tion won't be deductible, but qualified withdrawals will be tax-free down the road and you won't have to take distributions at any particular age.

3. **Go back to your company plan.** If you can, put more money into your company plan until you max it out.

4. **Save even more.** If you can save more (congratulations!), additional savings can go into a regular brokerage account. Another choice would be a nondeductible contribution to a traditional IRA. Realize, though, that this is probably not a great choice as compared to a brokerage account. You will have to pay ordinary income tax rates when you withdraw funds from a nondeductible IRA; when you withdraw funds held for a year or more from a brokerage account, you pay taxes at the lower, long-term capital gains rate.

⮕ SMART MOVE: Many people choose to have both tax-deferred and tax-free retirement accounts. This strategy can let you time your taxed and tax-free withdrawals, minimizing your income taxes in a given year. It's kind of like diversifying your taxes.

Next Steps

- Are you a sole proprietor or small business owner? See your retirement account options in **Question 15**.
- Curious about required minimum distributions? See **Question 23**.
- Ready to invest your retirement dollars? See **Question 5**.
- If you're thinking about converting your traditional IRA to a Roth IRA, see **Question 23**.

The stock market has me spooked. How should I invest as I get closer to retirement?

We've seen plenty of turmoil in the financial markets in the last several years. The market meltdown in 2008 destroyed $6.9 trillion of wealth, causing many investors to run for the hills. This was particularly traumatic for those nearing or in retirement. Millions of Americans lost their hard-earned savings—and along with that, their faith in the financial markets.

The good news, of course, was the subsequent recovery. Four years after the market crash, the broad market had not only recovered its losses but had reached new highs. Unfortunately, though, the investors who had bailed at the bottom didn't get to share in the good times. Their losses were sealed.

There's a tough lesson here. As an investor, we shouldn't overestimate our ability to handle downturns. If you know deep in your heart that you can't handle losses, invest more conservatively. The market will go up and then it will go down again. Your portfolio has to be constructed in a way that will allow you to hold on through thick and thin.

As painful as 2008 was, we can now look back and be reassured that our basic principles held true. Diversification matters. Asset allocation matters. Fees matter. And it is essential to keep a long-term view.

That said, financial markets continue to change, and our advice continues to evolve as well. In these pages I provide you with the most up-to-date thinking from the Schwab Center for Financial Research for building and maintaining your portfolio. Although individual securities often capture the headlines, these fundamentals are the most important keys to your success as an investor. And even though I'm aiming this at all of us who are in our fifties and sixties, everything I cover is essential for every investor at any age.

One more thing before we get started. Investing like a pro is complicated. Certainly there are ways to simplify the process, which is especially appropriate for those who are young and just getting started. But once you have built up some wealth, and you know that you're going to be relying on your portfolio for your "paycheck" in the not-too-distant future, there's more to think about. In the following pages I may provide more detail than some of you will want—or need—to read. In that case, skip the material set off in boxes. If you're working with a financial advisor—great! Let them sweat the details so you can focus on the big picture. But if you're investing on your own, or you want to engage your advisor in some good discussions, dig in!

Think Long-Term

I distinctly remember the look on my colleague's face when she came into my office. It was in the summer of 2009. The market was slowly recovering from the collapse the previous year, but we were all pretty frustrated. Part concerned, but also part amused, she told me that her husband had proclaimed that he was ready to bail out of the market "as soon as the Dow hits 10,000." Nearing retirement, he was understandably shaken, and had "had it."

We chuckled a little, but at the same time we both totally understood where he was coming from. Thankfully my colleague was able to convince her husband to hang in, and ultimately his portfolio rebounded. But this story illustrates a couple of important points.

The value of a dollar invested in stocks versus bonds from 1987 to 2012

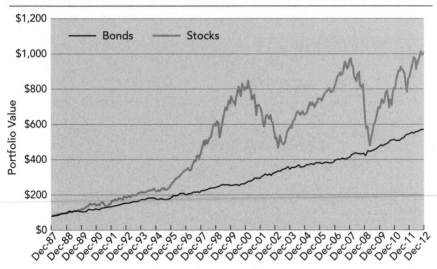

Source: Schwab Center for Financial Research, with data provided by Morningstar, Inc. The chart illustrates the growth in value of $100 invested in various financial instruments on December 31, 1987, through December 31, 2012. Results assume reinvestment of dividends, capital gains, and coupons, and no taxes or transaction costs. Stocks are represented by the monthly total returns of the S&P 500® Index, and bonds are represented by the monthly total returns of the Barclays U.S. Aggregate Bond Index. Indexes are unmanaged, do not incur fees or expenses, and cannot be invested in directly. Past performance is no indication of future results.

First, as an investor you need to keep a long-term view. The dramatic decline in 2008 was extraordinary and painful. But as the chart above shows, it's customary for the stock market to fluctuate year to year, month to month, or even day to day—and sometimes a lot! Unfortunately, if you jump ship after a steep decline, all you do is seal in your losses.

Part of thinking long-term is realizing that our emotions are not our friend. When the market goes up, we feel confident taking on more risk. When the market goes down, we feel burned and either look for safer investments or back out completely. This may be human nature, but it's not the way to manage a portfolio.

If this sounds familiar, take a step back and try to figure out how much risk you can handle in a "neutral market," or one that isn't moving dramatically in one direction or another. Use that as your guiding light, and be prepared to hold your course. Of course your circumstances or your goals may change, at which time you should reevaluate your decisions. But in the meantime, try not to react to each market trend.

➤ SMART MOVE: If you don't have a formalized retirement plan, make one—now! Studies have shown that investors who plan have significantly better outcomes in retirement.

◎ FACT: According to a 2013 study by the Employee Benefit Research Institute, 46 percent of workers have completed a retirement needs calculation, which involves determining how much money you are likely to need in retirement and how much you will need to save to meet that goal. More than half (53 percent) have not taken this important first step.

The second important point of this story is that both **asset allocation** (the way you divvy up your money among different categories of investments such as stocks, bonds, cash, etc.) and **diversification** (owning investments of different types within each asset class) are crucial for controlling risk—although neither, of course, can guarantee a profit or totally eliminate the risk of loss. I talk more about these concepts later, but my colleague knew that her husband had worked with their advisor to build a diversified portfolio based on his personal goals and time frame. It wasn't as if he had just selected a few random stocks and bonds. That ultimately gave him the confidence to hang on.

DON'T TRY TO TIME THE MARKET

It's understandable to want to be in the stock market when it's going up, and out when it's going down. The problem is that virtually none of us, even the most experienced investor, can accurately predict how much and when the market will move in a particular direction. The following chart, which reflects the annualized total return of the S&P 500 for the twenty-year period from 1993 to 2012, tells the story.

As you can see, missing just a few of the top performing days can dramatically lower your return. Many of the best performing days follow market dips. In fact, missing just the top 20 trading days during this twenty-year period (20 out of 5,041 days) would have resulted in a return below that of three-month T-bills (3.1 percent for the same time period).

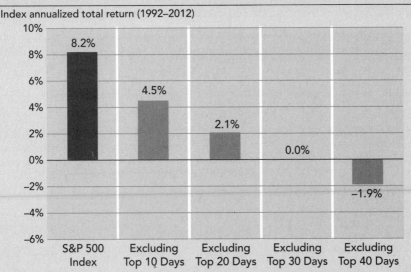

Time in the market is more important than timing the market

Index annualized total return (1992–2012)

- S&P 500 Index: 8.2%
- Excluding Top 10 Days: 4.5%
- Excluding Top 20 Days: 2.1%
- Excluding Top 30 Days: 0.0%
- Excluding Top 40 Days: −1.9%

Source: Schwab Center for Financial Research with data provided by Standard and Poor's. Return data are annualized based on an average of 252 trading days within a calendar year. The year begins on the first trading day in January and ends on the last trading day of December, and daily total returns were used. Returns assume reinvestment of dividends. When out of the market, cash is not invested. Market returns are represented by the S&P 500 Index, which represents an index of widely traded stocks. Top days are defined as the best performing days of the S&P 500 during the twenty-year period. Indices are unmanaged, do not incur fees or expenses, and cannot be invested in directly. Past performance is no indication of future results.

Understand Investment Risk: The Foundation for Your Portfolio

As investors, we know that the potential for higher returns generally comes with higher risk. And as a broad statement, that's true. Stock portfolios tend to have higher highs and lower lows than bond portfolios. Small company stocks tend to be more volatile than large company stocks. But there's more to it than selecting individual investments. What's most important is how these investments work together as a whole. One combination of investments (or, more accurately, categories of investments, otherwise known as *asset classes*) won't provide you with the same opportunity for growth and the same potential for loss as another combination. Modern portfolio theory (see **Behind the Scenes** on pages 53–54 for more) is built on this essential concept of an "efficient" portfolio, or one that combines asset classes (otherwise known as your *asset allocation*) in a way that can minimize risk while maximizing return.

RISK TERMINOLOGY

No need to memorize these terms! But the definitions might come in handy as you read on.

Asset allocation: The division of a portfolio into different asset classes (for example, stocks, bonds, cash, real estate, and commodities) with the goal of minimizing risk.

Beta: A measure of the volatility, or systematic risk, of a security or a portfolio in comparison to the market as a whole. Due to macroeconomic variables, it cannot be diversified away.

Correlation: The statistical strength of the relationship of the returns of two assets, ranging from −1 to +1. Perfect positive correlation (+1) implies that as one security moves up or down, the other will move in lockstep. Perfect negative correlation (−1) implies that if one security moves in one direction, the other will move the opposite way. Securities with a correlation of 0 have no relationship and move independently.

Diversification: The division of money *across* and *within* asset classes with the goal of reducing risk.

Efficient frontier: A graphical representation of a set of portfolios that provide the greatest expected return for a given amount of risk.

Sharpe ratio: A ratio that indicates whether a portfolio's or a fund's returns are due to smart investment decisions or are the result of excess risk. The higher the ratio, the better the risk-adjusted returns. A negative Sharpe ratio indicates that a risk-free asset would have performed better.

Systematic risk: The portion of total risk that is due to macroeconomic variables (for example, a change in interest rates), also called *beta*. Adding more securities to a portfolio will not eliminate it.

Total risk: The combination of systematic and unsystematic risk, measured by standard deviation. Once unsystematic risk has been diversified away, only systematic risk remains in a portfolio.

Unsystematic risk: The diversifiable portion of total risk that is specific to an individual investment. In theory it can be eliminated by increasing the number of securities in a portfolio.

Although modern portfolio theory has been challenged, particularly in light of the market collapse in 2008, its basic tenets—diversification and asset allocation—are as valid today as they were fifty years ago. What is changing, though, is the way we execute these principles to keep up with new market realities.

A CASE STUDY: DIVERSIFICATION AT WORK

Asset allocation and diversification are crucial to your long-term success as an investor. We've experienced two major bear markets in the last decade, and as painful as these times were, diversified portfolios fared much better.

From 2000 to 2002 the S&P 500 experienced a 45% loss, while a blended portfolio consisting of 60% S&P 500 and 40% Barclays U.S. Aggregate Bond Index experienced less than half of the decline (21% loss). In 2008, the S&P 500 had a meltdown of 51%, whereas a blended portfolio dropped only 31%.

In other words, having 40% of a portfolio invested in a diversified set of bonds could have substantially reduced losses. $100,000 invested in the S&P on December 31, 1999, would have ended with $123,886, while $100,000 invested in a blended portfolio ended with $167,683 over the thirteen years.

The following chart tells the story.

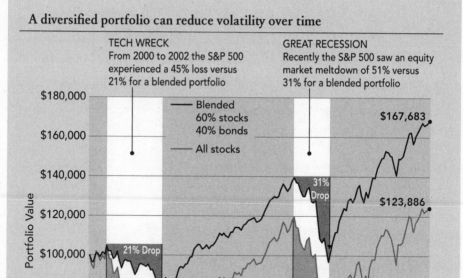

A diversified portfolio can reduce volatility over time

TECH WRECK
From 2000 to 2002 the S&P 500 experienced a 45% loss versus 21% for a blended portfolio

GREAT RECESSION
Recently the S&P 500 saw an equity market meltdown of 51% versus 31% for a blended portfolio

Source: Schwab Center for Financial Research, with data provided by Morningstar, Inc. Stocks are represented by total annual returns of the S&P 500® Index, and bonds are represented by total annual returns of the Barclays U.S. Aggregate Bond Index. The 60/40 portfolio is a hypothetical portfolio consisting of 60% S&P 500 Index stocks and 40% Barclays U.S. Aggregate Bond Index bonds. The portfolio is rebalanced annually. Returns include reinvestment of dividends, interest, and capital gains. Indexes are unmanaged, do not incur fees or expenses, and cannot be invested in directly. Diversification does not eliminate the risk of investment losses. Past performance is no indication of future results.

Unfortunately, though, in 2008, just when we needed the protection of diversification the most, we were disappointed. Large-cap stocks, small-cap stocks, international stocks—everything declined. One investment that was supposed to balance out another didn't. Partially in response to this across-the-board crash, "postmodern" portfolio theory, with a focus on downside risk, gained attention.

BEHIND THE SCENES: FROM MODERN PORTFOLIO THEORY TO POSTMODERN PORTFOLIO THEORY

In 1952, Harry Markowitz introduced the foundational concept of **modern portfolio theory** when he proposed that investors should be judging investment risk *not* on an individual security level, but instead by looking at how all of the investments in their portfolio work together. He proposed diversification as a way to manage risk, suggesting that by constructing a portfolio of investments that have a low correlation to one another, an investor could reduce overall risk.

The concept of an *efficient* frontier stems from this work. According to Markowitz, all portfolios that offer the highest return for a given amount of risk (or the minimum risk for a given return) are *efficient*. When you graph these theoretical portfolios, with one axis being risk and the other return, the resulting arc is the *efficient frontier*. By extension, any portfolio that doesn't fall on this arc is *inefficient*, and won't provide sufficient return for the risk (or enough safety for the return).

In 1964, Bill Sharpe expanded on Markowitz's work by introducing the **capital asset pricing model**, which computes the *expected* return of a security or a portfolio, given its risk. If this expected return doesn't meet or exceed an investor's *required* return, then the investment is not a good choice. He also introduced what became known as the **Sharpe ratio,** a measure that reveals a portfolio's risk-adjusted performance. In other words, it tells us whether a portfolio's returns are due to smart investment decisions or are the result of excess risk.

According to modern portfolio theory, investing risk can be divided into two big buckets: systematic risk (beta), the type of risk you can't avoid by diversifying your holdings; and unsystematic risk, the type of risk you *can* mitigate through diversification. If you own stocks, you can't avoid systematic risks such as interest rate risk, purchasing power risk, or political risk. But by buying more stocks with different characteristics (for example, large cap, small cap, international), or diversifying, you *can* minimize other risks such as business risk and exchange rate risk. As investors, our goal is to construct an efficient portfolio that will eliminate unsystematic risk while maximizing our potential for the greatest return.

Although the work of Markowitz and Sharpe was widely accepted in the academic world (and both ultimately won Nobel Prizes for their work), modern portfolio theory wasn't broadly adopted until the 1990s, when portfolio managers and institutions began to develop asset allocation strategies based on the efficient frontier.

There is no question that modern portfolio theory established a groundbreaking framework for portfolio construction. It can fall short in practice, though, because it uses the standard deviation of all returns (positive as well as negative) as its measure of risk. The problem is that this doesn't accurately reflect how humans experience risk. As behavioral economics has shown, our losses matter more to us than our gains. Our pleasure over a gain decreases as the magnitude of the gain increases. Conversely, we experience a sudden jump in anxiety when a loss exceeds a certain threshold.

Postmodern portfolio theory deals with these realities by focusing exclusively on downside risk, using standard deviation of negative returns as its measure. Although in development for decades, postmodern portfolio theory didn't gain much traction until 2008, when the old models fell short and failed to protect investors from the market collapse. In the intervening years, postmodern portfolio theory has garnered more support, and continuing research has advanced the science of asset allocation—to the ultimate benefit of all investors.

Build Your Portfolio

Traditional investing wisdom says that the older you get, the more conservatively you should invest (in other words, your portfolio would have a larger percentage of bonds and other fixed-income investments, and fewer stocks). And I agree, with a couple of caveats.

Yes, younger investors can handle more risk because they have more time to ride out market ups and downs. But it's important to think about inflation. If you're a healthy fifty-year-old with a family history of longevity, you could live another forty or more years. If you avoid stocks, you eliminate market risk, but at the same time you're taking on the very real risk that your money will lose considerable value after inflation.

INFLATION CAN SEVERELY ERODE PURCHASING POWER OVER THE LONG TERM

Although we are now in a low inflation environment, the years ahead may be different. The average annual rate of inflation over the last eighty-seven years has been roughly 3%, and the average for the 1970s and 1980s was 6.2%.

Even under rather mild inflation of 3%, $100,000 today will be worth only about $55,000 in twenty years: a 45% loss in value.

As the following chart shows, over time stocks have been the best hedge against inflation.

Equities have outperformed other asset classes

(1926–2012)

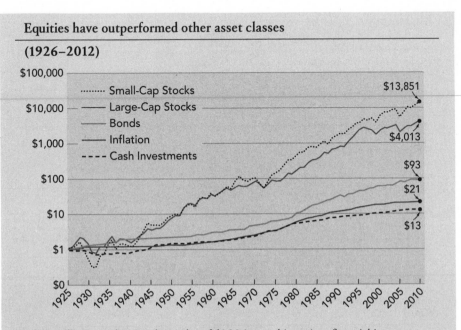

The chart illustrates the growth in value of $1.00 invested in various financial instruments on 12/31/1925. Results assume reinvestment of dividends, capital gains, and coupons, and no taxes or transaction costs. Generally, small-cap stocks are in the bottom 50% of publicly traded companies based on market capitalization. These stocks are subject to greater volatility. Source: Stocks, Bonds, Bills & Inflation® 2012 Yearbook, © 2013 Morningstar, Inc. Based on the copyrighted works of Ibbotson and Sinquefield. All rights reserved. Used with permission. The indices representing each asset class are S&P 500® Index (large-cap stocks); CRSP 6-8 Index (small-cap stocks); Ibbotson Intermediate U.S. Government Bond Index (bonds); and Ibbotson U.S. 30-day Treasury bills (cash investments). Indices are unmanaged, do not incur fees or expenses, and cannot be invested in directly. Past performance is no indication of future results.

The best asset allocation varies by individual, and will depend on your personal tolerance for risk, your wealth (and the degree to which you'll depend on your portfolio for living expenses), your anticipated longevity, and a host of other factors.

The following pie charts provide more detail on how you might design your portfolio, especially if you are investing on your own and want to keep

Classic Schwab model portfolios

Conservative

For investors who seek current income and stability, and are less concerned about growth.

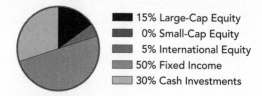

- 15% Large-Cap Equity
- 0% Small-Cap Equity
- 5% International Equity
- 50% Fixed Income
- 30% Cash Investments

Moderately Conservative

For investors who seek current income and stability, with modest potential for increase in the value of their investments

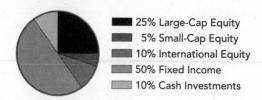

- 25% Large-Cap Equity
- 5% Small-Cap Equity
- 10% International Equity
- 50% Fixed Income
- 10% Cash Investments

Moderate Allocation

For long-term investors who don't need current income and want some growth potential. Likely to entail some fluctuations in value, but presents less volatility than the overall equity market.

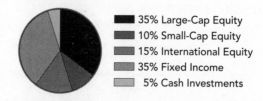

- 35% Large-Cap Equity
- 10% Small-Cap Equity
- 15% International Equity
- 35% Fixed Income
- 5% Cash Investments

Moderately Aggressive

For long-term investors who want good growth potential and don't need current income. Entails a fair amount of volatility, but not as much as a portfolio invested exclusively in equities.

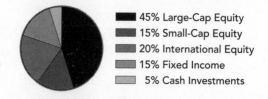

- 45% Large-Cap Equity
- 15% Small-Cap Equity
- 20% International Equity
- 15% Fixed Income
- 5% Cash Investments

Aggressive

For long-term investors who want high growth potential and don't need current income. May entail substantial year-to-year volatility in value in exchange for potentially high long-term returns.

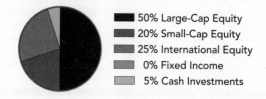

- 50% Large-Cap Equity
- 20% Small-Cap Equity
- 25% International Equity
- 0% Fixed Income
- 5% Cash Investments

things fairly simple. All five provide a good trade-off between risk and return; see **Behind the Scenes** on pages 53–54). Note that more aggressive portfolios include proportionately more stocks, and less fixed income and cash. As you approach the date when you will want to start withdrawing money from your portfolio, the percentage of stocks declines.

These models are a great start. However, if you have the time and interest to fine-tune your strategy (and especially if you are working with a

Enhanced Schwab model portfolios with nontraditional asset classes added

Conservative

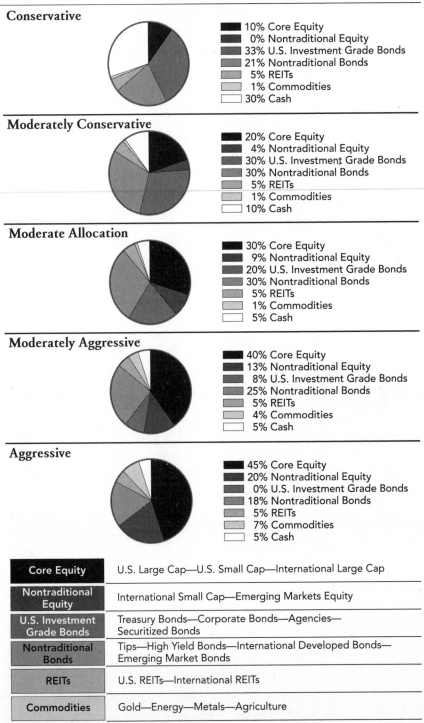

- 10% Core Equity
- 0% Nontraditional Equity
- 33% U.S. Investment Grade Bonds
- 21% Nontraditional Bonds
- 5% REITs
- 1% Commodities
- 30% Cash

Moderately Conservative

- 20% Core Equity
- 4% Nontraditional Equity
- 30% U.S. Investment Grade Bonds
- 30% Nontraditional Bonds
- 5% REITs
- 1% Commodities
- 10% Cash

Moderate Allocation

- 30% Core Equity
- 9% Nontraditional Equity
- 20% U.S. Investment Grade Bonds
- 30% Nontraditional Bonds
- 5% REITs
- 1% Commodities
- 5% Cash

Moderately Aggressive

- 40% Core Equity
- 13% Nontraditional Equity
- 8% U.S. Investment Grade Bonds
- 25% Nontraditional Bonds
- 5% REITs
- 4% Commodities
- 5% Cash

Aggressive

- 45% Core Equity
- 20% Nontraditional Equity
- 0% U.S. Investment Grade Bonds
- 18% Nontraditional Bonds
- 5% REITs
- 7% Commodities
- 5% Cash

Core Equity	U.S. Large Cap—U.S. Small Cap—International Large Cap
Nontraditional Equity	International Small Cap—Emerging Markets Equity
U.S. Investment Grade Bonds	Treasury Bonds—Corporate Bonds—Agencies—Securitized Bonds
Nontraditional Bonds	Tips—High Yield Bonds—International Developed Bonds—Emerging Market Bonds
REITs	U.S. REITs—International REITs
Commodities	Gold—Energy—Metals—Agriculture

financial advisor), Schwab has developed more complex models based on postmodern portfolio theory, designed to deliver more downside protection as well as the potential for a higher return.

Notice that these more sophisticated models differentiate between **core equity,** which includes U.S. large- and small-cap companies as well as international large-cap companies, and **nontraditional equity,** which includes international small-cap and emerging markets positions. Bonds are classified according to **U.S. investment grade** (Treasury bonds, corporate bonds, agency bonds, and securitized bonds) and **nontraditional** (TIPS, high-yield bonds, international developed bonds, and emerging markets bonds). Note also that each portfolio includes a 5 percent slice of **REITs** (both U.S. and international), a portion devoted to **commodities** (energy, gold, metals, and agriculture) as well as **cash.** Although more complex, and therefore requiring more work on the part of the investor, these portfolios provide more diversification and in some cases a higher expected return.

ARE REITs RIGHT FOR YOU?

REITs, or real estate investment trusts, are companies that own and often operate income-producing real estate such as apartments, shopping centers, office buildings, hotels, and warehouses. Some REITs specialize in particular property types or geographic locations, while others are widely diversified.

Individual REITs are traded on the major stock exchanges and you can also buy REIT mutual funds and ETFs that invest in a pool of REITs. Both individual REITs and REIT funds can give you a practical way to include professionally managed real estate in your portfolio, providing diversification, income in the form of dividends, and the potential for protection against inflation.

Select Your Investments

Once you've settled on an asset allocation, it's time to select investments. The good news, and the not-so-good news, is that you have literally thousands of choices. If you're up to the task of researching and selecting individual stocks and bonds, more power to you. That's the way to have maximum control and potentially lower overall costs. But if not, mutual funds and exchange-traded funds (ETFs) can be great tools for achieving cost-effective diversification without as much sweat and tears. And of course this isn't an all-or-nothing proposition. Many investors (and I count myself in this group!) find that they like to combine a selection of favorite stocks or a bond ladder (a series of bonds with a sequence of maturities) with a number of funds. All can work well together.

A CLOSER LOOK: DIVERSIFYING YOUR PORTFOLIO

One way to help achieve proper diversification is to break down your portfolio into layers, as illustrated in the following pyramid. Much as the familiar food pyramid did for our diet, this diagram shows the stock and bond components of a well-diversified portfolio.

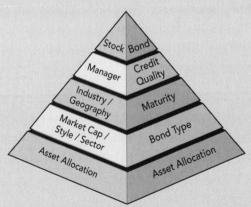

As you can see in the pyramid, asset allocation forms the foundation for your entire portfolio. Then, for the stock portion of your portfolio, you should think about diversifying according to:

- **Market capitalization.** This is the size of the company, measured by its stock price multiplied by the number of outstanding shares. Small-cap stocks tend to be riskier than large caps, but they also have the potential for more upside.

- **Style.** This indicates either a value or a growth orientation.

- **Sector.** There are ten sectors; for example, Consumer Discretionary, Consumer Staples, and Energy.

- **Industry.** The ten sectors include sixty-five industries. For example, Banks, Diversified Financials, Insurance, and Real Estate are all part of Financials.

- **Geography.** In addition to domestic companies, it is a good idea to include stock of companies from both developed and emerging markets around the world.

- **Manager.** It can be risky to have all of your actively managed funds with the same manager.

- **Individual stock.** Look out for overconcentration. See pages 65–66 for more.

In a similar vein, you should consider the following factors when building a diversified bond portfolio:

- **Type.** Primary types include U.S. Treasuries, government agency, agency mortgage-backed, corporate, and municipal. Other types are international bonds from developed countries, emerging market bonds, and high-yield "junk" bonds such as corporate bonds rated below "investment grade."

- **Maturity.** This is the time until your principal is repaid. Generally, the longer the maturity, the higher the interest paid. But risk also rises with maturity. Longer-term bonds tend to fall more in value than do shorter-term bonds when interest rates rise.

➡ **SMART MOVE:** When it comes to selecting bond maturity, a good balance can be "intermediate term," or five to ten years, when you average all of your bond investments. However, if you believe that interest rates will rise (causing bond prices to fall), or if you need your principal soon, you can lean toward shorter-term bonds. Or if you think that rates will fall, and you can accept some risk, you can include longer-term bonds.

- **Credit quality.** In general, the lower a bond's rating and the higher its risk, the greater its yield.

➲ SMART MOVE: For your core bond holdings, it's likely best to stick to high quality. More aggressive investors can consider bonds with a lower rating, keeping in mind the higher risk. In general, I don't recommend having more than 20 percent of your fixed-income portfolio in lower-rated, high-yield bonds.

- **Individual bond.** As a general rule, you should own bonds from no fewer than ten issuers for adequate diversification.

Note: Diversification cannot ensure a profit and does not protect you against losses in declining markets. Additionally, high-yield bonds are subject to greater risk of loss, including default risk, than higher-rated bonds and their prices may be volatile. International investments are also subject to additional risks such as currency fluctuation, geopolitical risk, and the potential for illiquid markets.

☎ TALK TO AN EXPERT. Overwhelmed by the vast number of investments? Think about working with a financial advisor to create a portfolio that matches your goals and risk tolerance. (I certainly do, as do many of my most savvy colleagues!)

As I mentioned earlier, many investors turn to mutual funds and exchange-traded funds (ETFs) for much, if not all, of their portfolio. Both allow you to purchase a basket of securities with a single investment.

➲ SMART MOVE. Before you buy a mutual fund or an exchange-traded fund, take the time to review its prospectus. Here you'll find essential information such as the fund's investment objectives and strategy, risk factors, financial history, fees, and management.

Mutual funds come in two flavors:

- **Actively managed funds** are run by a manager who analyzes and selects investments that he or she hopes will outperform a particular benchmark.
- **Passive (or index) funds** use a formula to select investments, with the goal of replicating the performance of a particular benchmark.

Each approach has its pros and cons. Passive management can be both tax- and cost-efficient but doesn't offer the potential for above-market returns. Active management can either outperform or underperform the market, at a higher cost.

- Most **ETFs** are essentially index funds that trade like stocks (there are just a few actively managed ETFs). The primary difference is the way you purchase and sell shares: With a mutual fund, your order to buy or sell shares is processed at the end of the trading day, and if you're buying a no-load, no-transaction-fee fund, there's no cost for the trade (although all funds have ongoing management fees and expenses). With an ETF, you can buy or sell shares at any time during market hours, and you generally pay a commission, just like any stock trade.

Following are some examples of when a mutual fund or an ETF might make more sense:

AT A GLANCE: RATIONALES FOR ETFS OR MUTUAL FUNDS

Consider an actively managed mutual fund if	• You want a fund that could potentially beat the market. • You want the broadest possible selection of funds.
Consider an index mutual fund if	• You make small, regular investments. Although some ETFs are available commission-free, many are not. • The comparable index mutual fund has lower annual operating expenses. • The comparable ETF trades infrequently.
Consider an exchange-traded fund (ETF) if	• You want to make a big long-term investment in an index-based fund. There may or may not be a commission, and expenses are generally lower. • You trade actively. Intraday trades, stop orders, limit orders, etc., are not available with mutual funds. • You want exposure to a sector or asset class at a relatively low cost. • You want niche exposure (e.g., to a particular industry or commodity) at a relatively low cost. • You're tax-sensitive. Although index funds tend to be tax-efficient, ETFs are generally even more so.

AN EXPLOSION OF ETFs

From only about 200 funds in 2000 to about 1,400 in 2012, the number of ETFs has grown by leaps and bounds. Basically, they come in three varieties: traditional, niche, and exotic.

Traditional ETFs tend to be low-cost, tax-efficient funds that provide access to a broad range of securities in an asset class like large U.S. stocks, small U.S. stocks, international stocks, or investment-grade bonds.

Niche ETFs focus on a narrow slice of a broader asset class—for example, sectors like health care, single countries like France, or narrow parts of the bond market like high-yield bonds. They tend to have somewhat higher expenses than traditional ETFs, can be more volatile, and often carry additional risk.

Exotic ETFs provide access to unusual asset classes or investment styles, typically at a premium price by ETF standards. Exotic ETFs include commodities such as gold, concepts such as clean technology, or leveraged securities that move twice as much as the market or in the opposite direction to the market.

BEWARE LEVERAGED AND INVERSE ETFs

All ETFs are subject to risk, but two types—leveraged and inverse ETFs—are especially fraught with danger. Leveraged ETFs seek to provide a multiple of the investment returns of a given index or benchmark on a daily basis. Inverse ETFs seek to provide the opposite of the investment returns, also daily, of a given index or benchmark, either in whole or by multiples.

Due to the effects of compounding, aggressive techniques, and possible correlation errors, both leveraged and inverse ETFs may experience greater losses than one would ordinarily expect. Compounding can also cause a widening difference between the performances of an ETF and its underlying index or benchmark, so that returns over periods longer than one day can differ in amount and direction from the target return of the same period. Consequently, these ETFs may experience losses even in situations where the underlying index or benchmark has performed as hoped. Aggressive investment techniques such as futures, forward contracts, swap agreements, derivatives, and options can increase ETF volatility and decrease performance.

Bottom line? Only purchase a leveraged or inverse ETF if you are prepared to take on a large amount of risk, and only if you are prepared to monitor them closely. If you own either type, check them frequently—as often as once a day.

BEHIND THE SCENES: FUNDAMENTALLY WEIGHTED INDEXING

For many years, academics have debated whether active or passive management (using index mutual funds or ETFs) is the smarter way to invest.

Passive management has traditionally used market capitalization to purchase securities. With this method, the largest companies have the largest weight in the index—and the largest impact on its performance. Examples of cap-weighted indexes include the S&P 500 Index, the Russell 3000 Index, the MSCI EAFE Index, and the Dow Jones U.S. Total Stock Market Index.

More recently another methodology, **fundamental weighting,** has gained support. Instead of giving the largest companies the largest weights, this approach weights securities on factors such as a company's profits, dividends, book value, cash flow, sales, or number of employees. If it's true, as some assert, that cap weighting puts too much money into overvalued companies, fundamentally weighted indexes would tend to perform better when the markets correct and market-cap indexes would excel during strong bull markets led by large companies.

The experts at the Schwab Center for Financial Research believe that a combination of these methodologies can provide the best overall risk-adjusted results for your portfolio. For example, although fundamentally weighted indexes have delivered excess returns over longer intervals, there are also market environments where market-cap strategies generate better results. In addition, in the most efficient markets (for example, domestic large cap), passive strategies (fundamental or market-cap) tend to outperform active management. In less efficient markets (for example, international small cap or emerging markets) active management has historically had an edge. (Of course, when it comes down to your own portfolio, you always have to remember that past performance does not guarantee future returns!)

⚠️ **CAUTION:** Overconcentration is a common and costly mistake. As many investors have learned the hard way, owning too much of any one company is risky business. Even if it's a great company—or the company you work for and therefore know well—you're taking on a lot of risk if its stock represents more than 20 percent of your portfolio.

The following table lists some previous corporate giants whose dramatic downturns cost investors dearly. These fallen angels were onetime industry leaders that were considered "safe" investments for the long term. In many cases, the financial condition of these companies deteriorated quickly and caught investors by surprise.

OVERCONCENTRATION CAN BE A COMMON, COSTLY MISTAKE

Chapter 11 Examples	Cause of Chapter 11 Filing
Enron Worldcom	Fraud
UAL Northwest Airlines	Business model
Polaroid	Technological obsolescence
Owens Corning W. R. Grace	Litigation
Washington Mutual IndyMac Bank	Credit management
Lehman Brothers Bear Stearns	Overleveraged
Delphi General Motors	Cost structure

FACT: A review of more than two million self-guided clients at Schwab found that nearly one-third of them had a concentrated stock position making up more than 20 percent of their portfolio.

WHICH IS BETTER: AN INDIVIDUAL BOND OR A BOND FUND?

As you likely know, individual bonds are designed for predictable payments and maturity values. A bond's market value can fluctuate during its term, depending on changes in interest rates, overall credit quality of the issuer, and other factors, but that will matter only if you need to sell prior to maturity.

A bond fund is a different animal. Although owning a fund is certainly easier and often more practical than managing a number of individual bonds, it is important to understand that a fund doesn't provide the predictable income or the principal protection of an individual bond. Because a fund typically invests in many individual securities and often trades them prior to maturity, its value will fluctuate with market conditions—sometimes dramatically. When you redeem shares, they may be worth more or less than you originally paid.

To help you sort through the pros and cons of each, the Schwab Center for Financial Research has created the following guidelines:

If you	then consider . . .
Are a new investor or have a small dollar amount allocated to bonds	Bond funds—more diversification for less money
Want to use an automatic investment plan	No-load, no-transaction-fee bond funds
Lack time to research and monitor individual bonds	Bond funds—for professional management
Need a specific level of income	A ladder of individual bonds
Don't want to incur unnecessary capital gains	Individual bonds
Seek predictable market value at maturity	Individual bonds

Note: Although bond funds are not subject to sales loads or transaction fees, other fees may be assessed for investment management and other on-going expenses.

Keep Some Cash

When you review the pie charts on pages 56–57, you can also see that every portfolio, even the most aggressive, has a portion in cash. In general, we tend to think of cash as the money we keep in our checking or savings accounts. But in your portfolio, cash can include short-term and relatively safe investments like money market funds, U.S. Treasury bills, and corporate commercial paper (none of which are FDIC-insured).

Although returns on cash are generally low, it still serves three important purposes in your portfolio:

1.   **Liquidity.** Everyone should have an emergency fund equal to at least three to six months of nondiscretionary spending. As you approach

retirement, it can be wise to gradually increase this pot—we recommend that you have at least one year's living expenses in cash by the time you retire. See **Question 22** for more.

⚠ **CAUTION:** Never invest in the stock market any money that you know you will need in the next two or three years. That's what cash is for.

2.   **Flexibility.** By holding a percentage of your portfolio in cash, you can take advantage of investment opportunities. A cash cushion can also come in handy when it comes time to rebalance your portfolio or pay investment fees. You don't want to be forced to sell an investment at the wrong time to raise cash.

3.   **Stability.** Depending on your risk tolerance, you might want to add cash to your holdings for stability. In other words, it can play defense as the rest of your portfolio is pushing for gains.

For ideas on where to keep your cash, see **Question 22**, pages 192–193.

Be Tax-Smart

As an investor, asset allocation and diversification are your top priorities. But when it comes to selecting individual securities, it's also important to consider tax consequences. After all, it's not just what you make, but what you keep after taxes, that counts.

In general, investments that tend to lose less of their return to taxes are good choices for taxable accounts. Conversely, investments that tend to lose more of their return to taxes should go in tax-deferred accounts. The next chart spells out which investments to put where.

AT A GLANCE: TAX-SMART WAYS TO INVEST

Taxable accounts may be the best place for:	Tax-deferred accounts such as traditional IRAs and 401(k)s may be the best place for:	A Roth IRA or Roth 401(k) may be the best place for:
• Individual stocks you plan to hold more than one year • Tax-managed stock funds, index funds, exchange-traded funds (ETFs), low-turnover stock funds • Stocks or mutual funds that pay qualified dividends • Municipal bonds/I Bonds	• Individual stocks you plan to hold one year or less • Actively managed funds that may generate significant short-term capital gains • Taxable bond funds, zero-coupon bonds, inflation-protected bonds, or high-yield bond funds • Real estate investment trusts (REITs)	• Assets that you believe have the greatest chance for the largest return

TAX DIVERSIFICATION: HEDGING FUTURE TAX RATES

Investing would be so much easier if we could predict our income tax rate. Higher than the current rate? Load up your Roth IRA or Roth 401(k). Lower than the current rate? Plow all your savings into tax-deferred accounts.

But as we all know, our future personal situation as well as the federal and state tax structures are uncertain. To counter this, your best strategy is to consider holding a variety of accounts with different tax characteristics, putting the appropriate kinds of investments in each one. Then, when you begin to tap your accounts in retirement, you can be strategic, maximizing after-tax returns. For more on turning your savings into a retirement paycheck, see **Question 23**, page 198.

Measure Your Performance

Investing doesn't stop with building your portfolio. Just like having an annual physical exam, it's important to periodically assess your portfolio's performance so that you know you're staying on the right track. And just like checking on your health, you have to look at your overall well-being as well as the health of your individual systems.

STEP 1: BIG-PICTURE VIEW

Before you can answer the question "How am I doing?" you have to answer the question "Compared to what?" The answer lies in consulting the appropriate benchmarks.

> *Example:* Let's say you're a moderate investor and your target asset allocation is 35 percent large-cap stocks, 10 percent small-cap stocks, 10 percent international stocks, 35 percent bonds, and 5 percent cash. In the previous year your portfolio grew by 8 percent.

To measure your personal performance, you'll need to first calculate the blended benchmark return that reflects your portfolio. As illustrated in the following, and continuing the example from above, you have to look up the return for each asset's benchmark index and multiply it by your percentage weight to get the weighted return. Then you can add up the results for your benchmark portfolio return.

Calculating Your Portfolio Return

Asset Class	Index Benchmark	2012 Market Return	Weighting	Your Weighted Return
Large-cap stocks	S&P 500 index	16%	35%	5.6%
Small-cap stocks	Russell 2000 index	16.35%	10%	1.64%
International stocks	MSCI EAFE index	17.32%	10%	1.73%
Bonds	Barclays U.S. Aggregate Bond index	4.32%	35%	1.51%
Cash investments	Citigroup 3-month Treasury Bill index	0.07	5%	0.0035%

Hypothetical moderate portfolio benchmark return = 10.48%.

After completing this calculation, you can see how your portfolio performed relative to the market. Continuing with our example from above, unfortunately you didn't fare so well. On the surface, an 8 percent return sounds good. But compared to the combined benchmark return of 10.45 percent, you fell short. Time to take a deeper look!

☎ **TALK TO AN EXPERT:** Calculating your return relative to the appropriate indexes is a key responsibility of an advisor. Also note that the previous calculation doesn't take into account deposits or withdrawals. If you either deposited or withdrew large sums during the year, you will get a more accurate result by calculating what is known as your *internal rate of return*. Your advisor should be able to help.

STEP 2: A CLOSER LOOK

Once you've got a sense of the big picture, you can look more closely at how your individual stocks, bonds, and funds performed relative to their indexes. Even if one category outperformed its benchmark, it's possible that there's a laggard dragging down your overall return. Deciding what and when to sell can be just as important as knowing what and when to buy.

Once you've completed these two steps, you'll have a very good idea of how your portfolio is performing. You now have the information you need to make changes as necessary.

Rebalance at Least Yearly

I've spent a lot of time talking about asset allocation and its importance in controlling risk. If you've gotten as far as constructing an efficient portfolio that matches your goals and risk tolerance, congratulations. Rebalancing is about maintaining that mix over time.

REBALANCING VS. REALLOCATING: UNDERSTAND THE DIFFERENCE

- **Rebalancing** means adjusting your portfolio through time to maintain your risk level. Let's say that you're a moderate investor with an asset allocation of 60 percent stocks, 35 percent bonds, and 5 percent cash. If your stocks gain in value and are now equal to 80 percent of your portfolio's value, you should consider selling some of your stocks to buy bonds. This rebalancing will restore your previous asset allocation and risk level.

- **Reallocating** shifts your portfolio to a new asset allocation and different risk level. Let's say that you select a moderate asset allocation when you're 60 years old. By the time you're 65 you want to reduce your risk and therefore shift, or reallocate, your investments so that you have only 40 percent in stocks.

Rebalancing provides the discipline to fight your own worst emotions. In rising stock markets, investors often take on more risk than is suitable. In the late 1990s, and again in the early 2000s, investors loaded up with stocks. Then, when the markets collapsed, they were pounded. Had they instead rebalanced out of stocks when the stock market climbed, they would have been somewhat protected.

In order to preserve your risk level, the Schwab Center for Financial Research recommends that you rebalance your portfolio at least annually, focusing on any asset class that has outgrown its target by more than 5 percent. By selling some of the asset classes that have performed well and buying more of the asset classes that have done poorly, you buy low and sell high. The process can feel counterintuitive, but it works.

⚠ **CAUTION:** If you don't rebalance your portfolio, in effect you are giving up control of your risk level and letting market forces take over. A moderate portfolio may become more conservative, but it is more likely that over time it will become more aggressive.

You can approach rebalancing in tax-smart ways. For example, you can:

- Sell assets from a tax-advantaged account to avoid taxable gains.
- Take dividends and capital gain distributions in cash, directing the funds toward underweighted asset classes.

> **SMART MOVE:** I like to plan my charitable contributions for the next year at the same time that I rebalance my portfolio. To read more about the benefit of donating appreciated stocks, see **Questions 10** and **25**.

Next Steps

- Thinking about working with an advisor? See **Question 6**.
- To learn about annuities, see **Question 20**.
- For ideas on where to keep your cash, see **Question 22**.
- To learn how to create your retirement "paycheck," see **Question 23**.

Important Disclosures

Diversification and asset allocation strategies do not ensure a profit or totally eliminate the risk of losses in declining markets.

High-yield bonds are subject to greater risk of loss, including default risk, than higher-rated bonds, and their prices may be volatile. International bonds are also subject to additional risks such as currency fluctuation, geopolitical risk, and the potential for illiquid markets.

Mutual fund and ETF returns and values will fluctuate, and shares, when redeemed, may be worth more or less than the original cost.

Q6.

I'm too busy to manage my money carefully. Are there any simple strategies for someone like me?

You might be surprised to learn that I have someone else manage my money. For me, it's not a matter of disliking money management (after all, personal finance is my chosen field!), but rather a matter of time. Like so many others of our age, I have a busy professional and personal life, and can't follow my investments as carefully as I know I should.

For me, it's also a matter of my nature. I love to collaborate, and I value others' expertise. And apparently I'm not alone. During the height of the recession my husband asked our advisor if his phone had been ringing off the hook. To our surprise, he said "no." In fact he had received only one frantic phone call—and that was from the client who *always* called. The rest, like us, were comfortable knowing that our advisor was keeping a watchful eye.

So whether your life is complicated, or you find the market ups and downs too frustrating, or you'd just rather spend your time doing something else—sometimes the best thing you can do is let someone else handle your money for you.

Now, some people might immediately think that it only makes sense to have professional management if you have a lot of money or a complicated financial life. After all, it's not free. But fortunately, money management comes in a lot of flavors—from a single fund you can invest all or part of your money in, to a financial advisor to consult with periodically, to a manager who will handle all your finances for you. Your choice depends on how involved you want to be and how much you're willing to pay.

One more very important point: Even though I have a money manager, I meet with him several times a year and both my husband and I are involved in all major decisions. My feeling is that, while you may choose not to manage every detail concerning your money, you can't afford to ignore it. It's up to you to establish and stay in touch with your goals, and then make sure that your investments are helping you reach them.

FACT: Schwab's 2013 Advice and the Affluent Investor Study shows that 74 percent of investors are confident making investment decisions working with an advisor while only 32 percent are confident making investment decisions on their own.

For a Simple, Low-Cost Solution, Consider a Target Fund

In today's increasingly complicated financial markets, a lot of people are looking for a way to invest that doesn't require a huge time commitment. They know they need to have a reasonable number of investments to make that happen; they want professional help in choosing investments; but they also don't want to pay a fortune for it. In response, fund companies have come up with a different breed of mutual fund: a **target fund**— which is a diversified portfolio of stocks, bonds, and cash managed by a professional investment manager to meet a specific goal. You might call it a single-portfolio solution.

Of course, no single portfolio is going to match the needs of every investor, so there are several different target funds to choose from. That's where your work comes in, because to choose the appropriate target fund, you have to think about how much risk you want to take and how long you have to invest. Here are the basic choices:

- **Target risk funds**—These funds are generally designated as aggressive, moderate, or conservative and typically invest in a mix of U.S. and international stocks, bonds, and cash investments to match. They can be a good choice if you believe your tolerance for risk will stay the same for a while. If and when it changes, you can invest in a different target fund. In the meantime, you can relax and let the fund manager handle the details.

- **Target date funds**—These funds can be a good choice if you have a good idea of when you'll retire. That's because they automatically become more conservative as you age. So let's say you plan to retire in 2025. You'd pick a 2025 target date fund. The fund would invest more aggressively (that is, more stocks) in the early years and progressively more conservatively (more bonds and cash investments) the closer you get to the target date. You just have to pick the date—the fund manager does the rest.

One of the beauties of target funds is that the minimum initial investment can be as low as $100. So you can test the waters with as little or as much money as you wish. And whether you choose a target risk fund or a target date fund, you pay for it through an **expense ratio**, which represents the fund's annual operating expenses as a percentage of the assets managed. You don't pay this fee directly. It is deducted from your returns.

⚠ **CAUTION:** It's always smart to keep in mind that like the value of any other mutual fund, the value of a target fund is never guaranteed, not even at the target date (the expected date at which many investors are likely to begin withdrawing from the fund). The value of the fund will fluctuate up to and even beyond the target date, and the asset allocation will change over time according to the fund's prospectus.

➲ **SMART MOVE:** Not all target funds are alike. When shopping for a target fund, be sure to compare past performance, asset allocation, and expense ratios. Also make sure that you understand the fund's time frame: Is it intended to take you "to" retirement, or all the way "through" retirement?

If You Have a Fair Amount to Invest,
Look into a Managed Account

A target fund is a type of mutual fund managed for a pool of investors. A managed account is a more personalized investment. It is actually a fund managed for a single investor. This is an important difference. When you invest in a mutual fund like a target fund, you own shares of a pool of securities with other investors. But when you invest in a managed account, you actually own the underlying stocks, bonds, and cash investments. It's like your own personal mutual fund.

This gives you a lot more control than you have with a regular mutual fund. For instance, you can customize your portfolio to include or exclude certain stocks. You can have your manager buy and sell stocks to control taxes specifically for your own situation. And you'll be kept up-to-date on all activity in the account on a more frequent basis.

Of course, this type of individualized management isn't for everyone. It usually takes a more substantial investment and costs more. Account minimums for managed accounts range from $25,000 upward, and fees are generally 1 percent or more of assets managed. But if you have a fairly large amount of money and want more personal management, it might be worth it.

Want One-on-One Advice? Find the Financial
Advisor Who's Right for You

Another option is working with a financial advisor. This is especially appropriate if your finances are complicated or if you have substantial assets. But others may also appreciate and benefit from the one-on-one advice of a financial advisor. Advisors offer a wide range of services, from one-time consultations to periodic check-ins to complete hands-on management. Following is a quick tour of the various services you could seek out:

- **Big-picture planning**—I think of financial health much as I think of physical health, in that it depends on the strength of several interrelated parts. Your retirement savings, your estate plan, your taxes, your insurance needs—as well as your portfolio—all need to work together. As you're starting to plan your retirement, this type of comprehensive review can be a great way to get on the right track. A comprehensive financial plan is not inexpensive, but it will most likely save you money (and time) in the long run.

- **Periodic consultation**—Anyone who wants to be hands-on with their investments but still wants a little help can simply check in with an advisor periodically. Once a year, or whenever you feel the need, you can discuss your strategy, review your mix of stocks, bonds, and cash, and make adjustments as necessary. For instance, as you get closer to retirement, you may want to move into more fixed-income investments—an area that can be particularly daunting even for experienced investors. In this situation, an advisor with fixed-income expertise could be a welcome partner.

- **Ongoing consultation**—If you would like more frequent advice but still want to maintain control of your accounts, you can work with a financial advisor who will keep an eye on your investments and meet with you on a regular basis. Your advisor would make recommendations, and you would make the final decisions. This way you'd always have someone to phone if the need arises.

- **Ongoing management**—If you want even more help, you can consider working with a registered investment advisor who will manage your account on your behalf (this is also known as a *discretionary* account). This type of arrangement is generally best suited for people with at least $250,000 in assets (different advisors may have different minimums). Although it is always smart to be involved in the decision making, you grant permission to your advisor to place trades and carry out your wishes.

NAVIGATING THE MAZE OF FINANCIAL ADVISORS

As you begin to look for a financial advisor, be careful. First, realize that *financial advisor* is a generic term and can include professionals with a wide variety of credentials, experience, and regulatory oversight. Before you select a financial firm or professional, make sure you understand exactly who and what you're paying for.

- A **broker** (or **registered representative**) is someone who works for a broker-dealer (such as Charles Schwab) who is registered to buy and sell securities on your behalf. Every broker must pass an exam, register with the Financial Industry Regulatory Authority (FINRA), and be licensed by the state in which they conduct business. A broker may also be called a *financial advisor,* a *financial consultant,* or an *investment consultant.*

- An **investment advisor** (also known as a **registered investment advisor** or **RIA**) is paid for providing advice, not for buying or selling securities. Unlike the generic term *financial advisor, investment advisor* is a legal term that identifies a professional who is registered with either the Securities and Exchange Commission or a state securities regulator. Registered investment advisors are held to a *fiduciary* standard, which is higher than a *suitability* standard, which means that they are required to act in the client's best interests at all times.

- A **financial planner** can provide a wide range of services, including creating a comprehensive, individualized financial plan. Although financial planners do not have separate regulation (they are registered in accordance with the other services they provide, such as investment advice), a Certified Financial Planner™ professional has completed extensive training, passed a rigorous test, and has ongoing continuing education requirements.

Take the Time to Find the Right Advisor

Whatever type of financial advice best suits you—and this may change over time—finding an advisor is a serious pursuit and you need to do your homework. You want someone you're comfortable with both professionally and personally; someone who will listen to your questions and provide clear, understandable answers; someone who truly has your interests at heart.

Here are some steps to help you:

- **Get referrals and make appointments.** Start with recommendations from friends, colleagues, or other financial professionals. This will give you insight into their experience with a particular advisor. Then make an appointment for a consultation. In addition to finding someone with the right kind of professional expertise, you want to make sure you and a potential advisor click personally. Most advisors are happy to give you a one-time consultation free of charge.

- **Prepare for the initial consultation.** Make a list of questions. You'll want to ask about background, experience, number of clients, assets managed, and types of services. I also suggest that you probe potential advisors about their investing philosophy. For example, do they prefer picking stocks or buying index funds? Do they think about tax efficiency? Do they have a special expertise in fixed income?

- **Ask about compensation.** Some advisors charge a *flat fee* for services; others charge an *asset-based fee*, a fee based on the size of your portfolio. The idea behind an asset-based fee is that the advisor is incentivized to grow your account. You'll also want to ask if the advisor receives any commission, reimbursement, or incentive for selling specific types of investments because that could present a conflict of interest.

- **Verify history, credentials, and experience.** Be sure to check on education and qualifications. Consider whether you're comfortable with a broker who primarily sells investment products or if you would prefer a professional whose primary business is giving advice. If you're talking to a registered investment advisor, ask to see Form ADV, which he or she is required to file with the SEC or with the state.

- **Get references.** Ask for a list of past and current clients—and don't hesitate to call them. This will give you a chance to ask about things like attentiveness and responsiveness as well as satisfaction with how their money is being managed.

QUESTIONS TO ASK A POTENTIAL ADVISOR

Ideally, your relationship with your advisor will be long-term. So whether you want day-to-day management or just occasional advice, it's important that the two of you have a good rapport. A financial advisor can be well worth the cost, both in terms of potential financial opportunity and your confidence in the future—as long as you take the time to find the advisor who's right for you. When you interview an advisor, be sure to ask:

- What's your educational background?
- How long have you been in business?
- How many clients do you have?
- How much money do you manage?
- What services do you offer?
- What is your guiding investing philosophy?
- Do you prefer specific types of investments?
- How are you compensated?
- Will I maintain control of my assets and where will they be held?
- How will we stay in touch?
- With whom will I be working?

No Matter What, Stay Involved

Whatever type of management help you choose, I can't emphasize enough how important it is to stay in touch with your money. Whether you decide on a solution like a target fund or full-time management, you'll receive periodic reports and updates on the progress of your portfolio. Don't just file them away—read them. At a minimum, you should be checking in with your accounts annually to review your investments and make sure you're still on target.

AT A GLANCE: INVESTMENT MANAGEMENT CHOICES

	Target Funds	Managed Accounts	Financial Advisor
Description	A type of mutual fund offering a professionally managed portfolio of stocks, bonds, and cash investments	An investment account owned by an individual investor looked after by a professional money manager	Can range from big-picture financial planning to periodic consultations to money management
Typical minimum investment	As low as $100	Upwards of $25,000	Depends on advisor and type of advice; often upwards of $250,000 for hands-on management
Type of management	Portfolio management to meet a specific goal or maintain a specific risk level	Individual management based on the account holder's goals and objectives	From full financial planning to periodic consultations, depending on type of advice wanted
Typical fees	Operating expense ratio, usually under 1%	Based on assets managed; usually starting at 1%	Flat fee or based on assets managed; usually starting at 1%

Next Steps

- Even if you choose some type of professional money management, it's good to have ideas on how you may want to invest. See **Question 5.**
- Whether or not you manage your own money, **Question 11** has some tips on how to get organized so you can more easily stay on top of all your finances.

Q7.

Is long-term care insurance worth the cost?

Long-term care insurance (LTCI) is a controversial topic. It's expensive, yes—but so is long-term care. And it's not just because we're living longer. The cost of care also depends a lot on where you live. For instance, according to a Genworth Financial survey in 2012, the average annual cost of a home health aide in Alabama was $36,608. In Minnesota that same care cost $57,772. When you get into nursing home care the differences are even more dramatic. A semiprivate room in a nursing home in Kansas averaged $54,750 a year, but in New York, that shot up to $118,625!

Because of these staggering costs, thinking about the cost of long-term care is an important part of your long-term financial planning. Without LTCI, your retirement savings could be in jeopardy. On the other hand, you may not need it. So before you can decide if LTCI is worth the cost, you have to take a look from both a personal and a financial perspective.

FACT: According to the National Bureau of Economic Research, in 2013 only 10 percent of the elderly had a private long-term care insurance plan.

Weigh the Odds You'll Need Long-Term Care

As I said at the beginning of this book, there's no way to know for sure whether you'll need long-term care. If you're generally healthy and you have good genes, you may be one of the lucky ones. But current statistics are sobering. According to the Department of Health and Human Services, about 70 percent of people over age 65 will require some type of long-term care during their lifetime.

Consider Your Options for Covering the Cost of Care

Many people don't realize that Medicare and other types of health insurance don't cover long-term care—what insurers call the "activities of daily living" such as bathing, dressing, eating, using the bathroom, and moving. For instance, Medicare will only pay for medically necessary *skilled* nursing and home care, such as giving shots and changing dressings, not assisted-living costs like bathing and eating. Social Security doesn't pay for any type of long-term care.

So if you need long-term care, how will you cover it? You could turn to your family—realizing, of course, that providing this type of ongoing hands-on care can be a huge task for anyone. You could decide to pay for it yourself if you have a lot of savings. Medicaid is an option for people with a low net worth. And then there's LTCI.

> ➲ **SMART MOVE:** If you have a Health Savings Account, you can use it to pay for long-term care. Yet another reason to amp up that account.

CAN YOU AFFORD LONG-TERM CARE?

The cost of long-term care can be staggering, and varies tremendously depending on where you live. A 2012 Cost of Care survey by Genworth Financial found that the median annual rate for a private nursing home room was $81,030. And the American Council of Life Insurers projects a 2.6-year stay in a nursing home will cost about $496,000 in thirty years!

THE COST OF CARE TODAY (NATIONAL MEDIAN RATES)

Licensed homemaker services	$18/hour
Licensed home health aide services	$19/hour
Adult day care	$61/day
Assisted-living facility (one bedroom, single occupancy)	$3,300/month
Nursing home (semiprivate room)	$200/day
Nursing home (private room)	$222/day

Source: 2012 *Cost of Care survey*, Genworth Financial

Be Sure to Comparison Shop

LTCI can cover a wide range of services, from home health care and nursing services to adult day care. But not all policies are equal, so it pays to comparison shop. Start by checking the quality of the insurer. This includes financial strength, rating, and length of time in business. Then review the terms of the policy. Be sure you understand:

- What's covered: skilled nursing, custodial care, assisted living?
- Specifically whether Alzheimer's disease is covered since this is a leading reason for needing long-term care
- Limitations on preexisting conditions
- Maximum payouts and whether payments are adjusted for inflation
- Lag time until benefits kick in
- How long benefits will last
- If there's a nonforfeiture benefit offering some coverage even if you cancel the policy
- Whether the current premiums are guaranteed in future years, or there are any constraints on future increases

- How many times rates have increased in the past ten years—this is especially important!
- If you buy a group policy through an employer, is it portable— meaning can you take it with you should you change jobs?

Determine the Best Time to Buy

LTCI can protect your retirement assets down the road, but you also need to consider the cost of premiums now—and in the future. Generally speaking, between ages 50 and 65 is the most cost-effective time to buy LTCI if you're in good health. According to the *2012 America's Health Insurance Plans: Guide to Long-Term Care Insurance,* the average annual premium for someone age 55–64 for a policy that covers about $150 per day for four to five years with a ninety-day deductible is $2,261. That premium goes up to over $4,123 for someone age 75.

As you can see, premiums tend to go up the older and less healthy you are; at some point you may become uninsurable if your health deteriorates too much. So, while it's not inexpensive, buying LTCI sooner rather than later may be a smart move.

COMMON MISTAKES WITH LONG-TERM CARE INSURANCE

- **Failing to comparison shop**—Prices can vary considerably company to company. Benefits vary, too. Look carefully!

- **Buying too soon**—At 40, premiums might be lower, but you'll be paying them for a much longer time. And there's no guarantee that the policy you buy today will be the right one for you 30 years from now. Between ages 50 and 65 tends to be the most cost-effective time to buy.

- **Not reading the fine print**—Every policy has exclusions. Make sure you understand what *isn't* covered by your policy as well as what is.

Next Steps

- Check out longtermcare.gov—a website developed by the U.S. Department of Health and Human Services (HHS). It's full of information and resources to help consumers plan for long-term care needs, including calculators on the cost of care in different states, how much to save, and more. Individual state websites may also provide valuable information. For example, the California Department of Health Care Services has extensive educational materials via its Partnership for Long-Term Care website.
- Make sure you don't pay for unnecessary insurance. See **Question 27.**
- Plan for out-of-pocket health-care costs during retirement. See **Question 37.**

Q8.

Does it make sense to borrow from my 401(k) if I need cash?

When cash is tight, your 401(k) can seem like a perfectly reasonable way to make life a little easier. The money is there and it's yours—so why not tap it to pay off debt or get out of some other financial jam? Or you might be tempted to use it to pay for that dream vacation you deserve to take.

Stop right there. The cash in your 401(k) may be calling you—but so is your financial future. The real question here: Will taking the money today jeopardize your financial security tomorrow?

I'm not saying a 401(k) loan is always a bad idea. Sometimes, it may be your best option for handling a current cash need or an emergency. Interest rates are generally low (1 or 2 percent above the prime rate) and paperwork is minimal. But a 401(k) loan is just that—a loan. And it needs to be paid back with interest. Yes, you're paying the interest to yourself, but you still have to come up with the money. What's worse is that you pay yourself back with after-tax dollars that will be taxed again when you eventually withdraw the money—that's double taxation!

If you're disciplined, responsible, and can manage to pay back a 401(k) loan on time, great—a loan is better than a withdrawal, which will be subject to taxes and most likely a 10 percent penalty. But if you're not—or if life somehow gets in the way of your ability to repay—it can be very costly. And don't think it can't happen. A 2012 study by Robert Litan and Hal Singer estimated defaults on 401(k) loans were up to $37 billion a year for 2008–2012 as a result of the recent recession. There's a lot to think about.

Find Out If Your Plan Allows Loans

Many 401(k) plans allow you to borrow against them, but not all. The first thing you need to do is contact your plan administrator to find out if a loan is possible. You should be able to get a copy of the Summary Plan Description, which will give you the details. Even if your plan does allow loans, there may be special conditions regarding loan limitations. While there are legal parameters for 401(k) loans, each plan is different and can actually be stricter than the general laws. So get the facts before you start mentally spending the money.

Understand the Limits on How Much You Can Borrow

Just because you have a large balance in your 401(k) and your plan allows loans doesn't mean you can borrow the whole amount. Loans from a 401(k) are limited to one-half the vested value of your account or a maximum of $50,000—whichever is less. If the vested amount is $10,000 or less, you can borrow up to the vested amount.

For the record, you're always 100 percent vested in the contributions you make to your 401(k) as well as any earnings on your contributions. That's your money. For a company match, that may not be the case. Even if your company puts the matching amount in your account each year, that money may vest over time, meaning that it may not be completely yours until you've worked for the company for a certain number of years.

Example: Let's say you've worked for a company for four years and contributed $10,000 a year to your 401(k). Each year, your company has matched 5% of your contribution for an additional $500 per year. Your 401(k) balance (excluding any earnings) would be $42,000. However, the company's vesting schedule states that after four years of service, you're only 60% vested. So your vested balance would be $41,200 (your $40,000 in contributions plus 60% of the $2,000 company match). This means you could borrow up to 50% of that balance, or $20,600.

Now let's say that after ten years of service, you're fully vested and your balance has grown to $120,000. The maximum you could borrow is $50,000.

The government sets these loan limits, but plans can set stricter limitations, and some may have lower loan maximums. Again, be sure to check your plan policy.

Factor in When—and How—You Have to Pay It Back

You're borrowing your own money, but you do have to pay it back on time. If you don't, the loan is considered a taxable distribution and you'll pay ordinary income taxes on it. If you're under 59½, you'll also be hit with a 10 percent penalty. Put that in real dollars: If you're 55, in the 25 percent tax bracket, and you default on a $20,000 loan, it could potentially cost you $5,000 in taxes and $2,000 in penalties. That's a pretty hefty price to pay for the use of your own money!

Before borrowing, figure out if you can comfortably pay back the loan. The maximum term of a 401(k) loan is five years unless you're borrowing to buy a home, in which case it can be longer. Some employers allow you to repay faster, with no prepayment penalty. In any case, the repayment schedule is usually determined by your plan. Often, payments—with interest—are automatically deducted from your paychecks. At the very least, you must make payments quarterly. So ask yourself: If you're short on cash now, where will you find the cash to repay the loan?

Think About What Would Happen If You Lost Your Job

This is really important. If you lose your job, or change jobs, you can't take your 401(k) loan with you. In most cases you have to pay back the loan at termination or within sixty days of leaving your job. (Once again, the exact timing depends on the provisions of your plan.) This is a big consideration. If you need the loan in the first place, how will you have the money to pay it back on short notice? And if you fail to pay back the loan within the specified time period, the outstanding balance will likely be considered a distribution, again subject to income taxes and penalties, as I discussed above. So while you may feel secure in your job right now, you'd be wise to at least factor this possibility into your decision to borrow.

> ⟫ **SMART MOVE:** To lessen the odds of having to take a 401(k) loan, try to keep cash available to cover three to six months of essential living expenses in case of an emergency. (When you're in retirement, you'll want to have funds on hand to cover a minimum of a year's expenses.)

Consider the Impact on Your Retirement Savings

Don't forget that a 401(k) loan may give you access to ready cash, but it's actually diminishing your retirement savings. First, you may have to sell stocks or bonds at an unfavorable price to free up the cash for the loan. In addition, you're losing the potential for tax-deferred growth of your savings.

Also think about whether you'll be able to contribute to your 401(k) while you are paying back the loan. A lot of people can't, possibly derailing their savings even more.

DO YOU QUALIFY FOR A HARDSHIP DISTRIBUTION?

If your plan allows it, you might qualify for a **hardship distribution**. But doing so isn't easy. First, you must prove what the IRS considers "immediate and heavy financial need." In general, the IRS defines this as:

- Medical expenses for you, your spouse, or dependents

- Costs directly related to the purchase of your principal residence (excluding mortgage payments)

- Postsecondary tuition and related educational fees, including room and board for you, your spouse, or dependents

- Payments necessary to prevent you from being foreclosed on or evicted from your principal residence

- Funeral expenses

- Certain expenses relating to the repair of damage to your principal residence

The amount of the distribution is limited to your own contributions to the plan and possibly your employer's contributions but doesn't include earnings or income on your savings. It can't be for more than the amount of the specific need—and you can't have other resources available to cover it. Plus, you'll have to pay both income taxes and a 10 percent penalty on the distribution.

Is There Any Way to Take an Early 401(k) Distribution Penalty-Free?

There are a few situations in which a penalty-free early distribution is allowed:

- You become disabled.
- You die and a payment is made to your beneficiary or estate.
- You pay for medical expenses exceeding 7.5 percent of your adjusted gross income.
- The distributions were required by a divorce decree or separation agreement ("qualified domestic relations order").

As you can see, the IRS doesn't make it easy to take your 401(k) money early under any circumstances!

AT A GLANCE : 401(k) LOANS

Pluses	Minuses
No application or credit check	Loss of potential tax-free growth
Quick approval and low fees	Potential for default if you lose your job, resulting in taxes and penalties
Comparatively low interest rates	Repayment through payroll deductions reduces take-home pay
Usually no prepayment penalty	The loan is paid back with after-tax dollars

BEHIND THE SCENES: MULTIPLE 401(k) LOANS

Some plans allow you to carry more than one loan at a time. However, the maximum loan limits still apply—the lesser of one-half of the vested value of your account or $50,000. It gets a bit tricky because the otherwise maximum permissible loan is reduced by the highest outstanding loan balance during the twelve-month period ending the day prior to when the current loan was due.

Example: Let's say you have $125,000 in vested benefits. You borrow $40,000 on January 1, 2014, and repay $25,000 on April 1. Then on December 1 of the same year, you want to take another loan. Even though you repaid part of your first loan, you would still be limited to a maximum second loan of $10,000 because your highest loan balance within the previous twelve months was $40,000 ($40,000 is subtracted from $50,000, or the maximum permissible loan amount). If you wait until April 2 of 2015, you'd be able to borrow $35,000 because your $25,000 payment would have been factored in and your highest loan balance in the prior twelve-month period would then be $15,000 ($15,000 subtracted from $50,000).

With multiple loans, it's not just a question of how often you can borrow but how much you can borrow at a given time.

Next Steps

- Keep your 401(k) growing. **Question 5** talks about ways to invest before you retire.
- Get a handle on debt before you retire. See **Question 13.**
- Think ahead. See **Question 14** for ideas on what to do with your 401(k) when you leave your job.

Q9.

My partner and I aren't married. What do we need to know about managing our finances as a team, especially when it comes to planning for retirement?

Planning and saving for your later years is a big challenge for everyone. But unmarried couples, whether of the same or opposite sex, are faced with a number of additional challenges. And with approximately seven million unmarried couple households in the United States in 2010, according to the Census Bureau, these issues need to be addressed by a significant percentage of our population.

On top of this, attitudes and laws are constantly changing. The Supreme Court ruling that struck down the Defense of Marriage Act paved the way for many same-sex couples to marry and claim the legal and financial benefits afforded heterosexual married couples. But many other committed same- and opposite-sex couples either can't or prefer not to marry—for a variety of reasons. For them, entering into a civil union or domestic partnership provides some benefits, but is recognized only on a state, county, or city level—not federal.

Of course taking care of oneself isn't just about what's legally recognized. Federal and state laws aside, when it comes to things like asset ownership and estate planning, there are things unmarried partners can do to protect themselves and each other. Regardless of your marital status, it's important to understand your choices and plan accordingly.

> ➲ **SMART MOVE:** Married or not, everyone should go through the steps in **Question 1** to decide if they're on track with their retirement savings.

Create a Domestic Partnership Agreement

When it comes to financial matters, there's nothing like having things in writing. A legally binding *domestic partnership agreement* (also known as a *cohabitation agreement*) can be the foundation of a financial relationship for new couples, much like a **prenuptial agreement**. But even couples who have been together for years can benefit by sitting down together to review their overall financial picture.

This is a chance to define (or redefine) roles and responsibilities, review and decide on shared and separate assets, and specify the distribution of assets should the relationship end. This is especially important in terms of spelling out ownership rights and percentages if you own a home or other significant property.

Some states will allow unmarried couples to officially register as domestic partners. But if your state doesn't, an agreement will help prevent painful financial misunderstandings, whether you're talking about daily finances or future planning. Also, even in states that don't officially recognize these relationships, many cities and counties within the states do.

WHAT DEFINES A DOMESTIC PARTNERSHIP?

There are several core elements that are generally accepted as the basis of a domestic partnership:

- The partners must have attained a minimum age, usually 18.

- Neither person is related by blood closer than permitted by state law for marriage.

- The partners must share a committed relationship.

- The relationship must be exclusive.

- The partners must be financially interdependent.

> **SMART MOVE:** Research current domestic partner laws in your home state, county, and city. Officially register as domestic partners if you can.

Know Which Retirement Benefits You Can Count On—and Which You Can't

The number one retirement rule applies to everyone: Save, save, and save some more. Each partner should contribute to an employer-sponsored retirement plan and/or an IRA if possible. (See **Questions 4** and **15** for more on types of retirement accounts.)

The tax-deferred growth of these plans is a plus individually. And there are a couple of ways that unmarried couples can get some tax savings as beneficiaries of each other's retirement plan:

- All qualifying retirement plans—including pensions, 401(k)s, stock ownership plans, profit-sharing plans, 403(b)s, and government 457(b) plans—allow a nonspouse beneficiary to roll over inherited retirement benefits paid in a lump sum to an IRA tax-free.
- A nonspouse beneficiary can choose to take required minimum distributions instead of a lump sum distribution. This allows for tax-deferred growth over a longer period of time.

Unfortunately, though, unmarried couples lose out on many valuable federal benefits and protections available to married couples. For example, Social Security provides spousal and survivor benefits only to married couples. Unmarried couples can pool their benefits while they're together, but neither partner can count on the other's benefits when one dies. In addition, military and veteran's benefits, favorable estate tax provisions, potential income tax advantages, and some employer-sponsored insurance and family benefits are available only to married couples.

Also, while you may have rights to certain benefits in your state, county, or city, some of these benefits may be subject to federal income tax.

CONTEMPLATING MARRIAGE? KNOW YOUR BENEFITS

Thinking of tying the knot? As you and your partner decide on whether you want to take this significant step, it's important to understand what marriage will mean for your finances. From owning property to retirement planning to estate planning to filing taxes, marriage changes things. There are literally more than a thousand financial benefits that come with marriage. In some cases a couple may get hit with a higher income tax bill (the infamous "marriage penalty"), but from a financial planning perspective, the positives far outweigh the negatives.

Thanks to the 2013 Supreme Court ruling, many same-sex couples also have this choice. The difference is that there are countless details that need to be resolved for same-sex marriages—especially where federal and state law intersect. For all of these reasons, I believe that all couples, but especially same-sex couples, need to take the time to familiarize themselves with these benefits and learn how to maximize their impact. Following are some of the highlights.

SOCIAL SECURITY BENEFITS

One of the most significant advantages of marriage is that **you will now be eligible for both spousal and survivor benefits from Social Security.** As a married couple, you will each be eligible to collect either a Social Security benefit based on your own work record, or up to 50 percent of your spouse's benefit, whichever is greater. And as I explain in **Question 30**, pages 255–

256, there are a number of strategies that can increase your combined benefit. In addition, as a widow or widower, each of you will be eligible to collect up to 100 percent of the other's benefit. And should you divorce, you may still be eligible for benefits as an ex-spouse.

> ➲ **SMART MOVE:** Married or not, take your time to determine when you should file for Social Security benefits! The financial implications can be huge.

FAVORABLE GIFT AND ESTATE TAX PROVISIONS

You will be able to take advantage of the unlimited estate tax marital deduction. A married person can leave an unlimited amount of money to a spouse without paying any estate tax. In addition, the surviving spouse can use any unused portion of the deceased spouse's lifetime estate tax exclusion upon his or her death. Under current law, this means that a married couple can pass on up to $10.5 million free of estate tax. See **Question 39,** page 309, for more on estate tax and the benefit of "portability."

> ➲ **SMART MOVE:** In light of potential estate tax savings, wealthy couples should revisit their life insurance needs.

Your gifts to each other won't be subject to gift tax. Married couples can transfer an unlimited amount of property to each other free of any reporting responsibilities or gift tax. In addition, you'll be able to use "gift splitting" when you both give to a third party. See **Question 41,** pages 321–322, for more.

> ☎ **TALK TO AN EXPERT:** As a married couple, you may want to create a life estate trust such as a QTIP trust. See **Question 42,** pages 329–330.

INCOME TAX IMPLICATIONS

You will be able to choose between filing a joint or separate income tax return. This doesn't mean that your combined tax bill will go down; in fact, you may see it go up—especially if you both earn a substantial and similar amount of money. It's probably best to run both scenarios to see which is best.

You won't have to pay tax on a spousal insurance benefit. When an unmarried person includes a partner on their health insurance plan, that benefit is taxable. For married couples, it is tax-free.

You will be able to defer distributions from an inherited IRA. If you inherit an IRA from your spouse, you can basically treat it as your own, and postpone taking required minimum distributions until the year you turn 70½. This can potentially allow your assets to continue to grow tax-deferred until they are withdrawn.

ERISA BENEFITS

If one of you participates in a qualified retirement plan through your employer, your spouse will be entitled to a number of benefits and protections. For example, your spouse is the automatic sole beneficiary of your retirement assets, and must consent in writing to waive this benefit. A spouse is also entitled to other benefits, including health-care coverage and family medical leave.

MILITARY AND VETERAN BENEFITS

As a military spouse, you may be eligible for a number of benefits, including health care and family separation pay. Spouses of deceased veterans are also entitled to health care, educational assistance, home loan guarantees, pensions, etc.

FEDERAL EMPLOYMENT BENEFITS

The federal government provides a broad array of benefits to the spouses of its more than 22 million employees, including health, retirement, and survivor benefits.

☎ **TALK TO AN EXPERT:** If marriage is on the horizon, consider meeting with an attorney as well as a financial planning expert. This is the ideal time to reevaluate your entire financial plan, including your investment accounts, income tax filing, insurance coverage, and estate plan. Depending on your situation, you may want to prepare a prenup. Any newly married couple can benefit from some advice as they join their finances.

Update Your Beneficiaries

One of the most important things unmarried couples can do is designate each other as beneficiaries on their retirement accounts. Update all beneficiary forms—employer plans, IRAs, annuities, life insurance—to make certain they reflect your wishes as an individual and as a couple.

> ⮕ **SMART MOVE:** Consider taking out a life insurance policy if your partner would be responsible for house payments or other major expenses.

Put Safeguards in Place

Also, no matter what state and federal laws allow, as an unmarried couple you can protect yourselves by putting certain safeguards in place:

- Each partner should make a **will** with specific instructions regarding the distribution of both financial assets and personal possessions. If you have young children, specify guardianship. You may also want to consider a living trust.
- Each partner should create a **durable power of attorney** so you can make financial decisions on each other's behalf should either of you become disabled.
- Likewise, each partner should create an **advance health-care directive**. This document specifies your preferences for end-of-life care and can grant each of you the right to make medical decisions for the other. Make sure that your directive is HIPAA-compliant to provide for hospital visits and access to each other's medical information. *Note:* This document goes by different names in different states; it may also be called a *living will* or an *advance medical directive.*

➡ **SMART MOVE:** If one of you has a large estate, that partner can make annual gifts of up to $14,000 (in 2013) tax-free to the other to pass on assets during your lifetimes. This amount will be periodically increased for inflation.

☎ **TALK TO AN EXPERT:** While it's possible to handle basic retirement and estate planning yourselves, if either of you has substantial assets, I'd suggest working with an attorney who specializes in domestic partnerships.

HOW YOUR HOME FITS INTO YOUR PLANS

While buying a home isn't necessarily about retirement planning, it can impact your mutual financial well-being. So while you're reviewing your finances, take a look at how you've titled your property to make sure it's fair to each of you—and reflects your wishes. For example, if one of you has sole title, the other could be left with nothing—and forced out of the house. Here are some scenarios to consider:

- If you want your partner to inherit your interest, probably the easiest solution is to own the home as joint tenants with right of survivorship. Or if you are registered as domestic partners and live in a community property state like California, you can own the home as community property with right of survivorship. Either way, your share of the house will pass to your partner outside of probate.

⚠ **CAUTION:** Unless both of your names are on the title to your primary residence, you will be able to exclude only $250,000 of the capital gain when you sell your home. If you jointly own the home, you will be able to exclude $500,000.

- If you want your interest to pass to someone else, you can own the home as tenants in common. As joint tenants with right of survivorship, you each own half the property and inherit the other half if one of you dies. But as tenants in common, you can each own any percentage of the property and sell or pass it on to whomever you wish.

- If you contribute unequally, and take title as tenants in common, be sure to keep careful track of each person's contributions to ongoing improvements and maintenance.

I highly recommend consulting an attorney to make sure you both understand the implications of your decisions.

Next Steps

- Talk to each other to make sure you share the same goals for this phase in your life.
- Make certain you have the right type of retirement accounts. See **Question 4.**
- Create or update your estate plans. **Question 38** covers the basics.
- Don't put off establishing an advance health-care directive. See **Question 38.**

Q10.

I want to contribute to a few charities. How can I make the most of what I have to give?

Philanthropy has always been a big part of my life. To me, it's important to give back, no matter the size of your budget. So I've given a lot of thought to the question of how an individual can have the greatest impact. And one thing has become very clear to me: Effective charitable giving isn't just about money. It's really about giving of yourself—your time, your expertise, even your thoughtful evaluation of which charities and organizations you want to support.

I like to think of charitable giving as part of your personal mission, or your vision of how you want to make a difference. It helps you focus more clearly not just on what you have to give, but also on where and how you want to give. Then, with your mission clearly defined, you can take a thoughtful approach to making the most of your donations, both in money and in time.

A little strategic thinking up front can make even a small gift go further—and make you feel even better about the effectiveness of the contribution you're making.

Start by Getting Involved

My first recommendation is to get involved. If there's a charity or organization that interests you, volunteer a few hours to get to know the people, what they do, and how effective their program is. With this first-hand experience, you'll be better able to decide if it's a group you want to contribute to financially.

And remember, while nonprofits depend on local generosity to fund their yearly budgets, most also depend on volunteers to accomplish their goals. Could you serve on a board of directors? Work at a local school? If you have a few hours a week to give, your time and expertise could be even more valuable than money—and will be an ongoing gift that may offer you a rewarding experience in return.

However, if your time is already stretched to the limit, or if you're unsure where to begin, here are a couple of ideas to help you focus on where and how much you want to give:

- **Look to your own interests or experiences**—Are you passionate about the arts? The environment? A particular segment of the population? Have you or someone you know been helped by a specific organization? Write down the top three areas or groups you'd like to support. Be clear on why you want to support them and how you'd like to support them. If you want to narrow—or expand—your list, that's fine. And it may very well change over time. The point is to be very certain about your choices.

⊃ SMART MOVE: If you're clear on what charities you want to support, when someone asks you to contribute to a different cause, you can honestly say you have other priorities. Rather than feel bad that you can't honor the request, you can feel good that you're supporting another cause that's meaningful to you.

- **Explore your community's needs**—From senior groups to art museums to homeless shelters, every community has programs and projects that need financial help. Where could your dollars make the greatest difference? You might decide to give a one-time gift or even set up an ongoing contribution that will continue to connect you to your own neighborhood or city.

Do More In-Depth Research

Even if you think you know a charity pretty well, it's always a good idea to dig a little deeper. How effective is the charity? Is it staying true to its purpose? Is the money being used wisely? Can it show measurable results?

A good place to get information is schwabcharitable.org, which has a number of resources all in one place. You can also consult an independent online rating service such as charitynavigator.org or charitywatch.org. You'll find helpful tips on how to research, evaluate, and compare charities.

RESEARCH A CHARITY AS IF IT WERE A POTENTIAL INVESTMENT

If you want your charitable donations to fulfill your personal philanthropic goals, a little due diligence up front will help ensure you get the results you want from the money you give. Approach each charity as if it were a potential investment. Here are some questions to ask a charity you're considering:

- What's the organization's mission?

- What has it accomplished over the last five years? What was the major accomplishment in the past year? How many individuals are served annually? What is the impact on their lives?

- Who are the directors and board members? Do you respect their credentials?

- Does the organization have a well-thought-out business plan?

- What percentage of each dollar donated goes toward program activities versus administrative overhead and fund-raising? For instance, CharityWatch recommends that an organization spend a minimum of 60 percent of funds—and ideally 75 percent or more—on charitable programs.

While there are no hard-and-fast guidelines for what makes a particular organization a good choice, you need to get answers that make you feel confident your contribution will lead to measurable results.

SMART MOVE: Once you've decided which charities you want to support and why, an easy way to give is to make a predetermined donation—a set dollar amount or a percentage of your income—every month or year.

Give Yourself a Tax Break

Giving is about helping others, but there's no harm in taking advantage of the associated tax breaks. (The IRS allows you to deduct up to 50 percent of your adjusted gross income [AGI] for most donations to qualifying public charities.) Here are some things to keep in mind that can help reduce your tax burden and may even allow you to give more:

- If you plan to deduct charitable contributions, you'll need to itemize deductions on your tax return.
- You need a receipt for donations of $250 or more to a single charity. You also need a receipt or a corroborating bank record for all cash donations no matter the amount.
- If you have appreciated stock (or bonds or mutual funds) that you've held for more than a year, consider donating that instead of cash. If you sell the stock first, you pay capital gains tax. But if you donate the stock to charity, there's no capital gains tax. Plus, the charity gets the full value of the stock—and you get to deduct the full value of your gift.
- Although volunteer hours worked for a charity aren't tax-deductible, you can deduct out-of-pocket expenses related to your volunteer work, such as for transportation.

➲ **SMART MOVE:** Many companies match their employees' donations to qualified nonprofit organizations. Don't miss this chance to supplement your giving!

HOW GIVING APPRECIATED STOCK CAN BE A WIN-WIN

When we think of giving, our first impulse is often to pull out the check-book. But cash may or may not be the most effective way to give. Although a cash donation is always well received, giving a gift of appreciated stock that you've held for a year or more is even better—not only for your tax situation, but for the charity's bottom line as well. Here's why.

Example: Let's say that several years ago you bought 100 shares of a stock at $10 a share and it's currently worth $50 a share. Now you want to make a gift to your alma mater. If you sell the stock first, you'll have a long-term capital gain of $4,000. Assuming you're in the 15 percent federal long-term capital gains tax bracket, that takes a $600 bite out of your donation (not including state income taxes, if applicable)—lowering the value of your gift (and your tax deduction) to $4,400. You and the charity both lose out.

However, if you were to give the appreciated stock directly to the university, the university would get the total $5,000 market value of the stock—and you could claim the total amount as a charitable contribution on your tax return. Plus, if your alma mater hangs on to the stock and it goes up in value, so much the better for the school.

However, as always, there are a few caveats to consider:

- Be sure you've held the appreciated stock for more than a year. Otherwise, it's considered a short-term holding and you'll be able to deduct only the purchase price, not the full market value.

- Make sure the charity or organization is approved by the IRS so you can get the tax deduction.

- Ask if the organization is set up to receive the stock. Your broker can help you with any necessary paperwork.

- If you're considering making a large donation, be aware that the IRS has limits on how much you can donate relative to your adjusted gross income.

⚠ **CAUTION:** If a stock has gone down in value, it's better to sell the stock first and then donate the proceeds. You can claim the loss on your tax return and still claim the full value of the gift as a charitable deduction. If you give the depreciated stock directly, you won't be able to claim the loss.

Be Aware of Deductibility Limits

You also need to realize that not every contribution is fully tax-deductible. The form of the contribution matters. IRS Publication 526 gives you all the details, but here are the essentials:

- **Cash**—Usually fully deductible up to 50 percent of your AGI.
- **Tangible personal property (used clothing and household items, even cars)**—Deductibility allowances depend on the usefulness of the item to the charity. For instance, the current reasonable value of old clothing or household goods donated to Goodwill is usually fully deductible because they relate directly to the charity (as long as the items are in good condition). Similarly, if you donate a painting to a museum, you can deduct the painting's full market value. But if an object doesn't relate directly to the charity (for example, if you donate a painting to a hospital), you may deduct only the amount you paid for it or its current reasonable value, whichever is less.

⚠ **CAUTION:** Donating a car can be especially tricky if your claim is for more than $500. IRS Publication 4303, "A Donor's Guide to Vehicle Donations," is a good source of information.

- **Ordinary income property**—Items from a trade or business, such as a painting that would normally be sold for income, are usually fully deductible. *Short-term stocks held for less than a year are included in this category. However, you can deduct only what you paid for the stock, not the market value.*

- **Appreciated long-term assets**—You can usually deduct the full market value of stocks, bonds, and mutual funds you've held for more than one year. An added plus is that you pay no capital gains taxes. *However, the deduction is limited to 30 percent of your AGI, rather than the 50 percent limit that applies to other contributions.*

➲ **SMART MOVE:** Make certain a charity is tax-*deductible*, meaning that you can deduct contributions on your federal income tax return. Some charities are only tax-*exempt*, which means that the organization doesn't have to pay taxes—not that you get a tax break.

AT A GLANCE: IS YOUR CONTRIBUTION TAX-DEDUCTIBLE?

To be tax-deductible, your contribution must be:	
To a qualified organization	An organization must be what the IRS has designated as a *qualified* organization for your contribution to be tax-deductible. Examples include churches, schools, hospitals, organizations like the American Red Cross and Boys & Girls Clubs of America, and private foundations.
In an accepted form	Accepted forms include cash; tangible personal property such as household items, clothes, and cars; ordinary income property used in a trade or business (including stocks held short-term); and long-term capital gain property such as appreciated stocks, bonds, or mutual funds. (See "Be Aware of Deductibility Limits.")
Without benefit to you	If you receive a benefit from your contribution, you can deduct only the amount that exceeds the benefit.

Properly documented	• For any cash contribution you need a receipt or corroborating bank record that includes the date, amount, and name of the charity.
	• Noncash contributions also require documentation:
	  • For a donation over $250, you need a receipt that shows the organization's name, date, and place of the contribution, and a description of what you gave.
	  • If your combined contributions for the year are over $500, you'll need to file Form 8283 with your taxes.
	  • Noncash contributions worth over $5,000 require a written appraisal.

☎ **TALK TO AN EXPERT:** If you go beyond the deductibility limit (up to 50 percent of your adjusted gross income depending on the type of contribution and the type of organization), there is a five-year carryover of any unused charitable deduction for a given year. This usually affects only large donors. Best to check with your tax professional.

A CHARITABLE GIFT ACCOUNT: ONE OF THE BEST-KEPT SECRETS FOR EASY, TAX-SMART GIVING

One of the best-kept secrets for making the most of your giving is a Charitable Gift Account (also known as a donor-advised fund), offered by many major financial institutions (including Schwab Charitable). In the interest of full disclosure, I serve as chairman of the board of Schwab Charitable—but my enthusiasm for Charitable Gift Accounts far precedes that role.

You can open a Charitable Gift Account with a tax-deductible contribution of as little as $5,000 and then use the funds to make grants to any public charity over the course of years. You can choose to make additional tax-deductible contributions to the fund—often as little as $100 at a time.

Here's a quick look at how it works:

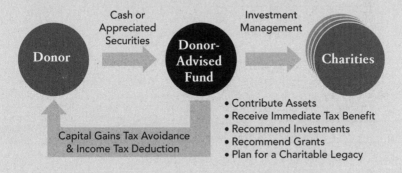

As you can see from the chart above, you can even open an account with appreciated stock. For instance, a friend of mine used a small amount of appreciated stock to initially fund her account with Schwab Charitable. After opening the account, all she had to do was a simple online transfer from her brokerage account to her Charitable Gift Account. She paid no capital gains taxes, and all the related reporting was taken care of for her. She could then focus on where to direct her donations.

One of the reasons I love donor-advised funds is that they provide average Americans all the convenience and support that otherwise is available only to major philanthropists. Not only do you get the immediate tax deduction, but the fund takes care of the bulk of the record keeping and maintains a complete history of your giving. Here's another great example from my friend. When she was asked if she was planning to make her annual donation to a certain charity, she was sure she'd already done it. But when she went online to look at her giving history, she saw that it had been a year since her last donation! She quickly made another donation with the click of her mouse.

That's another great benefit of a Charitable Gift Account. You can do almost everything online, including recommending grants of various sizes to a variety of recipients. Plus, you'll have the ability to invest your money, potentially increasing its value over time.

➲ SMART MOVE: Consider your charitable giving goals when you rebalance your portfolio. For instance, every year I work with my advisor to come up with a charitable giving budget. Then when we rebalance at the end of the year, we take that into consideration and often transfer appreciated stock to my Charitable Gift Account. It's an easy, tax-smart way to give.

Next Steps

- To make certain you're giving within your means, review your budget. See **Question 2** for tips on budgeting and managing cash flow.
- Get the facts on charities you're considering. Make use of online resources such as schwabcharitable.org, charitynavigator.org, and charitywatch.org.
- Consider making charitable giving part of your estate plan. **Question 43** discusses ways to do this.

Important Disclosures

Schwab Charitable is the name used for the combined programs and services of Schwab Charitable Fund, an independent nonprofit organization. The Fund has entered into service agreements with certain affiliates of the Charles Schwab Corporation.

Schwab Charitable accepts contributions of real estate, private equity, or other noncash assets via a charitable intermediary, with proceeds of your donation transferred to your donor-advised account upon liquidation. This intermediary considers donations on a case-by-case basis, and assets typically must be valued at $250,000 or more. Call the Fund for more information at 800-746-6216.

A donor's ability to claim itemized deductions is subject to a variety of limitations depending on the donor's specific tax situation.

Q11.

I'm drowning in financial paperwork. How can I get organized?

There's no doubt that the more your financial life becomes filled with things like owning a home, insurance policies, investment accounts, and retirement savings—not to mention income taxes—the more organized you need to be.

The beauty of today's electronic world is that you don't necessarily have to keep hard copies of every document. You can often access things like account statements and canceled checks from your financial institution's website. You can choose to scan and save your documents on a computer or in "the cloud." But whether you keep paper or electronic files, you still need to know what documents you have and where they are, not only for your own sense of security but also for the security of your loved ones should something happen to you. And that requires organization. Here's what I suggest to get started.

Put Your Paperwork into Categories

First, it helps to think of your financial life in terms of basic categories. For example, you likely have:

- Bank accounts—checking and savings account statements
- Debt—credit card statements, car loans, student loans, personal loans
- Home—lease and security deposit receipt if you rent; mortgage, title, or deed and final settlement statement if you own your home; home improvement receipts
- Car—sales receipt or lease, title, warranties, and repair records
- Taxes—Completed returns and receipts for charitable contributions, business, and other deductible expenses
- Insurance—health, auto, homeowner's/renter's, life, umbrella, and disability policies; sales receipts for insured big-ticket items
- Personal—birth certificate, marriage certificate, passport, pre-nup, divorce decree, health records, educational records, military service records
- Retirement—401(k) and IRA statements, pension agreement, Social Security statements
- Investments—statements for taxable brokerage accounts, trade confirms, children's accounts
- Wills and trusts—a current copy of your will, trust(s), durable powers of attorney for finances, advance health-care directive

Once you have the categories, it's easier to create a filing system to match.

➲ **SMART MOVE:** Be sure to keep all of your home improvement receipts. Substantiated capital improvements (not repairs or maintenance) will increase your cost basis when you go to sell your house. See **Question 18** for more on taxes when you sell your house.

Decide What to Keep and What to Toss

Now look at what's essential to keep and for how long—and what you can safely get rid of. Personal documents should be kept pretty much forever. Keep insurance policies as long as they're active. The IRS suggests that you keep your tax returns for seven years. Also, keep satisfied loan documents for seven years. It's wise to keep records involving the purchase, sale, improvements, and taxes on your home for at least three years after you sell the property. These are all important papers to store in an easily accessible, physical location.

A lot of folks fill their file cabinets with everyday bills, credit card receipts, and monthly bank, credit card, and investment account statements—much of which can be gotten rid of sooner or accessed online. For instance, you can toss your utility bills at the end of the year, unless you're using them as a tax deduction for a home office. You need to keep monthly bank and credit card statements only until you get your annual statements. The same goes for quarterly investment statements. And there's no need to hold on to sales receipts once your check has cleared or a sale shows up on your statement, unless there's a tax purpose.

AT A GLANCE: DOCUMENT STORAGE

What to Keep	How Long to Keep It
Bank statements	1 year, unless needed for tax information
Birth certificates, marriage licenses, divorce papers, passports, education records, military service records	Forever
Contracts	Until updated
Credit card records	Until paid, unless needed for tax information
Home purchase and improvement records	At least 3 years after you sell the property
Life insurance policies	Forever
Car and homeowner insurance policies	Until you renew the policy
Investment statements	Keep monthly or quarterly statements until you get your annual statement; keep annual statements until you sell the investment
Loan documents	Keep satisfied loan documents for 7 years
Real estate deeds	As long as you own the property

What to Keep	How Long to Keep It
Sales receipts	Until check has cleared or credit card statement arrives, unless needed for tax information or return
Service contracts and warranties	As long as you own the item
Social Security card	Forever
Social Security statement	Until you receive a new one
Tax records	7 years from the filing date
Utility bills	1 year; 3 years if used as tax document for home office
Vehicle titles	As long as you own the car
Will	Until updated

➲ SMART MOVE: To help protect against identity theft, be sure to shred any document that contains a Social Security number, account number, or other financial information before tossing it.

Create a Home File for Everyday Management

Once you've gotten rid of the paperwork you no longer need, put the documents and information you use more regularly in an active file in your home. This file might contain bank statements, credit card information, bill payment receipts, bills that need to be paid, tax receipts, warranties, appliance manuals, loan information, health-care information—anything that you may need to refer to on a regular basis. And don't forget to include a list of your passwords!

➲ SMART MOVE: When you have a filing system in place, make sure everyone in the family knows where the important papers are. Consider appointing one family member to keep the files up-to-date.

Put Important Dates on Your Calendar

Once your paperwork is organized, do the same for your calendar. Late fees and penalties are just money down the drain. You'll be wise to mark all important financial dates on your calendar. For example, include:

- Due dates for estimated taxes, both federal and state
- Due dates for property taxes
- Date for your required minimum distributions (see **Question 23, page 200,** for more on RMDs)
- If you've sold stocks, a reminder to do your annual tax-loss harvesting (see **Question 25,** pages 220–221, for more)
- A reminder to make your charitable contributions

Put Special Docs in a Safe Place

Certain documents need added security. Consider keeping your birth certificate, marriage certificate, prenup, Social Security card, passport, and automobile titles in a safe-deposit box at your bank. You might want to keep current insurance policies there as well. If you'd rather keep your documents at home, purchase a fireproof/waterproof safe.

> **SMART MOVE:** Make copies of your most important papers and put them in a safe, easily portable "emergency kit." You never know when you'll have to grab them and go!

PLACES TO STORE YOUR IMPORTANT PAPERS

There's no one perfect storage system for your documents. Your system depends largely on what's most comfortable for you. But today, there are a few more choices to consider.

- **Hard copies:** This is the tried-and-true method. And a lot of people feel most comfortable keeping hard copies of all their documents. However, even the IRS now accepts electronic documents, so if you're tired of sorting stacks of paper, you might look into electronic options, at least for certain financial papers.

- **On your own computer:** Scanning and organizing your important papers takes time, but once it's done, you have a simple storage system. You can keep your documents on your home computer, an external hard drive, a flash drive, or a combination of these choices. Nothing is foolproof, so always make sure you have a backup system. An easily portable electronic filing system can be a good emergency backup even if you keep hard copies.

- **On a Web-based storage service:** There are a number of companies that now offer online storage services on external servers. Some are free; some charge a small monthly fee. Privacy and security are concerns with this type of storage, so be sure to check out any online storage service carefully before entrusting it with your important documents. Also, choose a company that you believe will be around for a long time; otherwise your data could go the way of the company.

Make a List of Locations and Contacts

Once you have your paperwork organized, make a master list of all of your accounts, policies, and important documents, and indicate where everything is located. This should include your credit cards, bank accounts, investment accounts, insurance companies, safe-deposit box information, wills, and trust documents.

Then make a separate list of whom to contact in case of emergency: family members, employers, financial advisors, insurance agent, attorney, accountant, and banker. Keep these lists in a secure place and make sure the appropriate individuals know how to access them.

⊃ **SMART MOVE:** Keep your location and contact lists easily accessible— not in a safe-deposit box. Consider keeping one at home and perhaps a copy with another responsible family member.

SIMPLIFY WHERE YOU CAN

Once you've gotten a handle on your financial paperwork, simplify your finances. Here are some ways to make staying on top of things even easier:

- Use direct deposit wherever possible—for your pay, pension, and Social Security benefits

- Have one primary bank account and only one or two credit cards

- Set up automatic payments for recurring bills

- Consolidate brokerage accounts

- Use online banking tools

- Set up automatic deposits to your savings and retirement accounts

Next Steps

- Make sure your estate planning papers are in good shape. **Question 38** reviews basic estate planning documents.
- Reviewing your insurance documents? See **Question 27** for insights on the type of insurance you need at this point in your life.
- Interested in creating a turnkey system for your spouse? See **Question 29.**

PART II

Getting Closer: Transitioning into Retirement

We baby boomers are known for our independence. We have a strong and proud history of reinventing ourselves and our lifestyles. And of course the way we choose to live our lives in "retirement" is no different. Many of us continue to work at least part-time—or intermittently. Those of us who are healthy and financially secure will continue to challenge ourselves and lead fulfilling lives, whether that involves working or not.

So how do we get to that point? As dry as it may sound, much of financial security is based on preparation. We all know people who had outsized paychecks for decades—and lifestyles to match. Generally, though, it's the men and women who save and plan who get to reap the benefits later in life.

As you get closer to retirement, you'll need to take your planning to a new level. Do you know where and how you want to live, and how much that will cost? You've been saving, but do you need to ratchet it up? What about your debt? Or insurance? This section addresses these and other issues that you'll face in the two to three years leading up to retirement.

It's also not too early to start thinking about Social Security and Medicare, which are covered in Part IV. Estate planning is covered in Part V.

If you've never worked with a financial advisor, now could be the ideal time to forge that relationship. He or she can work with you as you shape your future and prepare your finances for what hopefully will be the best time of your life.

Q12.

Can I keep contributing to my retirement accounts indefinitely?

The age and income requirements for contributing to a retirement account are pretty straightforward. But you also have to think about what makes sense for your circumstances. Let's take a look at the rules first, and then take a closer look at your choices.

See If You Meet the Income and Age Requirements for Contributing to Tax-Advantaged Accounts

First the rules, which vary by account. **Question 4** goes into more detail on account details, but I'll give you the top line here.

- **IRAs**—To contribute to either a traditional or a Roth IRA, you must have earned income. For instance, if you're no longer working and have only investment income, you can't contribute to an IRA. (There is an exception for a nonworking spouse as long as the working spouse has earned income equal to any contributions for both.) If you do have earned income, the yearly maximum you can contribute to either type of IRA is $5,500—plus an additional $1,000 catch-up contribution if you're 50 or over.

There are income ceilings for being able to contribute to a Roth IRA. For 2013, a single person can't earn more than $127,000, and the amount you can contribute is gradually reduced starting at $112,000. Married people can't earn more than $188,000 to be eligible, and the allowed contribution is reduced starting at $178,000.

While there's no age limit for contributing to a Roth IRA as long as you have earned income, with a traditional IRA you can't make contributions past age 70½ even if you continue to work. In fact, you're required to take minimum distributions (RMDs) from your traditional IRA beginning the year after you turn 70½. See **Question 23** for more on RMDs.

⚠ **CAUTION:** Before contributing to a traditional IRA, make sure your contribution is tax-deductible. See **Behind the Scenes** on page 42 for how income and participation in an employer-sponsored plan affect tax deductibility. If it isn't deductible, you will likely be better off putting that money into a taxable account.

- **Employer-sponsored plans**—As long as you're working and your employer offers a plan such as a 401(k) or 403(b), you're eligible to contribute to it. The amount you can contribute depends on your income and the specifics of your company's plan, but theoretically, you could sock away up to $23,000 each year in your 401(k). For 2013, workers of any age can contribute up to $17,500. Those 50 and over can contribute an additional $5,500 as a catch-up contribution. And there's no RMD as long as you're still employed.

⧗ **DEADLINE:** The IRS gives you the choice of taking your first RMD either by the end of the year you turn 70½ or by April 1 of the year following. (If you delay to year two, you'll have to take two withdrawals that year.) Don't be late. The penalty for failure to take your RMD on time is *50 percent* of the amount that should have been withdrawn— and you'll still owe taxes on it. Be sure to see the details in **Question 23**.

Think About Taxes as You Decide Where to Put Your Savings

It's satisfying to reduce your current tax bill by contributing to a 401(k) or traditional IRA, but that doesn't always make the most sense from a long-term perspective. So before you automatically continue to direct your savings to a tax-deferred account, take a step back.

In **Question 5** I talk about the importance of tax diversification. Your opportunity to spread your assets among accounts with different tax rules is clearly greater when you're younger and have more years to save. However, as you continue to put money aside in your fifties, sixties, and even later, you still have the opportunity to maximize your after-tax returns by spreading your savings between tax-deferred, tax-free, and taxable accounts.

As you decide how to divvy up your savings, consider the following:

1. **Always start with your company plan.** Whether that's a 401(k), a Roth 401(k), or a 403(b), never walk away from your employer match. Always contribute enough to your company plan to capture the maximum match.

2. **Make sure you have enough cash.** If retirement is only two or three years away, start to build up your liquid reserves to cover a minimum of one year of expenses.

3. **Cover your bases, tax-wise.** In general, if you believe that your income tax rate will be **lower** once you're retired, you should direct your savings to tax-deferred accounts like a traditional 401(k) or a traditional IRA. If you believe that your income tax rate will be **higher** once you're retired, you should direct your savings to a Roth 401(k), or a Roth IRA, if you qualify. But since your own future circumstances and the future of taxes are, to a certain extent, unknowable, it's smart to have your money in a variety of accounts with different tax consequences. That will give you the most flexibility in the future.

4.   **Save more.** Once you've maxed out your retirement accounts, invest your additional savings in a taxable account.

➲ **SMART MOVE:** If you divide your savings between a tax-advantaged retirement account and a taxable account, it's also a good idea to divide your investments between them in a way that maximizes the tax benefits. See **Question 5,** page 69, for the best type of investments for each type of account.

MANAGING YOUR CASH FLOW

Once you're retired, it pays to think carefully about the best time to tap each of your accounts. In general, it may make more sense to withdraw money from your taxable accounts first and pay the lower capital gains taxes rather than pay ordinary income taxes on IRA withdrawals. (See **Question 23** for more on which accounts to draw on first.)

But a lot depends on your cash needs and your tax bracket. Talk to your tax advisor before making any decisions. It will be worth the effort to help ensure you have retirement income that's both tax-smart and secure.

Next Steps

- Review your current savings plan to see if you're on track to meet your goals. **Question 1** has guidelines to help you.
- For more detail on the ins and outs of retirement accounts, see **Question 4.**
- Make sure your savings are working for you. **Question 5** looks at ways to invest before retirement.
- Go to **Question 14** for ideas on what to do with your 401(k) when you leave your job.
- Consider whether converting your traditional IRA to a Roth makes sense for you. **Question 23,** pages 205–206, helps you weigh the pros and cons.

Q13.

Should I be debt-
free before I retire?

There's no doubt that not having any debt can give you a certain sense of freedom. When you don't owe anything to anybody, the money you have is yours to do with as you wish—a great retirement dream scenario. But as we all know from experience, reality can be a bit different.

In an ideal world, none of us would have any debt—ever. And we'd certainly pay off our mortgages, credit cards, and car loans before we retire. But that's not always possible. And sometimes, it's not even the best thing to do. As I discussed a bit in **My Top Ten Recommendations** on page 3, debt isn't necessarily negative. In fact, in the financial world there's a common distinction made between "good debt" and "bad debt." But you have to know the difference. And to keep debt from ruining your plans, you also have to figure out how much debt you can comfortably handle on your retirement income. Here are some ways to go about it.

Put Your Debt in Perspective

Debt that creates opportunities can actually work for you. If it's also low cost and has tax advantages, so much the better. For instance, with mortgages or home equity lines of credit, you're borrowing to own a potentially appreciating asset. On top of that, home loans may be tax-deductible. So they fall into the category of good debt.

On the other hand, there's nothing positive about debt that's high cost, isn't tax-deductible, and is taken to buy an asset that will likely depreciate. Things like credit card debt and car loans fall into the "bad debt" category. The image of taking on high monthly payments for a new car that decreases in value the minute you drive it off the lot is probably one of the clearest examples of debt that works against you.

What should you do? If the ideal scenario of being debt-free is out of reach, your practical goal should be to pay down any bad debt while keeping the good debt working for you.

> **⊙ FACT:** The average debt held by families headed by individuals 55 and older stood at $75,082 in 2010, up more than $1,300 from 2007, according to Federal Reserve data crunched by the Employee Benefit Research Institute.

HOW MUCH DEBT CAN YOU AFFORD? THE 28/36 RULE

- **28%**—An industry rule of thumb suggests that no more than 28 percent of your pretax household income should go to servicing home debt (principal, interest, taxes, and insurance).

- **36%**—No more than 36 percent of your pretax income should go to all debt: your home debt plus credit card debt and auto loans.

As you look ahead, I think you should be even more conservative. While these percentages may be manageable when you're working, I suggest keeping debt much lower in retirement.

Safe Debt Guidelines

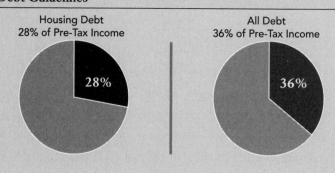

Housing Debt	All Debt
28% of Pre-Tax Income	36% of Pre-Tax Income
28%	36%

Prioritize Your Payments

Don't try to tackle all your debt at once. You'll likely just become frustrated and discouraged. Instead, prioritize.

If you have credit card debt, that's your first priority. Make a list of your credit cards and balances, from the highest-interest card to the lowest. Focus on highest-interest debt first, increasing the payment if you can, while continuing to at least make minimum payments on the rest. Work your way down until everything is paid off. And give yourself a pat on the back as you eliminate one debt after another.

Another way to approach multiple credit card debts is to consolidate them on a low-interest card and pay the maximum that you can afford each month. But be very wary of loan consolidation offers. While some are legitimate, others have up-front fees and hidden costs.

BEHIND THE SCENES: WHAT CREDIT CARD DEBT REALLY COSTS YOU

When you want that new top-of-the-line flat-screen TV, it's easy to whip out the plastic and figure you'll pay if off over time. But when you stop to calculate what that single purchase can cost you if you don't pay it off right away, the numbers could make you think again before you buy. Here are three eye-opening scenarios:

COST OF TV: $5,000; INTEREST RATE: 14%

- Make the **minimum payment** each month (usually interest plus 1%) and it will take you **264 months** (22 years!) to pay it off. During that time you'll pay **$5,333.30 in interest,** more than doubling the original cost of the TV.

- Make a fixed monthly payment of **$200** and it will take you **30 months** to pay if off with **$946.23 in interest.**

- Up your monthly payment to **$500** and you'll have your TV paid off in **11 months** and pay only **$348.12 in interest.**

Of course the best scenario of all is to pay cash to avoid any interest charges. The numbers speak for themselves!

⚠ **CAUTION:** Once you've finally paid off your credit card debt, keep your guard up! It's way too easy to fall back into bad habits and run up your balances again.

DON'T LET DEBT PAYMENTS DERAIL YOUR SAVINGS

Paying down debt and saving for retirement doesn't have to be an either/or proposition. The two can work together. Once again, you have to prioritize. Here's what I recommend:

1. Save enough in your retirement accounts to capture the entire employer match.
2. Pay off high-interest consumer debt.
3. Create an emergency fund to cover necessary expenses for a minimum of three to six months.
4. Save more for retirement.

After that, prioritize other savings and debt reduction goals according to your own situation.

And Finally, Assess Your Mortgage

For most of us, our mortgage is probably our largest debt. And eliminating your monthly mortgage payment before you retire is a worthy goal. But deciding whether to pay off your mortgage is more difficult because there can be a psychological as well as a financial aspect to your decision.

The financial side is pretty straightforward. First, what's the interest rate? Is it adjustable or fixed? Next, factor in tax deductibility.

Example: Let's say that you have a 5% fixed loan and your combined federal/state income tax bracket is 30%. Assuming your mortgage interest is fully tax-deductible, your mortgage is really costing you only 3.5%. On the one hand, paying it off is equivalent to a risk-free 3.5% return on an investment. If you're happy with that return, pay off the mortgage. If you think that you can earn more from another investment, then it probably makes sense to keep it.

Note: As you reach the end of your mortgage term, you're paying less interest and more principal. Only the interest portion is tax-deductible.

➲ **SMART MOVE:** If you have a high interest rate mortgage or an adjustable mortgage, think about refinancing to a lower, fixed rate. You might also consider a shorter term (say fifteen years), which will carry a lower interest rate.

On the psychological side, you need to weigh the value of having more money in the bank (or in your portfolio) versus being mortgage-free. Only you know which will ultimately give you more peace of mind. It could also be a matter of proportion. For example, if you have a $250,000 portfolio and a $100,000 mortgage, it's probably not prudent to deplete your assets by 40 percent to pay it off. But if you have $1 million in assets, paying off a $100,000 mortgage is more reasonable.

Finally, you can always decide to split the difference—pay off half your mortgage and refinance the rest. It all depends on what you can handle on your retirement income and what makes you feel the most secure.

➲ **SMART MOVE:** One way to pay down your mortgage more quickly is to make additional annual payments. Even one extra payment a year can cut significant dollars off your debt and time off your mortgage.

WHEN DOES IT MAKE SENSE TO PREPAY YOUR MORTGAGE?

If you have the money to prepay your mortgage in a lump sum, consider these points before writing that big check:

- **After-tax opportunity cost.** Consider the after-tax cost of money. As I mentioned in the example, a 5% mortgage loan actually costs you only 3.5% on an after-tax basis if you have a combined marginal income tax bracket of 30% (assuming full deductibility). Can you do as well or better with an alternative use of your money—risk-free?

- **Liquidity preference.** If you have a low-rate mortgage, you might prefer to keep this money liquid. It might also be a question of keeping your money diversified.

- **Income tax considerations.** Remember, you can deduct the interest on mortgage debt of up to $1.1 million (in 2013) on your primary and/or secondary residence for purchase or capital improvement. Once you've paid off the original mortgage, you'll be limited to the $100,000 home equity debt ceiling unless you make capital improvements or buy another home.

- **Psychological considerations.** Does your desire to be debt-free trump these other considerations? If so, put your peace of mind first and make the big payment.

SMART MOVE: If you own your home and don't already have a home equity line of credit (HELOC), consider opening one now. You're much less likely to qualify when you don't have a regular income, and it can be a great backup in case of an emergency. Plus, you can deduct the interest on up to $100,000 of home equity debt used for any purpose. So it could also be a tax-deductible way to consolidate your higher interest loans.

Next Steps

- If you're thinking about borrowing money from your 401(k) to pay off debt, don't miss **Question 8.**
- Retiring early and need to cut expenses? **Question 24** has some practical tips.

Q14.

What should I do with my 401(k) when I leave my job?

Sometimes getting ready to retire can seem like a lot of work. It's not as easy as just clearing your desk and walking out the door. Especially if you have a 401(k), you've got some planning to do and some choices to make. But look on the bright side: The more effort you make now, the more you can relax later on.

It's wise to think about it ahead of time because your choice will impact not only the potential continued growth of your retirement savings but also your income taxes. To me, that makes it worth the effort.

Review Your Basic Choices

Generally, there are four things you can do with a 401(k) when you leave your job. One in particular—rolling it over to a new employer—doesn't apply if you're planning to retire. But the other three merit consideration.

Basically, when you retire you can:

- **Take the cash**—At age 59½ there's no penalty for taking a lump sum payment from your 401(k)—but there are tax consequences.

Withdrawals from a 401(k) are taxed as ordinary income, so this could be a big initial hit. The IRS withholds 20 percent right off the top (this is mandatory), and any remaining taxes will be factored in when you prepare your return for the year in which you take the distribution. On the plus side, you'll have immediate access to your money. On the minus side, your savings can no longer grow tax-deferred. There is a sixty-day window in which you can still choose to move your money into a tax-deferred IRA, but after that time your only choice is to put it in a taxable account.

- **Keep your 401(k) with your former employer**—This is probably the easiest and does have some benefits. You avoid income taxes and the mandatory 20 percent withholding; your money can continue to grow tax-deferred; and you maintain the option of rolling it over should you ever decide to go back to work. The main potential drawback is that your investment choices are limited to what's available in the plan. If you have fifteen or so funds to choose from, that could be just fine. But if you're limited to three or four investment selections, you might be better off moving your money elsewhere. There also may be limitations on transactions, so get the details from your employer's plan administrator. And finally, another consideration is tracking. It will be easier to integrate this money into your planning for the rest of your portfolio if you house it at the same financial institution.

- **Roll it over to an IRA**—Like a 401(k), an IRA allows your money to keep growing tax-deferred. It also gives you greater flexibility to choose the types of investments that you deem best. Plus, you can invest and access your money whenever you want (withdrawals before age 59½ may be subject to tax penalties, however). Those are significant advantages. However, there are potential drawbacks, too. For example, a qualified employer plan, such as a 401(k), may have more legal protection from creditors than an IRA. And institutional share classes, generally available only in qualified plans, may have lower expenses than the same or similar funds purchased in an IRA. Also, an IRA generally requires you to wait until age 59½ before you can take penalty-free distributions. With a 401(k) you may be able to take penalty-free distributions at age 55 if you lose your job.

AT A GLANCE: 401(k) CHOICES WHEN YOU RETIRE

	Take the Cash	Keep with Former Employer	Roll Over to an IRA
Advantages	Immediate access to your money	Easy No taxes or penalties Savings keep tax-deferred status Option of rolling it over if you go back to work	Money can continue to grow tax-deferred More investment choices Easy access to your money No taxes or penalties for a direct rollover
Disadvantages	Taxed as ordinary income Mandatory 20% withholding 10% penalty if you're under age 59½ Savings no longer grow tax-deferred	Limited investment choices Possible limits on transactions	Less legal protection from creditors than a 401(k) Potentially higher investment expenses Generally cannot take penalty-free distributions at age 55 if you lose your job

LET YOUR BROKER OR BANK HANDLE YOUR ROLLOVER

If you decide to roll over your 401(k) to an IRA, it's a good idea to let your broker or bank handle the details. A financial institution can work with your employer's plan administrator to do a direct rollover, saving you unnecessary hassle, and ensuring you don't get hit with a big tax bill.

If you do the rollover yourself, meaning you personally take a lump sum from your employer and then put it into an IRA, you end up with a potential tax burden. That's because your employer would be required to withhold 20 percent in taxes when making a distribution directly to you.

Example: Let's say you have $250,000 in your 401(k), and plan to roll it over yourself into an IRA. Your employer would be required to withhold 20%, or $50,000. So you'd get a lump sum distribution of $200,000. In order to make this a completely tax-free transaction, you'd have to put that $200,000 *plus* an additional $50,000 from some other source into an IRA within sixty days. On your next tax return, you could then file for the $50,000 that was withheld. But if you put only the $200,000 you received into your IRA, you'd have paid $50,000 in taxes just to roll over your money.

However, if you do a direct rollover from your employer to your financial institution, there'd be no withholding. You just fill out some paperwork and your financial institution will do the rest. You'll have the full $250,000 working for you until you decide to make withdrawals at some later date.

⏳ **DEADLINE: 60 DAYS**—The amount of time you have to put a lump sum distribution from your 401(k) into another tax-advantaged account to avoid paying income taxes on the total.

Decide Between a Roth and a Traditional IRA

You can roll over a 401(k) directly into either a Roth IRA or a traditional IRA. There are no income limitations on a rollover, so the main consideration is whether you want to pay income taxes on the money now—or later.

- **Roth IRA—taxes now:** Contributions to a 401(k) are made with pretax dollars, meaning you didn't pay income taxes on the money. The taxes are "deferred" until you take withdrawals, at which time you pay ordinary income taxes on whatever you withdraw. When you roll over a 401(k) to a Roth IRA, you have to pay those income taxes *up front*. That's because withdrawals from a Roth are income-tax-free—and Uncle Sam is not about to let you get away without paying taxes indefinitely. A rollover to a Roth can mean a big tax bite now.

- **Traditional IRA—taxes later:** A traditional IRA works just like your 401(k)—taxes are deferred until you make a withdrawal. So if you roll over to a traditional IRA, it won't cost you anything now, but you'll pay ordinary income taxes on your money later, when you withdraw it.

Either way, you end up paying taxes at some point. The question is, will you be in a higher or lower tax bracket when it comes time to make withdrawals? If you think you'll be in the same or a higher tax bracket, rolling over to a Roth could make sense, as long as you have the cash available to pay the income taxes now.

However, if you think you'll be in a lower tax bracket when you make withdrawals, a traditional IRA would be a better choice. You'll pay nothing now, and possibly less in taxes later.

⬭ **SMART MOVE:** Thinking about passing on your IRA to your heirs? That could factor into your decision between a traditional or Roth IRA. When someone inherits a traditional IRA, they're responsible for the income taxes. With a Roth IRA, the inheritance is tax-free.

Consider What to Do with Company Stock

If you have company stock in your 401(k), you have another decision. You can roll it over to an IRA with the rest of your 401(k), in which case all of your eventual withdrawals will be subject to taxation at your ordinary rate. But if the stock has appreciated since you acquired it, you have another choice that could not only save you money on taxes but also be a boon to your heirs. See **Behind the Scenes** on pages 138–140 for details.

☎ **TALK TO AN EXPERT:** If you're expecting a distribution of company stock from a 401(k) or other retirement plan, talk to your tax or financial advisor about your options.

BEHIND THE SCENES: NET UNREALIZED APPRECIATION

Instead of rolling company stock into an IRA, you can transfer it into a taxable account to take advantage of what's known as **net unrealized appreciation (NUA)**. Using this strategy, you pay ordinary income taxes only on the **cost basis** of the stock (its value at the time you received it) at the time of transfer. Appreciation beyond the cost basis (the NUA) isn't taxed until you sell the securities. Plus, the NUA will be taxed at the long-term capital gains rate. If you wait to sell, additional appreciation (after the distribution) will be taxed at either the short- or the long-term capital gains rate, depending on your holding period.

Example: You have $100,000 in company stock in your 401(k) when you decide to retire. Your cost basis is $40,000, and you're in the 25% tax bracket. You have two choices. You can either:

1. Roll the stock into an IRA and pay ordinary income taxes on the entire value when you eventually withdraw it ($25,000).

2. Transfer that stock into a taxable account and pay $10,000 in ordinary income taxes on the cost basis of $40,000 at the time of the transfer.
   - If you sell your stock right away, you'll pay a long-term capital gains rate of 15% (or 20%, depending on your income) on the $60,000 of NUA, which would be another $9,000. Total tax bill? $19,000. You've saved $6,000 in taxes.
   - If you decide not to sell right away, you pay the initial $10,000 in taxes when the stock is distributed. Later, when you sell, you pay taxes on the NUA at the long-term capital gains rate plus either short- or long-term capital gains taxes on any additional appreciation. So, for example, if you hold the stock for an additional two years and the stock grows to $150,000 at the time of sale, you will pay long-term capital gains on both the NUA and the additional $50,000 of appreciation.

Tax payable at distribution	Cost basis—$40,000	Taxed at ordinary income rates
	NUA—$60,000	Tax-deferred until sale of stock
Tax payable at sale—stock valued at $150,000	Cost basis—$40,000	Already taxed at distribution, not taxed again

| | NUA—$60,000 | Taxed at long-term capital gains rate regardless of holding period |
| | **Additional appreciation—$50,000** | Taxed at either short- or long-term capital gains rate, depending on holding period |

NUA can also benefit your beneficiaries or heirs. For example, if you die while you still hold employer stock in your retirement plan, your beneficiary can also use NUA tax treatment to reduce taxes. Or if you die after you've received a distribution but before you sell the stock, any appreciation as of the date of your death in excess of NUA will escape taxation due to a step-up in basis.

Example: Continuing the example from above, let's say you've transferred your stock to a taxable account and it has grown to $150,000 when you die. Your heir will receive a step-up in cost basis for the $50,000 of appreciation over NUA at the time of your death, which means that it won't be taxed. In other words, he or she will pay long-term capital gains tax on the $60,000 of NUA, but no tax on the $50,000. However, if your heir holds the stock beyond your death, he or she will pay additional short- or long-term capital gains on additional appreciation.

BEFORE YOU DECIDE, NOTE:

- NUA works to your advantage only if the stock has appreciated in value above its cost basis. It makes more sense the larger your NUA and the smaller your cost basis.

- Stock held in an IRA or a 401(k) has more protection from a creditor than stock held in a taxable account.

- Depending on the amount of cost basis relative to total fair market value, you may be better off rolling the stock into an IRA if you have a long time horizon, because 100% of your money will continue to work for you (there is an opportunity cost involved with paying taxes early). Of course, if you're going to spend the money right away, then an NUA election almost always makes sense. Keep in mind, it's not an all-or-nothing decision. You might elect NUA treatment on some stock and roll over the rest.

- If you own a lot of company stock, it may make more sense to sell in order to diversify your investments, in which case rolling over into an IRA to defer taxes would make sense.

Don't Forget to Factor in Social Security

Whether you take your entire 401(k) in cash at once or withdraw from it over time, the distributions will be added to your ordinary income. This, in turn, can impact how your Social Security benefits are taxed.

Currently, single filers could pay income taxes on up to 85 percent of benefits if their modified adjusted gross income (MAGI) is over $34,000. For married filing jointly, the MAGI threshold is $44,000.

☎ **TALK TO AN EXPERT:** Look at your 401(k) in conjunction with your other sources of retirement income. It's a good idea to sit down with your tax or financial advisor to review your entire financial picture before deciding what to do with your 401(k).

Next Steps
- Take a look at **Question 4** for more details on the differences between types of retirement accounts.
- See **Question 22** for ideas on how to manage your money once you're retired.
- Wondering how your income taxes may change in retirement? See **Question 25.**
- Give some thought to how you'll create an income stream from your retirement accounts. Go to **Question 23** for guidelines.

I'm thinking of leaving my nine-to-five job to become a consultant, working from home. What's the cost of being my own boss?

When thinking about working at home, most people focus only on the pluses: no commute, flexible schedule, more personal time, little or no cost for things like transportation, wardrobe, and eating out. It all sounds great. And it can be a great transition into retirement. In fact, you may like it so much you'll decide to keep working from home and never fully retire.

However, while working for yourself means a lot of freedom, it also means a lot of financial responsibility. So you want to be sure you're not making this leap too soon. By working as a consultant from home, you'll certainly cut down on a lot of work-related expenses. But what might you be giving up? Most full-time jobs come with a package of benefits that may far outweigh the everyday costs of going to work. And what additional expenses might you be taking on?

Here are some things to consider before you start planning your going-away party.

You Are Your Own Benefits Provider

This is probably one of the biggest costs. If you've had group health insurance through your employer, you may be in for a shock at just how expensive an individual policy can be. You can get insurance through your state's exchange, or the federal exchange, but chances are it will still be considerably more than you're used to paying.

Likewise, if you've been getting life insurance through work, you'll now be on your own for that as well. At 55, even the cost for a term-life policy can be significant. Private disability policies are also quite costly.

And what about sick days and vacation pay? When you work for yourself, there's no one to cover for you.

⊃ SMART MOVE: When shopping for health insurance, consider a high-deductible policy that allows you to contribute to a Health Savings Account (HSA). Contributions are tax-deductible, just like for an IRA.

You Pay All Social Security and Medicare Taxes

Working for a company, it's easy to forget that your employer picks up half the bill for Social Security and Medicare taxes. And we're quite used to having the other half deducted from our paycheck. But working for yourself, you pay the whole amount in the form of self-employment taxes. For 2013, that tax is 15.3 percent on earnings up to $113,700. If you earn more than that, you'll still pay a 2.9 percent Medicare tax on any additional earnings—plus a 0.9 percent sur-tax on incomes over $200,000 for singles and $250,000 for married filing jointly. You get to deduct half of your self-employment tax as an above-the-line deduction (lowering your adjusted gross income, before you take other deductions), but this can still add up to quite a tax bite.

The Cost of Doing Business Can Increase Your Bills

Insurance and taxes are probably the biggest costs, but the everyday cost of doing business can add up, too. Since you'll be working from home, you'll use more water, heat, and electricity. Utility bills are bound to go up.

You'll also have to pay for office equipment, supplies, and any additional computer and Internet needs. Generally, an employer has experts available to help with downed computers or malfunctioning printers. Once again, you'll have to be your own resource and foot the bill for both purchase and repairs.

☎ **TALK TO AN EXPERT:** Make friends with a good accountant and bookkeeper, especially if this is your first foray into self-employment. He or she can help you set up your books, advise you on which expenses are tax-deductible (for example, home office, health insurance premiums, even a portion of the self-employment tax), calculate your maximum retirement plan contribution, and help you file your tax return.

COLLECTING SOCIAL SECURITY WHILE YOU'RE WORKING

First, just to be clear: You're free to earn as much as you like at any time during your retirement. But if you take Social Security benefits before you reach your **full retirement age (FRA),** you'll be dinged for earning above a certain threshold.

In 2013, if you're a Social Security recipient and haven't yet reached your FRA, you can earn up to $15,120 with no impact on benefits. But above that modest amount, you'll temporarily lose $1 for every $2 earned (eventually you'll be paid back). In the year you reach your FRA, you can earn up to $40,080 (again, this is for 2013) free and clear, but your benefits will be reduced by $1 for every $3 you earn above that limit.

Once you reach your FRA you can earn any amount without having your benefits reduced. And eventually you'll be repaid for the benefits that were withheld. See **Questions 30–34** for more on Social Security.

Saving for Retirement Is Up to You

With no 401(k) contribution automatically deducted from your paycheck—and no employer match—you'll have to be especially vigilant about saving for retirement. There are several small business retirement plans available whether you work on your own or have employees. It's up to you to figure out which plan is best suited to your needs.

- A **SEP-IRA (Simplified Employee Pension)** can be a great choice for saving a lot and keeping paperwork to a minimum whether or not you have employees. It also allows for a lot of flexibility in the amount you contribute annually. However, only the employer makes contributions, and as an employer you are required to contribute the same percentage for your employees as you contribute for yourself. You can decrease that percentage in any year, or decide not to contribute at all.

- An **Individual 401(k)** or an **Individual Roth 401(k)** is a great choice if you work on your own or if your only employee is your spouse. It requires more paperwork than a SEP but allows even higher contributions. You can also borrow against your savings.

- A **SIMPLE IRA (Savings Incentive Match Plan for Employees)** is a good choice if you have one hundred or fewer employees and want them to make their own contributions. As the employer, you're required to make only a small matching contribution (1 to 3 percent of their compensation). However, the contributions you make for yourself are significantly lower than for a SEP or an Individual 401(k).

- A **Keogh plan** is a qualified retirement plan for the self-employed. As the employer, you make all of the contributions. It requires more paperwork than a SEP and allows for equivalent contributions.

▶ **SMART MOVE:** If you have a regular job plus self-employment income on the side, you can set up and fund a SEP-IRA or an Individual 401(k) in addition to your company plan—and save even more.

AT A GLANCE: MAJOR TYPES OF SMALL BUSINESS PLANS

Tax-Deferred	Tax-Free	Good For	2013 Contribution Limit	Withdrawal	Required Minimum Distribution	Special Feature
SEP-IRA		Business owners with few or no employees	Up to 25% of compensation (20% of net self-employment income) or $51,000, whichever is less	Ordinary income tax rate; 10% penalty if you are under 59½, with exceptions	Yes	Employer required to provide benefits to almost all employees
Individual 401(k)		Business owners with no employees (other than a spouse)	Up to 25% of compensation (20% of net self-employment income), plus additional $17,500 for a maximum of $51,000 *plus* catch-up of $5,500 if you are 50 or older	Ordinary income tax rate; 10% penalty if you are under 59½, with exceptions	Yes, unless still employed	
	Roth Individual 401(k)	Business owners with no employees (other than a spouse)	Up to 25% of compensation (20% of net self-employment income), plus additional $17,500 for a maximum of $51,000 *plus* catch-up of $5,500 if you are 50 or older	Contributions tax-free; 10% penalty on earnings if under 59½ and haven't held account for five years	Yes, unless still employed or rolled into a Roth IRA	Unlike a Roth IRA, no income restrictions. Can be rolled over to a Roth IRA
SIMPLE IRA		Small companies with 100 or fewer eligible employees	Up to 100% of compensation or $12,000, whichever is less; catch-up of $2,500 if you are 50 or older	Ordinary income tax rate; 10% penalty if you are under 59½, with exceptions	Yes	25% penalty for withdrawal in first two years
Keogh plan		Business owners with few or no employees	Up to 25% of compensation (20% of net self-employment income) or $51,000, whichever is less	Ordinary income tax rate; 10% penalty if you are under 59½, with exceptions	Yes	

➲ SMART MOVE: Before you decide on a plan, calculate (or have your accountant calculate) the maximum amount that you'll be able to contribute, based on your age and your income.

BEHIND THE SCENES: CALCULATING YOUR MAXIMUM CONTRIBUTION TO A RETIREMENT PLAN

If you're self-employed, calculating your maximum contribution to a SEP-IRA, Individual 401(k), or Keogh plan is not straightforward. This is because your contribution is based on your *earned* income, which the IRS defines as your earnings from self-employment reduced by one-half of your self-employment tax and the amount of your retirement plan contribution. So while you're allowed to contribute 25 percent of earned income, this really means 20 percent of net self-employment income less one-half of self-employment tax.

There is some logic to this. In effect, the IRS is trying to treat self-employed individuals as if they were corporations. Both employers and employees pay one-half of FICA taxes (6.2 percent for OASDI [Old-Age, Survivors, and Disability Insurance]—up to $113,700 in 2013 and 1.45 percent on all income for Medicare). But the self-employed have to pay both halves. If their company were a corporation, it would deduct one-half of the taxes. Similarly, it would deduct a contribution made to a retirement plan. The IRS is giving self-employed individuals the opportunity to do the same thing.

Most of us will want to leave the calculation up to our accountant. But just in case you want to figure it out on your own, here is one way to do it. In this example, let's assume that you have net income of $150,000 and you plan to contribute the full 25 percent allowed.

STEP 1. CALCULATE YOUR CONTRIBUTION RATE

The formula is contribution rate to other participants ÷ (1 + contribution rate to other participants) = self-employed contribution rate

Therefore, your self-employed contribution rate is: 25% ÷ 1.25% = **20%**

STEP 2. CALCULATE YOUR SELF-EMPLOYMENT TAX

$150,000	Net self-employment income
× 92.35%	Subtracting one-half of FICA tax, or 7.65%
$138,525	Net earnings subject to self-employment tax

× 15.3% up to $113,700 + 2.9% over $113,700 (15.3% x $113,700 + 2.9% x $24,825)

$18,116	Self-employment tax ($17,396 + $720)

STEP 3. CALCULATE YOUR MAXIMUM CONTRIBUTION

$150,000	Net self-employment income
− 9,058	Half of self-employment tax
$140,942	Adjusted net self-employment income
× 0.20	Self-employed contribution rate from Step 1
$28,188	Your maximum plan contribution

Reversing this calculation, you can see:

$150,000	Net income
− 9,058	Subtracting one-half self-employment taxes
− 28,188	Subtracting contribution
$112,754	Earned income
× 0.25	Multiplying by 25% to determine contribution
$ 28,188	Maximum contribution

➲ **SMART MOVE:** Even if you contribute to a small business plan, you can contribute to a traditional IRA or a Roth IRA in the same year. Do both if you can!

Next Steps

- Review your insurance needs. See **Question 27.**
- Consider disability insurance. **Question 17** talks about why this is a good idea even if you're in good shape.
- For things to think about if you decide to go back to work during retirement, see **Question 28.**

Q16.

My kids are grown. Do I still need life insurance?

With all the bells and whistles attached to different types of life insurance policies, it's easy to forget that at its core, life insurance serves one purpose: to compensate for an economic loss in the event of the insured's death. Some insurance salespeople may tell you that life insurance can be a great investment, a way to save for retirement or college—even a good way to build up cash. In my opinion, there are far better choices for investing—from stocks, to bonds, to real estate, to CDs, to you-name-it. But not life insurance.

Now that's not to say that life insurance isn't important. In fact, for many people it's critical. If there's someone who depends on you, whether a family member or a business partner, life insurance can be key. Or if your estate will get hit with a big tax bill, life insurance can lessen the impact.

Selecting a policy from the myriad of choices depends on the particulars of your situation. But speaking broadly, I believe that term insurance makes the most sense most of the time, particularly if you don't need coverage indefinitely. Permanent insurance, on the other hand, is appropriate if you have an ongoing need.

And it's true that as you move beyond the child-rearing years, you may no longer need life insurance at all. In fact, my husband and I have a term policy that will expire when our youngest is off on her own. But that may not be the best decision for you. Let's go over several scenarios where life insurance could still make sense, and then offer some possible strategies.

LIFE INSURANCE 101

At its most basic, life insurance falls into two categories: *term* (or *temporary*) and *permanent* (or *cash value*). Of the two, term insurance is by far the least expensive. It is pure insurance: You purchase a policy for a set length of time (the term) at a preestablished premium. Depending on the policy, the premium can increase, stay the same, or decrease over time. Unless you renew when the term is over, you no longer have coverage. Although it's the least expensive way to purchase life insurance, it can be very expensive (or impossible) to renew as you get older or develop health problems.

With *permanent* insurance, as long as you continue to pay your premiums, you have coverage for life. It is much more expensive than term insurance, partly because a portion of your premium goes toward building cash value, but also because of embedded commissions and fees. Traditional permanent insurance builds up cash value on a tax-deferred basis. Depending on the policy, you can either borrow against this cash value or apply it to future premiums.

Universal life insurance is a type of hybrid policy that provides a flexible premium structure with a cash-value component. In addition, there are many other variations of permanent policies. Always be sure that you understand all the terms and risks before you purchase.

AT A GLANCE: TYPES OF LIFE INSURANCE

	Term	Permanent	Universal Life
Premium	Generally low; depending on policy, may increase or decrease over time	Generally high; fixed	Generally high; flexible
Death benefit	Fixed during term, then none	Fixed minimum amount	Variable
Coverage	Renewable	For life	For life
Guaranteed cash value	No	Yes	Yes
Flexible payments	No	No	Yes
Loans allowed*	No	Yes	Yes
Invests in stock market	No	No	No

* Loans will reduce the cash value by the amount of the loan outstanding plus interest.

Ask Yourself These Questions

Whether or not life insurance will still make sense once the kids are grown requires a closer look at your overall financial situation. For instance:

- **Do you have a financial obligation?** You may not need to provide ongoing support for your kids, but you don't want to leave your family in a bind, either. For example, if you still have responsibility for a mortgage or other large debt—and you don't have other assets to cover it—life insurance can fill the gap.
- **Do you have a spouse or other dependent with ongoing needs?** If you want to provide for your spouse, or if you have a child or

other family member who will never be able to provide for themselves, you probably still need life insurance. For example, if your pension pays only during your life, insurance could provide your spouse with retirement funds. Or you may want a policy to help cover the years before Social Security kicks in.

- **Are estate taxes a concern?** A life insurance policy can be a good safety net. If your estate is primarily illiquid—for example, if it is tied up in something like a family business, real estate, or a farm— a life insurance policy could cover the estate tax bill.
- **Do you want to leave a large portion of your estate to charity?** If you want to leave a sizable portion of assets to charity, you can still provide for your heirs through life insurance.
- **Do you own a business?** Life insurance can play an important part in providing cash flow in the event of the death of a business owner. If you have your own business or have a business partner, talk to your financial advisor about how life insurance factors into your long-range plans.

☎ **TALK TO AN EXPERT:** A beneficiary doesn't pay income tax on life insurance proceeds, but the value of a life insurance policy is included in your gross estate for estate tax purposes if you are the policy owner at your death (or if you transferred the policy within three years of your death). If this is a concern, talk to an estate planning attorney about an *irrevocable life insurance trust (ILIT)*. With an ILIT, the trust owns the policy and the proceeds remain outside the estate.

Determine How Much You Need

If you answered yes to any of the questions above, the next step is to decide how much coverage you need. An industry rule of thumb says you should have life insurance equal to six to eight times your annual salary, but I think it's smarter to make a calculation based on your individual need. While every situation is unique, here's a simple way to look at it:

- Calculate your projected financial need. This could be either a fixed amount (for example, a mortgage) or the amount of money needed to fund living expenses over a number of years.
- Subtract your accumulated assets.
- If you have coverage through your employer, subtract that amount, too.
- The remainder is roughly the minimum amount of life insurance you should consider.

☎ **TALK TO AN EXPERT:** There are many online calculators that can help you determine how much insurance you need. I especially like the one provided by the American Institute of Certified Public Accountants at 360financialliteracy.org. However, because life insurance is both complicated and costly, I highly recommend that you consult with a fee-only insurance expert or other financial advisor before making a final decision.

Figure Out Your Next Move

Depending on your situation, you have several choices:

- **Need some coverage but can't afford the premiums?**
  - Turn your cash-value policy into a smaller, paid-up policy.
  - Have your adult children pay the premiums, particularly if they're the ones who will ultimately benefit.
- **Need a new policy?** If you're 50 or 60 years old and healthy, you'll have to pay more than a 30- or 40-year-old, but you'll likely qualify. First decide whether you want term or permanent coverage, and then do your homework comparing costs and features. With a permanent policy, it generally takes somewhere between eight and ten years to build cash value.

⊃ **SMART MOVE:** Buying a new life insurance policy involves passing a physical. So if you're a smoker, do your best to stop. Need to lose some weight or lower your blood pressure? Give yourself a few months to get in shape before you apply, and you could save thousands of dollars in premiums.

- **No longer need your term policy?** Consider canceling it and directing the amount you've been putting toward premiums to a savings or investment account.
- **No longer need your cash-value policy?** You can consider:
    - Canceling it and moving the cash value to your investment account. Caution: You will have to pay ordinary income taxes on the balance that exceeds your cost basis. Some policies also have a surrender charge.
    - Using the cash value to buy either an immediate or a deferred annuity. If you do this through a 1035 exchange, you won't have to pay taxes.
    - Using the cash value to buy a long-term care policy, again through a 1035 exchange to avoid taxes.

Next Steps
- Consider the benefits of disability insurance. See **Question 17.**
- Don't forget about long-term care insurance. **Question 7** gives you some food for thought.
- For more information on annuities, see **Question 20.**
- Review and refine your estate plan. **Question 38** covers the basics.

Important Disclosure
The death benefit and any other guarantees provided under a life insurance policy are subject to the financial strength and claims-paying ability of the issuing insurance company.

Please be aware that there are a number of important factors to consider before initiating a 1035 exchange that could reduce or eliminate the benefit of the exchange. These include surrender charges on your existing contract, loss of guaranteed benefits, and differences in features, costs, services, and company strength.

Q17.

I'm fit as a fiddle.
Do I really need
disability insurance?

You're out jogging, the sun is shining, and you're feeling great. You decide to sprint home, and with a burst of enthusiasm you take a flying leap off a curb, land on a rock, and end up with a severely broken ankle that requires surgery. Can it happen to you? As the saying goes, it could happen tomorrow. Unfortunately, being fit doesn't mean being risk-free.

According to the Council for Disability Awareness, more than 37 million Americans are classified as disabled, about 12 percent of the total population. More than 50 percent of those disabled Americans are in their working years, from 18 to 64. Yet the Social Security Administration reports that only 31 percent of the private sector workforce has long-term disability insurance. These are pretty sobering statistics for anyone who depends on earned income for their livelihood—whatever their fitness level.

Disability insurance provides a portion of your income if you can't work because of an illness or non-job-related injury. To me, being over 50 doesn't lessen the need for it. On the contrary, it may increase it. Many people in their fifties are in their peak earning years and building their retirement nest egg. An extended disability at this time of life could completely derail their financial future.

So ask yourself, how long could you survive without your income? If you have an emergency fund in place, that would carry you for a while. But what would you do when that's gone? The last thing you want to do is tap into your retirement funds—that would be raiding your future to pay for the present. So the question isn't so much whether you need disability insurance, but rather *how much* disability insurance you need. Once you're retired, you're in the clear.

Start with Your Employer

Many people just assume they have disability insurance through their work, but that's not always the case. If you live in California, Hawaii, New Jersey, New York, or Rhode Island, you're in luck. These states (as well as Puerto Rico) require employers to provide short-term state disability insurance. In some states it's provided through an insurance company; in others it's provided by the state and paid for through payroll taxes. On average, benefits are offered for six months, with California providing benefits for up to a year. The percentage of salary covered varies by state.

Even if it's not required, many employers (especially large companies) offer some type of short-term disability coverage for a specified period of time—a few weeks or months and possibly up to two years. With any short-term policy, there may be a waiting period before benefits begin.

Long-term disability is a different story. There's no requirement for employers to provide long-term coverage. If yours does, that's a plus. Long-term benefits begin once short-term benefits run out. Coverage can be anywhere from two to five years, or even up to age 65.

Getting disability insurance through your work is likely your most cost-effective choice because it's purchased through a group plan. An employer may pay the premiums or pass a percentage of the premiums on to you. Even if your employer doesn't specifically offer the insurance, you may still have the opportunity to voluntarily buy into a group plan at significant savings. One drawback is that, should you change jobs, you can't take your policy with you.

Look at All Your Sources of Income

Disability insurance through your work or your state is a step in the right direction, but it's not the complete answer. That's because these policies usually replace only about 55–65 percent of your income. Many policies have a benefit cap of around $5,000 a month, or $60,000 a year.

How will you cover any shortfall? Social Security Disability Insurance (SSDI) currently averages about $1,100 a month (and is very difficult to qualify for). If your spouse has an income or your savings are extensive, that may help. But is it enough?

WHY YOU SHOULDN'T COUNT ON SOCIAL SECURITY DISABILITY INSURANCE (SSDI)

According to the Social Security Administration (SSA), the number of work credits you need to be eligible for disability benefits depends on your age when you become disabled. Generally, you need 40 credits, 20 of which were earned in the last ten years, ending with the year you become disabled.

While you may have enough credits to be eligible for SSDI, qualifying for it is another story. The SSA has a very strict definition of disability:

- You must not be able to do the work you did before

- Your medical condition prevents you from adjusting to another type of work *and*

- Your disability is expected to last for at least one year or result in death

Even if you qualify, SSDI has a five-month waiting period, and the amount of your benefit will most likely fall far short of your needs. While your exact benefit will depend on your work history and income, average SSDI monthly payments are around $1,100. You can get more information at ssa.gov, but the bottom line is that you really should consider other sources of income in case you become disabled. See **Question 33** for more.

Consider a Private Policy

If your employer doesn't offer disability insurance, or you're self-employed, a private long-term disability policy—which can boost coverage to 80 percent of income—may be worth the cost. Besides a bigger benefit, private insurance has the advantage of being portable; you can take it with you wherever you go. Plus, benefits are tax-free as long as you paid the premiums with after-tax dollars.

To keep costs down, consider the following:

- Check into professional associations related to your line of work to see if you can buy into a group plan.
- In general, disability policies are more expensive for women than for men. As a result, women can benefit from being in a group plan that includes both men and women.

FACT: Disability insurance rates for women run 40–50 percent higher than for men. The reason for the difference? Women tend to file more disability claims and are disabled for a longer period of time. Statistically speaking, a 35-year-old professional female has three times the chance of being disabled for a period of more than ninety days than a male, says the *Journal of the American Society of Chartered Life Underwriters.*

- Look into increasing the waiting period from 90 to 180 days. This is a lot like increasing the deductible on your auto insurance; you absorb more risk so the price goes down.
- Look into decreasing the term. It may not be ideal, but it could lower the price.

SMART MOVE: If you're highly skilled (and can afford it), you should try to purchase "own occupation" as opposed to "any occupation" coverage. This would mean you wouldn't be forced to take a job outside your area of expertise.

WHAT TO LOOK FOR IN A PRIVATE DISABILITY INSURANCE POLICY

As with all insurance products, there can be substantial differences from one company to another. It's important to comparison shop. And be sure to read the fine print before you buy. Here are things to look for:

- **Is the policy for "own occupation" or "any occupation"?** One pays benefits if you can't perform a job in your area of expertise. The other pays only if you can't perform any job suitable to your education and experience. Premiums for an "own occupation" policy are generally higher.

- **What's the benefit period?** This is the amount of time you will receive monthly benefits. It's recommended that you get a policy that will pay at least until you reach age 65.

- **What's the waiting period before benefits are paid?** Policies have a waiting period before benefits start. The longer you wait, the lower the premium. The ideal is between 60 and 90 days, provided, of course, that you have an emergency fund to see you though.

- **Is there a cost-of-living clause?** A cost-of-living clause increases the amount of your benefits with inflation—but it also increases premiums.

- **Is the policy noncancelable?** A company can't cancel a noncancelable policy if you pay your premiums on time, *nor* can the company change the benefit or the premium.

- **Is the policy guaranteed renewable?** A guaranteed renewable policy can't be canceled by the company provided that you pay your premiums on time, *but* the premium can be raised.

Last, but not least, check on the financial stability of the insurance company. There are several ratings companies that will provide this information, including Moody's Investors Service and Standard & Poor's Ratings Services.

SMART MOVE: The older you are, the harder (and more expensive) it is to get disability coverage. If you think it's something you need, do it now. You likely won't be able to buy a new policy once you're close to 60.

☎ **TALK TO AN EXPERT:** Private policies are complicated, so get referrals to reputable insurance agents in your area and work with one you trust.

Next Steps

- Review all of your insurance policies to see if you're properly protected. Check out **Question 27** for tips on types of insurance you may—or may not—need.
- **Question 16** helps you zero in on your need for life insurance.
- Think seriously about long-term care insurance. See **Question 7**.

Q18.

I'm thinking of downsizing once I retire. Will I get hit with a tax bill when I sell my house?

There's a fair amount of confusion over this topic, probably because the rules changed dramatically back in 1997. Many of us baby boomers still remember the old rules about trading up to a more expensive home within two years to postpone taxes, or the once-in-a-lifetime exclusion for those who were 55 or older.

But it's a new day, with completely new (well, newish) rules. And quite frankly, it's one of the best tax deals around.

Under current law, if you sell your principal residence for a profit, up to $250,000 of that capital gain is tax-free. Married couples filing a joint return can exclude up to $500,000.

This means that most people will have no capital gains tax bill at all. (Unfortunately, though, if you sell your home at a loss, you cannot deduct that loss.)

But, of course, it's not quite that simple. In order to claim the maximum exclusion, you first have to pass what the IRS calls the ownership and use tests. This means:

1.   You must have owned the house for two years.

2.   You must have lived in the house as your principal residence for two out of the last five years, ending on the date of the sale.

There are a few exceptions to these rules—for example, if you had to move before owning the home for two years because of a job change, or because you experienced what the IRS designates as an "unforeseen circumstance," such as a divorce or natural disaster. In these situations the IRS will allow you to prorate the exclusion.

And interestingly, the two years' residency doesn't have to be consecutive—you just have to have lived in your home for a total of twenty-four months out of the five years prior to the sale. Even more interesting is that you can claim this exclusion on multiple sales—as long as each home was your principal residence for at least two of the last five years.

In terms of your own tax bill, if you pass the ownership and residency requirements, you can fairly accurately determine your potential taxes.

WHEN TIMING IS CRITICAL

The ownership and use tests may seem fairly straightforward, but there are situations when timing is a critical factor in whether or not you have to pay capital gains taxes. Consider this situation:

Two and a half years ago, Matt and Nancy moved to a new city for her job. They bought a new home and decided to rent their old one. They now want to sell their former home, which they've owned for ten years. They easily pass the ownership test, but what about the use test?

Remember, to claim the full capital gains exemption, you have to have lived in your house as your principal residence for two out of the past five years. In another six months, Matt and Nancy will have been out of their former house for three years. If they don't complete the sale before then, they'll no longer meet the two-out-of-five-year residency requirement for the capital gains exclusion—and they'll potentially have a hefty tax bill. There's no time to lose. They need to get their house on the market ASAP!

Calculate Your Cost Basis

To determine **capital gains** on the sale of your home, you simply subtract your cost basis from the selling price. But what exactly is your **cost basis?** It's not just the purchase price. It also includes the fees associated with both the purchase and the sale, that is, settlement fees, closing costs (not including escrow amounts related to taxes and insurance), commissions, etc. Add to this the cost of improvements (but not repairs) you made over time: upgrades, additions, roofing, landscaping, plumbing, etc. All of these improvements will increase your cost basis, therefore lowering your potential tax liability. Hopefully you've kept good records because this can add up!

On the other side of the equation, there are a few things that can reduce your cost basis. A lower basis will increase your profit, and potentially your tax. For example, if you have a home office and have claimed depreciation over time, you now have to subtract those deductions from your cost basis. Or if you received tax credits for energy-related improvements, you have to subtract that amount as well.

☎ **TALK TO AN EXPERT:** It's important to note that any depreciation taken after May 6, 1997, will be recaptured and taxed at a rate of 25 percent—even if your overall gain is less than your exclusion amount. Best to talk to your tax advisor. You can also see IRS Publication 523 for details.

BEHIND THE SCENES: CAPITAL IMPROVEMENT OR REPAIR?

Tax rules let you add the cost of a capital improvement to your cost basis, but not the cost of a repair. The difference? A capital improvement increases the value of your property. A repair simply restores your property to its original condition. A new deck is a capital improvement. Fixing your plumbing is a repair. Sometimes, though, the distinction is less clear. For example, if you replace your entire roof, that's a capital improvement. But if you simply replace some of the shingles, that's a repair.

SMART MOVE: Keep all records of capital improvements to your home. If your record keeping has been less than perfect, do your best to get back copies of bills and receipts.

Estimate Sale Price and Capital Gains

Now estimate your sale price and subtract your cost basis.

Example: Let's say you bought your house for $350,000, put in $50,000 in improvements, and had related fees and costs of another $15,000, giving you a cost basis of $415,000. Now let's say you expect to sell the house for $850,000. Your potential capital gain would be $435,000.

The next step is to factor in the exclusion.

Continuing our example: If you meet both the ownership and the use tests—and you own the home jointly with your spouse—you could claim the $500,000 exclusion and exclude the entire gain from your taxable income. You wouldn't even have to report the sale on your tax return. However, let's say your capital gain turned out to be $525,000. In that case, you'd have to report the sale and pay long-term capital gains on $25,000. (If you're single and your capital gain is $435,000, you'd have to pay capital gains taxes on $185,000; on a $525,000 gain, you'd pay taxes on $275,000.)

⚠ **CAUTION:** While your profit on the sale of your home can be taxable, a loss on the sale generally isn't deductible. However, special rules apply if the house has been turned into rental property. Check with your accountant.

A SAMPLE TAX BILL

Tracy and Jim bought their home in 1988. Now in their mid-sixties, they decide to downsize. They sell their home for $875,000.

Over the years, Tracy and Jim did a lot of remodeling and made considerable home improvements. Because Tracy has been working out of the house, they've claimed depreciation on their income tax return (which now has to be added back to the cost basis). They are in the 25 percent tax bracket and pay a 15 percent long-term capital gains tax rate. Here are the numbers:

Sales price:	**$875,000**
Initial cost of home:	$ 250,000
Settlement fees and closing costs:	$ 12,500
Kitchen and bath remodels:	$ 50,000
New roof:	$ 20,000
Landscaping:	$ 15,000
Selling costs:	$ 55,000
Depreciation (subtract)	($ 50,000)
Cost basis:	**$352,500**

Capital gain (sales price minus cost basis: $875,000 − $352,500): $522,500

Capital gains exclusion (for a couple):	$ 500,000
Capital gains subject to tax:	$ 22,500
Capital gains tax due (15% tax rate):	$ 3,375

Note: Tracy and Jim must also include the $50,000 depreciation deduction on their tax return as "unrecaptured section 1250 gain." It will be taxed at a rate of 25% ($12,500). They would have to do this even if their capital gain was less than their $500,000 exclusion.

⚠ **CAUTION:** As a result of the Affordable Care Act there is also a 3.8 percent tax on investment income for couples with adjusted gross income above $250,000 (or $200,000 for singles). A gain on the sale of your home above the exclusion could be subject to this tax.

> **BEHIND THE SCENES: MORE THAN ONE HOME**
>
> If you own more than one home, you can exclude the gain on the sale of only your "principal" residence, or the one you live in most. However, if you sell your primary home and then make your other home your primary residence, you will be able to exclude the gain on the sale of that home after two years.

Plan Your Next Move

Your next big decision will be figuring out where to live. Downsizing may mean buying a smaller house or moving to a less expensive area. Alternatively, you could decide that it would make more sense to rent and invest the bulk of your money.

There's a general own-to-rent ratio that can provide a ballpark way to compare the costs of buying versus renting. Simply divide the sales price of a home by the annual rent of a comparable home in the same area. A high rent ratio (above 20, generally speaking) means the cost of ownership exceeds the cost of renting. A ratio under 15 would indicate that it might make more economic sense to buy.

> *Example*: If a condo sells for $350,000 and a comparable condo rents for $1,400/month, the own-to-rent ratio is $350,000 ÷ $16,800 ($1,400 × 12) = 20.8. In this case, it would most likely be more cost-effective to rent. However, boost that rent up to $2,000 and the ratio drops to 14.5. Buying now becomes more attractive.

Of course, there are other things to consider. On the plus side, renting releases you from worry about things like property taxes and upkeep, potentially giving you more freedom both economically and emotionally. On the minus side, if you rent you won't be building equity and you'll be subject to the whims of a landlord. There's no right or wrong answer. You just need to think it through. A lot will depend on where you live and whether you plan to stay in your next home long-term. Websites such as zillow.com and trulia.com can help you get more precise information on the rent-versus-buy comparisons in your area.

☎ **TALK TO AN EXPERT:** If you make a considerable profit on the sale of your home, talk to your financial advisor about the best way to invest this money in light of your overall financial situation. An advisor can help you decide whether it makes more sense to reinvest in real estate or to add this money to your retirement savings.

Next Steps

- Go to **Question 25** for ways to lower your tax bill in retirement.
- Review your investment strategy. See **Questions 5** and **22.**
- Put mortgage debt in perspective. See **Question 13.**

Q19.

Should I take my pension as a lump sum or monthly payments?

If you're faced with answering this question, the first thing I want to say is "congratulations." You're among the lucky few who still have a traditional defined-benefit pension plan. Many people who are struggling to fund and invest their 401k(s) might envy the fact that you can count on a certain sum of money for the rest of your life.

But you can't just sit back and relax. Choosing between a lump sum or monthly payments is a big decision. There are pros and cons to consider when making your choice.

First Look at All of Your Choices

If you decide on the lump sum, that's generally straightforward. Your company will provide you with a dollar figure based on your life expectancy, and you can compare it to your other choices.

When it comes to a monthly payout, though, you will likely have several options. For instance, your company may offer:

- **Single life payment**—This will usually give you the highest monthly payment.

- **Single life with term certain**—This will lower your monthly payment a bit but, in return, if you died before the specified term was over, your beneficiaries would receive your payments for the length of the term. Say you choose 20 years. If you live longer than 20 years, payments will continue until you die. But if you die in 6 years, your heirs will receive payments for another 14 years.
- **50% joint and survivor**—You get a lower monthly payment and your surviving spouse will get 50 percent of your payment for the rest of his or her life.
- **100% joint and survivor**—This lowers your payment even more, but your surviving spouse will get 100 percent of your monthly payment for life.

Another important consideration is whether your pension has a cost-of-living adjustment (COLA), which will increase your monthly payments to keep up with inflation. This is huge. See "The Impact of Inflation" for examples.

THE IMPACT OF INFLATION

We all know that $1,000 in ten years won't have the same purchasing power as $1,000 today. But just how big a bite will inflation really take? The future is impossible to predict, but in the last one hundred years, the U.S. inflation rate has averaged just about 3.35 percent.

Using a 3.35 percent average rate, we can calculate the following:

- To purchase the equivalent of $1,000 worth of goods in ten years, you will need $1,390.

- To purchase the equivalent of $1,000 worth of goods in twenty years, you will need $1,932

- To purchase the equivalent of $1,000 worth of goods in thirty years, you will need $2,687.

Of course, averages can be misleading, because the actual rates can vary dramatically from decade to decade, or even from year to year. Nonetheless, unless your pension has a cost-of-living adjustment, you will lose significant purchasing power over time.

⮕ **SMART MOVE:** If you choose a single life payment to maximize your monthly income, you could also purchase life insurance to cover your spouse's needs should you die first. See **Question 16** for more on life insurance.

Do the Math

At first blush, a lump sum can be very tempting. But before you take the money and run, it's important to crunch some numbers. The longer you live, the more valuable the annuity option becomes.

> *Example:* You're 65 and have a choice between a lump sum of $300,000 and a single life annuity of $2,000 per month ($24,000 a year). If you live to 78½, you'll get the same amount of money either way ($24,000/ year for 12½ years, potential investing gains or losses aside). If you die earlier, you'll get more with the lump sum. You'd have the money in hand for as long as you live, and then be able pass on anything that's left to your heirs. If you live longer than 78½, you'll get more by taking monthly payments. Of course, the break-even points are different if you select a different monthly payment structure.

BEHIND THE SCENES: CALCULATING ANNUITY RETURNS

When you think of a rate of return, it seems pretty straightforward. But calculating a rate of return on an annuity is a bit more complicated. To do the calculation, you need to use a financial calculator or a spreadsheet. Let's go back to the example I gave earlier:

- You're 65 and you have a choice between a $300,000 lump sum and a single life annuity of $2,000 a month ($24,000 a year). If you take the lump sum, how much will you have to earn on average to get a return equivalent to the annuity?

- On the surface it looks like you're making 8% ($24,000 ÷ $300,000 = 8%). But an annuity is structured to pay out both interest and return of principal, leaving a zero balance, based on an assumption about how long you will live.

- If you assume that you will live another 20 years, the annuity's actual return is 4.96%. In other words, if you were to take the lump sum and invest it on your own, you would have to earn an average annual return of 4.96% to do as well.

- The longer you live, the higher the annual return turns out to be. If you assume that you will live another 25 years, the return increases to 6.24%. If you die sooner, the return goes down. For example, if you only live 15 years, the annuity's return falls to 2.37%. If you live less than 12½ years, the annuity return is negative.

☎ **TALK TO AN EXPERT:** Choosing between a lump sum and a monthly payment is a huge decision. I strongly recommend that you review your calculations and assumptions with a financial advisor before you make your choice.

Look at the Big Picture

As you can see, there's a lot to think about just in terms of dollars and cents. But there are several other factors to consider as well.

- **Be honest about your health and longevity.** We may be known as the generation that's "forever young," but when it comes to a pension payout, we have to come to terms with our mortality. As the previous example shows, the longer you live, the more sense it makes to annuitize your pension. Take an honest look at your health and your family history of longevity before you make your decision.
- **Consider the rest of your finances.** A monthly pension check combined with Social Security income could allow you to leave your IRA or 401(k) intact and growing tax-deferred. On the other hand, if you have several other sources of income—Social Secu-

rity, real estate, Roth accounts—it could be to your advantage to take the lump sum and invest it. Also take into account that you will be required to start taking distributions from your traditional IRA or 401(k) starting the year after you turn 70½. See **Question 23** for more on RMDs.

☎ **TALK TO AN EXPERT:** Your pension payout—whether a lump sum or an annuity—should be viewed as part of your overall financial plan. A financial advisor can help you look at how your pension payout fits into the bigger picture.

- **Think about taxes.** The money from your pension is taxable income. If you take it monthly, your payments are taxed as ordinary income in the year you receive them. However, with a lump sum, you have some additional choices. If you just take the money, the whole amount is taxable at once. But you can also choose to roll the lump sum directly into a traditional IRA and avoid paying income taxes until you take withdrawals at a future date. In the meantime, your money can continue to grow tax-free. You can also choose to roll your pension payout into a Roth IRA. In this case, you'd pay income taxes up front on the total amount, but future withdrawals would be tax-free. If you're considering a rollover, see **Question 14** for important details on timing and taxes when rolling over to either type of IRA.
- **Do you want to leave an inheritance?** With an annuity, you may choose to have payments continue for a spouse or other survivor. But after that, the payments end. A lump sum could provide for other heirs.
- **Weigh the risks.** Both choices involve risk. If you choose monthly payments, the risk is that your employer or the insurance company managing the annuity could go under. You can do a bit of due diligence by looking into the credit rating of the annuity provider or pension fund. Plus, the federal Pension Benefit Guaranty Corporation (PBGC) provides a certain amount of protection for private sector pension participants. (See "Is Your Pension Protected?" on

this page for more on the PBGC.) State laws generally protect the benefits earned by public sector workers.

- **Be honest about your investing skills and interest.** While it may seem smart to take the money and run, managing a lump sum for retirement income takes careful planning, budgeting, and discipline. If you're an experienced investor and are willing to put in the time and effort it takes to manage your money, no problem. But if you're uncertain about your investment ability, are uncomfortable with market risk, or would rather spend your time doing other things, you probably should think twice.

➲ **SMART MOVE:** Considering a lump sum? Be sure to use a reasonable estimate of your potential investment return. The Schwab Center for Financial Research estimates that a conservative portfolio of 20% stocks, 50% bonds, and 30% cash could grow 3.5% on average annually over the long term. Increase your stock allocation to 40% and you might be able to get a 4.3% annual return. Of course, there are no guarantees.

IS YOUR PENSION PROTECTED?

The Pension Benefit Guaranty Corporation is a federal government agency that guarantees basic benefits should a private sector pension plan terminate or go bankrupt. According to the agency, basic benefits include:

- Pension benefits at normal retirement age

- Most early retirement benefits

- Annuity benefits for survivors of plan participants

- Disability benefits

There are strict limits on how much the PBGC will pay monthly. Limits are determined each year by ERISA and vary according to your age. You can find Maximum Monthly Guarantee Tables at pbgc.gov. Just as an example, the 2013 maximum monthly single life annuity payment for a 65-year-old is $4,789.77, or about $56,000 a year. For a 75-year-old, that maximum goes up to $14,560.90 per month, or about $175,000 a year.

Consider the Best of Both Worlds

It would seem that if you're more comfortable with monthly checks, don't like risk, and don't want the responsibility of investing, your better choice is monthly payments. Conversely, if you prefer to have control over your money and feel you can handle investing a lump sum yourself (or with the help of an advisor), then that should be your choice.

But actually, there's a third option: Take the lump sum, roll it over into an IRA, and then invest a portion of it in a high-quality fixed immediate annuity. A fixed annuity is designed to pay you guaranteed monthly income immediately. So you'd get the best of both—monthly checks from your annuity to cover expenses plus additional assets to invest for growth and diversification or anything else you choose. (Always keep in mind that annuity guarantees are subject to the financial strength of the issuing insurance company.)

☎ **TALK TO AN EXPERT:** An advisor can help you run the numbers to see what option or combination of options would work best for you. But be sure to consult with someone who doesn't have a vested interest either in managing your investments or selling you an annuity.

AT A GLANCE: LUMP SUM VS. MONTHLY PAYMENTS

	Pros	Cons
Lump sum	• Control and flexibility • Can choose and change beneficiaries • Won't stop at death; remaining funds can pass on to your heirs • Pay taxes only on withdrawals if rolled over into a traditional IRA	• Responsible for investing to create own income stream • Assume investment risks and costs • May be smaller amount than sum of monthly payments • Could run out before you die
Monthly payments	• Guaranteed income for life • Possible guaranteed income for the life of your spouse • No investment responsibility or risk • Convenience	• Monthly checks taxed as ordinary income • Won't keep up with inflation unless there's a cost-of-living adjustment • Concern about financial health of the pension fund

Talk to Your Spouse

As with all retirement decisions, be sure to include your spouse. The choice you make will affect both of you, for the short and the long term. And remember, these decisions aren't just about dollars; they're also about your attitudes, your goals, and how you want to spend all the good years you have ahead of you.

Next Steps
- If you're considering rolling a lump sum payout into an IRA, see **Question 4** on types of retirement accounts and **Question 14** on rollovers.
- Interested in purchasing your own annuity? **Question 20** discusses things to consider.
- To see strategies for taking monthly withdrawals from your various accounts during retirement, see **Question 23**.

Q20.

Should I buy an annuity?

With apologies, I'm going to start my answer to this question with another question: *As you contemplate the time when you'll no longer be earning a regular paycheck, how confident are you?*

According to the annual national survey on retirement confidence conducted by the Employee Benefit Research Institute, in 2013 only about 13 percent of Americans responded to this question by saying that they were "very confident" about their prospects. In other words, if you have a hefty portfolio or a pension, you're among the lucky few. And if you have minimal savings, you probably shouldn't tie up your cash in an annuity. But if you fall somewhere in between—that is, you have a fair amount of savings, but not enough to guarantee a comfortable retirement—an annuity might be the answer.

In essence, annuities are investment and insurance products rolled up into one. There are many different types of annuities, but in general you give up the potential for outsized gains in return for a predictable income stream for life. Because of this, annuities are best suited for those who are either in or approaching retirement.

Over the years annuities have developed a somewhat bad reputation, certainly not without cause. Not only do many carry hefty fees and commissions, but they can be so complex that it's almost impossible to understand exactly what you're getting for your money—or to compare your return to another investment.

⊙ **FACT:** Close to half (44 percent) of Americans grade themselves a D or F on their annuities awareness, according to a 2013 Charles Schwab Retirement Survey.

That said, some annuities are better than others—and there are definitely circumstances when purchasing one can be a smart financial move. For example, consider the following:

Terry is 65. She has $1 million of assets and wants to spend $60,000 a year in addition to Social Security. As I discussed in Question 1, she should withdraw only about 4% of her portfolio each year ($40,000) if she wants to be 90% confident that she won't run out of money. Instead, she decides to put $400,000 into an annuity that pays $36,000 a year for life, with cost-of-living adjustments. She can then withdraw $24,000 from the remaining $600,000 (which is 4%). Combined, she has $60,000 of income that will grow with inflation.

In this case, the math works. But you have to compare policies and do your own calculations—most likely with the help of an objective and trusted financial advisor. In the following pages I review two different types of annuities that may be worth considering.

☎ **TALK TO AN EXPERT:** Annuities can be extremely complicated! Before you commit, talk it over with a trusted, objective advisor who understands your complete financial picture. Don't rely exclusively on a commissioned salesperson for advice.

ANNUITIES 101

Annuities can be divided into two broad categories: *fixed* and *variable*. Both are contracts with an insurance company. You pay a premium (or series of premiums) and then receive payments at regular intervals for a stated period of time.

Contributions to an annuity are not tax-deductible, but taxes on earnings are deferred until you make a withdrawal—at which time you pay ordinary income taxes on your gains. There is a 10 percent penalty for withdrawing earnings before age 59½.

Both fixed and variable annuities can be either deferred or immediate. An immediate annuity will start to pay out right away, continuing for a specified period of time or for life. Deferred annuities have two phases: accumulation, when you earn interest on your investment, and distribution, when you take withdrawals at a predetermined future date.

Immediate fixed annuities behave much like a pension. Provided the insurance company remains solvent, you can count on receiving payments for a set number of years, for life, or for the life of a beneficiary.

Variable annuities are somewhat like other tax-deferred investments but with extra protections and extra fees. You invest your money in a "subaccount" composed of stocks, bonds, or other vehicles, and your return will vary depending on their performance. For that reason, payments aren't as predictable as they are with a fixed annuity (however, as discussed below, you can also purchase a rider that guarantees a minimum payment, generally subject to certain restrictions and conditions).

Start by Asking Yourself a Few Questions

Intrigued? Before you get immersed in too many details, consider the following:

1.   **How important is it to you to guarantee income for life?** The whole point of an annuity is a reliable income stream. If you're confident that you'll be able to generate enough money from your portfolio, you don't need an annuity. But if you're concerned that your portfolio and other investments won't be able to sustain you, an annuity could make sense.

2.   **Do you want to leave your assets to your children?** Annuities are designed primarily to protect you, not your heirs. If you want to pass on these assets, an annuity is probably not the best vehicle.

3.   **Have you maxed out your retirement accounts?** If you're still working and you haven't contributed the maximum to your 401(k) or

IRA, it's probably best to start there. Otherwise you're walking away from tax benefits that can save you big in the long run. However, if you have contributed the maximum to your retirement accounts or you're no longer working, and you want to supplement your retirement savings, an annuity could make sense.

⚠ **CAUTION:** The experts at the Schwab Center for Financial Research generally recommend that you not put more than half of your assets in an annuity. That way you will retain some liquidity and the potential for growth on top of the security of a reliable income stream.

Two Options Worthy of Your Consideration

Of the literally dozens of different kinds of annuities available, the Schwab Center for Financial Research has given its conditional approval to two: **single premium immediate fixed annuities (SPIAs)** and **variable annuities,** particularly those that have an optional guaranteed lifetime withdrawal benefit (GLWB). An SPIA is most appropriate for someone who is either on the cusp of retirement or is already in retirement. A variable annuity with a GLWB rider might make sense if your retirement is five to ten years away.

- **Immediate fixed annuities:** With a single premium immediate fixed annuity (SPIA), you irrevocably turn a lump sum over to an insurance company in exchange for an immediate stream of guaranteed income for a set number of years or for life, depending on the annuity. In other words, you're buying a reliable cash flow, much like a pension. The biggest downside is that once you commit, you can't change your mind and get your money back.

  With an SPIA, like a fixed pension, the longer you live, the more you benefit. Your payment will be based on the insurance company's calculation of your life expectancy. Therefore, if you live longer than your cohorts, you'll collect payments for a longer time, increasing your rate of return. Also, the older you are at the time of purchase, the higher your monthly payment will be, because the insurance company anticipates paying you for fewer years.

An immediate fixed annuity makes the most sense for someone who wants income *now* without having to worry about the stock market. If you're one of the many people who lost sleep during the market crash of 2008, and you're concerned about outliving your portfolio, the security of an SPIA could be worth the cost.

Alternatively, if your primary fear is living into very old age (what actuaries call "longevity risk"), you can consider purchasing an annuity that won't start payments until you reach a certain age—say 80 or even 85. This will be a lot less expensive than purchasing an annuity that starts paying you earlier.

⚠ **CAUTION:** With interest rates at historic lows, this may not be the ideal time to put a big chunk of your money into an annuity. Instead, consider staggering your purchase over time so that you can potentially get a better return. One caveat is that annuity contracts can have "break points"; if you buy a smaller contract you may not get the best rate.

- **Variable annuities:** Our research shows that we're most vulnerable to the impact of a prolonged market downturn during the last five to ten years before retirement. On the other hand, you probably don't want to be out of the market, either, because your retirement could last for several decades.

  One way to resolve this conflict is with the protection of a variable annuity, which offers professionally managed investments along with a guaranteed stream of income for life (subject, of course, to the insurance company's financial strength and ability to pay claims). Adding an optional guaranteed lifetime withdrawal benefit (GLWB) rider, available at an additional cost, provides added protections by guaranteeing your income against market risk.

  Under the terms of a GLWB, you don't have to "annuitize" your contract—or irrevocably hand it over to an insurance company in order to receive a guaranteed stream of income for life. You retain control of your money and, at retirement, you can withdraw a guaranteed minimum level of income each year regardless of how the investments that are held within the variable annuity perform.

You should be aware, however, that the GLWB does not protect the value of your investments held in the annuity. It only protects the guaranteed minimum level of income that you can take from the annuity (for life, even if the promised minimum withdrawals and market losses deplete the value of the investments held in the annuity to zero). The actual value of the investments will fluctuate based on the performance of the market and will be reduced with each withdrawal. Also, if you withdraw more than the minimum level promised in your particular annuity contract in any year, that may decrease the minimum amount of future annual income.

On the surface, this may sound like a win-win. You're guaranteed to receive a set level of income no matter how the portfolio performs, and you also have the potential for growth if the investments do well. But be aware that all of this comes at a cost. In general, a variable annuity with a GLWB provides a lower guaranteed payment than an SPIA. In effect, you may be exchanging a higher guaranteed payment from the insurance company for upside potential as well as access to the investments held in your annuity if you need them.

No matter how you slice it, these vehicles come with a lot of fine print. Be sure to talk to an advisor who has experience with these products before you move ahead.

➲ **SMART MOVE:** Before you purchase an annuity, check out the credit rating of the insurance company. The FDIC does not insure annuities. Therefore, if you're investing a very large sum in annuities, consider diversifying between several companies. Even if you have to give up a little on return, buy only from the highest rated companies.

Calculate the Return

Before you purchase an annuity, it's important to understand how its return compares to another annuity's or to another secure stream of income—say from a laddered portfolio of CDs or high-quality bonds. I'll give a simplified example for an immediate fixed annuity here, but there can be a number of variables that make the calculation much more complicated (for example, a cost-of-living adjustment, available at an extra cost). Unless you're extremely adept at number crunching, I highly recommend that you enlist the help of your financial advisor or CPA to run various scenarios.

Example: Let's say that you're 65 and have $300,000 to purchase an immediate fixed annuity. You are quoted an annual payment of $24,000 per year for the rest of your life.

At first glance, $24,000 a year seems like an 8 percent annual return. But the payment is made up of the return of your principal as well as interest, so the actual return is lower—and will vary depending on how long you live.

For example, if you live for another 18 years, this annuity's annual yield is 4.45%. If you live to 90, the annual return goes to about 6.6%. If you live to 95, it's 7.3%.

Once you have a good sense of the return, you can then compare one annuity to another as well as to other investments.

⚠ **CAUTION:** Most deferred annuities have a surrender charge for the first six to eight years of the accumulation phase. You'll be able to withdraw your money, but you'll pay a penalty. Often that fee will decrease each year until it disappears. You may also pay a penalty for withdrawals before age 59½, plus taxes. Also note that a 1035 exchange will allow you to transfer from one annuity to another without tax implications, but you may still have to pay a surrender charge. There could also be a loss of guaranteed benefits or other factors that could reduce or eliminate the benefits of the exchange.

Shop Around

If you think an annuity is for you, compare products and their expenses from a number of highly rated companies before you commit. Because annuities can come with a dizzying array of features (all of which up the price), be sure you're making an "apples-to-apples" comparison by using the same set of scenarios for each quote.

Next Steps
- For thoughts on turning your portfolio into a monthly draw, see **Question 23.**
- Nervous about switching over to becoming a spender after having spent your whole life saving? See **Question 22.**
- Thinking about working part-time? See **Question 28.**

Important Disclosures
Variable annuities are long-term investment vehicles intended for retirement purposes. It is important to carefully consider the investment objectives, risks, charges, and expenses of the annuity and its underlying investments before purchasing it. Be sure to request a prospectus from the issuer and read it carefully before you invest. Also, be sure to keep the following in mind:

- The value of the annuity may be more or less than the premiums paid, and it is possible to lose money.
- Withdrawals prior to age 59½ may be subject to a 10 percent federal tax penalty in addition to applicable income taxes.
- Variable annuities are subject to a number of fees, including mortality and risk expense charges, administrative fees, premium taxes, investment management fees, possible surrender charges, and charges for additional optional features.
- Under the terms of a guaranteed lifetime withdrawal benefit (GLWB), your investment choices in the contract may be limited to a prespecified selection of options.

Q21.

I'm 60 and way behind in my savings. Will I ever be able to retire?

We baby boomers have always been known for doing our own thing and, as retirees, we continue to live up to that reputation. Our parents may have retired in a certain way, but we're determined to retire *our* way. So before you can answer the question of whether you'll ever be able to retire, you have to decide just what retirement means to you. Do you have a specific date in mind? A certain lifestyle?

In many ways, whether or not you'll be able to retire depends not only on how much you've managed to save, but also on how well you can manage on what you have. You have to be flexible, and you have to be focused, but as long as you're still working and saving, you can make decisions today that may make tomorrow a bit easier.

Start by Getting a Handle on Current Spending

Unfortunately, there's no magic formula. The only way you can save more—or survive on less—is to spend less. So if your savings are coming up short, you have some serious budget crunching to do right away. In **Question 2,** which is primarily addressed to someone who hasn't even started to save, I go into detail about creating a budget and managing cash flow. The same advice holds true for you. It's important to take a close look at how you're spending your money now to figure out 1) where you can cut back to save more, and 2) how you could realistically live on a smaller retirement income down the road.

Start with some simple accounting:

- Divide your expenses into two categories: nondiscretionary and discretionary.
- Compare your projected expenses to what you actually spend.

Now with this information in front of you, get practical. Find ways to cut back. Reprioritize your spending, putting savings at the top of your nondiscretionary expenses. If you spend less than projected in one area, put that extra money toward your savings.

➡ SMART MOVE: Live below your means both before and in retirement. You'll not only be able to save more; you also won't need as much to support yourself during retirement. This also allows you to build up a cushion in case you have unexpected expenses. When it comes to money, most surprises work against you rather than for you; without shock absorbers, the ride can get bumpy.

Lower Your Debt

Excessive debt can derail the best-laid retirement plans. If you're already in the hole, the first thing to do is stop digging! Then do your best to pay off as much debt as you can as soon as you can. If you expect you'll have to live on less in retirement, you don't want your precious dollars going toward interest payments. Start with your credit cards and move on to things like car payments and eventually your mortgage. While **Question 13** talks about the pros and cons of being debt-free before you retire (and not all debt is categorically bad), with a limited retirement income, the fewer bills you have to pay the better.

Make Saving Your Number One Goal

There's no time to lose. Put every dollar you can in your retirement accounts. Max out your 401(k) or other retirement plan contributions. Contribute to a deductible traditional IRA or a Roth IRA. (See **Question 4** for more on types of IRAs.) Once you've maxed out your tax-advantaged retirement accounts, save more if you can in a taxable account.

Whatever you do, don't get discouraged. Instead, make a commitment to use every possible means to increase your savings. **Question 2** gives you additional ideas on how to save more.

➲ **SMART MOVE:** Don't forget about catch-up contributions for people over 50 for both 401(k)s and IRAs. They work! See **Question 2.**

CREATIVE WAYS TO INCREASE YOUR SAVINGS

Increasing your savings takes discipline as well as a little creativity. Here are some ideas:

- **Increase your 401(k) contribution in increments.** Aim for the full 401(k) contribution of $17,500 plus a catch-up contribution of $5,500. If you can't reach it right away, start smaller. Up your contribution by a percentage point this year. Do the same each year until you retire and whenever you get a raise.

- **Turn back the clock on spending.** Think back on what you did when you had less money. Could you go out for lunch instead of dinner? Have friends over for an old-fashioned potluck? Give up the gym and start exercising outdoors? These are small changes that can really add up. They might even be more fun.

- **Use your age to your advantage.** Being over 50 has its perks. Take advantage of them. Join AARP and use your card in drugstores, car rental agencies—anywhere that offers a discount. And proudly ask for any senior discount. You've earned it!

- **Eliminate hidden expenses.** Periodically check your service plans (phone, cable, etc.) to make sure that you're actually using everything you're paying for. I'm a big fan of automated payments, but sometimes they make you lose track of where your money is going.

➲ **SMART MOVE:** To help yourself feel more in control, go to an online calculator like the one on schwab.com and explore different retirement savings scenarios. You might be amazed at how much difference a few extra dollars and a few extra years of saving can make.

Don't Be Discouraged by the 4 Percent Guideline

You've probably heard about the 4 percent guideline, which I discuss in greater depth in **Question 1.** This guideline, which is somewhat of an industry standard, can be a real heart-stopper for someone who feels they haven't saved enough. The rule says that you should aim to withdraw only 4 percent of your portfolio's value in your first year of retirement, then increase that amount every year for inflation. It assumes that you have a conservative to moderate portfolio (20–60 percent in stocks) and will have a thirty-year retirement.

But what does that mean to real people in real dollars?

Example: Let's say that you and your spouse expect to spend $65,000 the first year in retirement and anticipate $30,000 in combined Social Security benefits. If you have no other sources of income, you'll have to withdraw $35,000 from your portfolio to meet your income needs. Now multiply that figure by 25 to come up with a rough estimate of your target retirement portfolio (not taking into account portfolio growth or inflation). In this case, you'd need to aim for a portfolio of $825,000 to be able to follow the 4 percent rule.

If this example has you shaking your head in disbelief, don't despair. While withdrawing 4 percent of your portfolio each year is a good ballpark, it's not set in stone. You can adjust it according to your own situation. For instance, might your retirement be longer? Withdraw less. If you think it will be shorter, withdraw more.

Also, realize that this rule is designed to give you a 90 percent chance that your money will last as long as you do. If you can live with a lower probability that your portfolio will last, say 80 percent or even less, how much you withdraw is up to you. But having a guideline may help keep you from going through your money too soon.

In the meantime, review your current investments. Are you being too conservative? Too aggressive? **Question 5** goes into detail on how to invest when approaching retirement and how you might shift your investments over time.

⚠ **CAUTION:** Growing your savings is a worthy goal, but so is protecting it. Don't take on more investment risk than you can live with comfortably. Shoot for a realistic rate of return—which is probably lower than the high single digits we expected in the past. See **Question 5** for more on risk and return. And keep saving!

Be Realistic About Retirement Timing

Savings guidelines aside, you have to be realistic about your own retirement timeline. You may need to postpone retirement. Or transition from full-time to part-time work. More and more people are planning to work into their seventies. And many recent retirees have found that a part-time job keeps them happy, engaged, and on budget.

Maybe you'll need to adjust your lifestyle expectations as well and learn to live on less overall. If you're in good health and you're content to live more simply, your savings may go farther than you think.

WHEN DO YOU PLAN TO RETIRE?

According to the 2013 Employee Retirement Confidence Survey, conducted by the Employee Benefit Research Institute, in 1991 just 11 percent of workers expected to retire after age 65. In 2013, 36 percent of workers expected to wait until after age 65 to retire. And 70 percent plan to work for pay after they retire.

➲ **SMART MOVE:** Postpone taking Social Security if you can. For every year you delay past age 62 (up to age 70, when you max out), your benefit goes up anywhere from 6⅔ to 8%. Not a bad return! See **Question 30** for more.

Consider Tapping Into Your Home Equity

Your home may be your castle, but it can also be a source of retirement income. If you still have a mortgage, downsizing to a smaller home or a less expensive area could lower your expenses significantly, in terms of both mortgage payments and property taxes. And if you've owned your home for a number of years, you may also benefit from generous capital gains tax exclusions. **Question 18** has lots of practical information on selling your home.

If you have your heart set on staying in your current home, you might still tap into your equity through a reverse mortgage. While it's not for everyone—and you have to be cautious—it may be a viable way to supplement your monthly income. See **Question 26** for the pros and potential pitfalls of a reverse mortgage.

Next Steps
- Do a more detailed estimate of how much money you'll need in retirement. See **Question 1.**
- Review your insurance coverage to make sure you're not paying for something you don't need. **Question 27** has some tips.
- If you're considering a reverse mortgage, read **Question 26** before you take action.
- For practical guidelines on how to create a retirement income stream, see **Question 23.**

PART III

Life in Retirement

I have a friend who is now in his fourth "retirement." Every time he finishes up one job, opportunity comes knocking. Within the next few months, he's involved in the next challenge—which may last for six months or a year. For him, work is not a negative. It's interesting and fun—and provides some income to boot.

Welcome to the new retirement. You may be working part-time or on-and-off, but it's different. You're more independent in terms of both your finances and your lifestyle. You call your own shots.

The only catch is that with this freedom comes extra work and responsibility. You may have to manage your financial life more carefully than in the past. You have to stay on top of your investments, your insurance, and your tax bill. You're also responsible for paying yourself enough to sustain your lifestyle, but not so much that you deplete your savings too soon.

This section contains what we at Schwab call our "income fundamentals." Developed by the Schwab Center for Financial Research, they provide a concise and practical framework for managing your money in retirement. You'll also find advice on going back to work, insurance, and charitable giving.

All of this is essential to your well-being. But that said, I hope that concerns about money don't rule your life. Numerous studies have shown that we all need a baseline amount of money to be happy. Add more, and you don't get proportionately happier. Family, friends, creativity, fun—to me, that's what really matters. But no matter how much money you have, handle it wisely. And at the same time, I hope that you can harness your wisdom, your strength, and your sense of purpose to enjoy this very special time in your life.

Q22.

Now that I'm retired, how should I manage my money to make it last?

You've been building and protecting your retirement nest egg for de-cades. You've been anticipating the day when you could say goodbye to the nine-to-five grind and finally have time for whatever activities or challenges come your way—whether that's working part-time, volunteer-ing, or traveling, or even starting a new business. Whatever your dreams, this is your time. What surprises you, though, what you hadn't antici-pated, was how tough this transition would be psychologically—and how vulnerable you would feel.

I've heard variations of this story so many times that I know it isn't necessarily a function of one's wealth. Switching from being a saver to being a spender means having an entirely new approach to your money. It can be tough regardless of the size of your portfolio.

To ease this transition, my colleagues at the Schwab Center for Fi-nancial Research have come up with some pretty straightforward guide-lines. They aren't intended to be rigid directives. But our experience has shown us that these fundamentals can help reduce your financial stress and support whatever retirement lifestyle you choose.

Also, I hate to sound like a broken record, but think about consulting an objective financial planner as you transition into retirement. This is one of those times in your life when some professional guidance can go a long way.

#1: Review Your Situation

No matter how much or how little you've saved, make sure you know exactly where you stand. Gather the latest statements from all of your accounts, and as I recommend in **My Top Ten Recommendations** on page 1, create a net worth statement (your assets minus your debts). Then take a look at your cash flow (money in, money out) for the last couple of years, and use this information to create a projection for the future.

⚠ **CAUTION:** If you want your portfolio to last for thirty years, plan to withdraw no more than 4 percent of its value in the first year of retirement. After that, you can adjust the amount for inflation. See **Question 1** for more.

#2: Maintain at Least a Year of Cash

Set aside enough cash to cover at least one year of spending. This is the amount that you'll need in addition to the income you can count on—for example, from Social Security, a pension, or real estate investments.

Following are some good places to keep your cash. None will provide a great return, but that's okay. This is about safety and liquidity—not income.

WHERE TO STASH YOUR YEAR'S WORTH OF CASH

Investment	Liquidity	Market Value	Credit Quality
Bank checking and savings accounts (preferably interest-bearing)	Immediate	Stable	FDIC-insured
Money market funds	Generally immediate (may be limits on writing checks)	Generally stable but could fluctuate	Not FDIC-insured

T-bills	At maturity	Fluctuates prior to maturity	Backed by U.S. Treasury
Certificates of deposit (CDs) (perhaps laddered with three-, six-, and nine-month maturities)	Bank CDs may have penalties for early withdrawal	Stable	FDIC-insured

Note: Money market funds are neither insured nor guaranteed by the Federal Deposit Insurance Corporation or any other government agency. Although the fund seeks to preserve the value of your investment at $1.00 per share, it is possible to lose money by investing in the fund.

SMART MOVE: If possible, you'll also want to have enough cash to cover an additional one to four years in your portfolio. See #4 below for details.

#3: Consolidate Income in a Single Account

Combine all of your nonportfolio income—which could come from Social Security, a pension, an annuity, whatever—into one account. You can also put portfolio income—for example, interest and dividends—into this account. This account will be your primary source of cash, allowing you to more easily track your income and spending over time.

#4: Match Your Investments to Your Goals and Needs

In **Question 5**, I talk about selecting a mix of investments in keeping with your personal goals, time frame, and risk tolerance. For most people this means gradually moving away from stocks and toward bonds and other fixed income as well as cash. But it's important not to abandon stocks altogether, since they can help your portfolio keep up with inflation. Bonds not only will provide you with income, but also will act as a buffer against market volatility. Cash investments protect you from having to sell your stocks or bonds at a bad time.

For example, you might follow the following path:

	Pre-retirement	Early Retirement	Late Retirement
Portfolio	Moderate	Moderately conservative	Conservative
Percentage of stocks, fixed income, and cash	60% stocks 35% fixed income 5% cash	40% stocks 50% fixed income 10% cash	20% stocks 50% fixed income 30% cash

CREATING A LADDER

A short-term ladder (maturities of one to four years) of CDs, Treasuries, or the highest-rated bonds can be a sound way to cover your living expenses for the next several years. (A ladder is made up of individual securities with a sequence of maturities over a series of years. This way, some will always be maturing, while others invested for the longer term generate higher income.)

For example, you could create a ladder something like the following:

Amount Invested	Maturity	Type	Other Considerations
Two to four years of expenses	• 6 months • 1 year • 1 year, 6 months • 2 years • 2 years, 6 months • 3 years • 3 years, 6 months • 4 years	Mix of FDIC-insured CDs, Treasury bills and notes, and municipal bonds	A ladder can include multiple CDs or bond types, depending on interest rates. Also consider municipal bonds rated AA or higher by Moody's and Standard & Poor's, but only in taxable accounts.

#5: Cover Essentials with Predictable Income

In #1 you reviewed your income and expenses. We also recommend that you divide your expenses according to whether they're essential or discretionary. Ideally you'll be able to cover all of your essentials with predictable income. That way you can cut back on nonessentials in a lean year.

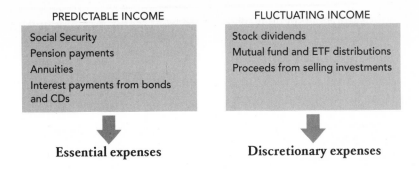

Note: Annuity guarantees are subject to the financial strength and claims-paying ability of the issuing insurance company.

➡ **SMART MOVE:** Don't have enough predictable income to cover your essentials? Consider purchasing an immediate fixed annuity. See **Question 20** for more.

#6: Don't Be Afraid to Tap Into Your Principal

It's the rare individual whose portfolio is large enough to live off dividends and interest alone. Your goal isn't to avoid tapping into your principal at all, but to do it in a prudent way.

First, review the 4 percent guideline from **Question 1.** In essence, you can withdraw up to 4 percent of your portfolio's value each year, increasing with inflation, and have 90 percent certainty that it will last for thirty years—provided that you are invested in a well-diversified portfolio with at least 40 percent stocks.

➡ **SMART MOVE:** If you have mutual funds in taxable accounts, consider having the distributions automatically swept into a money market fund. You may not have to sell as many shares that way.

#7: Follow a Smart Portfolio Drawdown Strategy

When it comes to creating your retirement "paycheck," tax-efficiency is king. I go into more detail in **Question 23,** but the short version is as follows:

1. First draw down your principal from maturing bonds and CDs.

2. Then, if you're 70½ or older, take your required minimum distribution from your IRAs or other tax-deferred accounts, focusing on **overweighted** and lower-rated assets.

3. Next sell overweighted and lower-rated assets in your taxable accounts.

4. And finally sell overweighted and lower-rated assets in your tax-deferred accounts. Sell from your traditional IRA before you move on to your Roth IRA.

The rationale behind this order is that withdrawals from traditional IRAs and 401(k)s are taxed as ordinary income, typically at a higher rate than the long-term capital gains rate that you'd pay when you sell investments held for more than one year from your taxable accounts. Also, leaving more money in your IRA or 401(k) provides more time for tax-deferred compound growth.

#8: Rebalance to Stay Aligned with Your Goals

As I discuss in **Question 5,** it's important to review your portfolio's asset allocation at least annually. If one asset class has grown beyond your plan, it's time to pare it back. Once you're retired, this can be a prime opportunity to sell assets to generate cash.

> *Example:* Let's say that your target asset allocation is 40% stocks and 60% bonds, but your portfolio has drifted to 45% stocks and 55% bonds. You can sell some stocks to generate income, and reallocate anything that's left over to bonds until you're back on target.

#9: Stay Flexible and Reevaluate as Needed

Life doesn't just stop changing once you're retired. Let's say you want to sell your house and travel the world. Perhaps you've received an inheritance. Or maybe you're starting a business or going back to work. As your needs change or your feelings about risk change, your portfolio and the amount you withdraw should reflect your new realities.

➡ **SMART MOVE:** Review your budget at least once a year, reassessing whether each expense is discretionary or nondiscretionary.

Next Steps

- For more on how to create your retirement "paycheck," see **Question 23.**
- Wondering when you should start collecting Social Security? See **Question 30.**
- For the lowdown on RMDs, see **Question 23.**
- To refresh your memory on the 4 percent guideline, see **Question 1.**

Important Disclosure

Rebalancing does not protect against losses or guarantee that an investor's goal will be met.

I just retired. What's the smartest way to draw income from my portfolio?

You have a half dozen or so accounts ranging from your 401(k) to your IRA, to your Roth IRA, to your brokerage accounts, each with different rules and regulations. Each also holds a variety of investments, from individual stocks and bonds to mutual funds and ETFs. So, yes—it can be very confusing to know what to take from where.

Thankfully, my colleagues at the Schwab Center for Financial Research have created a priority system. Their goal is to help you make decisions that minimize your taxes while also protecting your portfolio for the future. In **Question 22**, #7, on page 195, I gave you the CliffsNotes version. Now I'll go into some more depth.

Before I get started, though, I want to reiterate a few essentials for managing your portfolio at this point in your life:

1. Give very careful thought to your asset allocation. You probably shouldn't be taking on as much risk as you did when you were younger, but I caution you not to avoid stocks, either.

2. Figure out how much money you need to withdraw to supplement your income from Social Security, a pension, real estate investments, or

any other source. If you want your portfolio to last for thirty years, it's prudent to cap withdrawals at roughly 4 percent.

3.   Keep your most tax-efficient investments in your taxable accounts and your least tax-efficient investments in your tax-deferred accounts. See **Question 5,** page 69.

⚠ **CAUTION:** Stocks are the best protection against inflation—so unless you have a very large portfolio, and are certain that you can live on fixed income alone, don't avoid stocks.

1. First, Draw Down Principal from Maturing Bonds and CDs

In **Question 22** I talked about creating a short-term ladder of bonds or CDs. If you've done this, your first step can be to tap the principal of each bond as it matures. If this is enough to supplement your other income, congratulations—you're done. Chances are, though, that you'll need to press on.

2. If You're 70½ or Older, Take Your RMDs

Once you reach 70½, the IRS *requires* you to take a yearly required minimum distribution (RMD) from all of your retirement accounts except a Roth IRA (a Roth 401(k) and a Roth 403(b) have RMDs that kick in once you turn 70½—unless you're still working). Whether you need this money or not, you've still got to take it.

THE SKINNY ON RMDs

Starting at age 70½ you are required to begin withdrawing money from most of your retirement accounts—traditional, SEP and SIMPLE IRAs, and 401(k)s. (However, you can delay taking an RMD from your 401(k) if you're still employed.) If you have a Roth IRA, you're in the clear. There is no RMD for a Roth IRA.

While the concept of an RMD is simple, there are rules you need to abide by to avoid substantial penalties. Here are a few things to keep in mind.

Don't be late: Technically, you have until the year *after* you turn 70½ to take your first RMD. The IRS gives you the choice of taking it either by the end of the year you turn 70½ or by April 1 of the year following. For instance, if your 70th birthday is on December 1, 2013, you turn 70½ on June 1, 2014, so you could delay taking your first RMD until April 1, 2015. All subsequent RMDs must be taken by December 31 of each year.

This timing is no casual matter. The penalty for failure to take your RMD on time is *50 percent* of the amount that should have been withdrawn.

Factor in taxes: While delaying your first RMD may seem to make sense if you don't need the money, there's another consideration. Even if you wait until the April 1 deadline, you still have to take your second RMD by December 31 of that same year—two distributions in one year. Distributions are taxed as ordinary income, so taking two in one year could bump you into a higher tax bracket.

Calculate correctly: You must calculate an RMD for each of your retirement accounts, not just one. Your RMD is based on the value of your account on December 31 of the previous year, so start by listing the fair market value of your IRAs as of that date. Next, determine your life expectancy using appropriate Life Expectancy Tables from the IRS. You can find them in Publication 590, available at IRS.gov. The basic formula: Fair market value divided by life expectancy equals RMD.

⚠ **CAUTION:** Your RMD will change every year, so don't just use last year's figures. Given the size of the penalty, you want to get it right!

Example: Say your IRA is valued at $100,000. Using the Uniform Lifetime Table, the first year you would divide that by 27.4 years. Your first RMD would be $3,649.64.

To make it easy, the financial institution where you keep your IRA may calculate your RMD for you (Schwab does!), but it's good to know the formula yourself.

Decide how to take your distribution: While you calculate an RMD for each retirement account, you don't have to take the distribution specifically from each. You can take the sum total of your RMDs from any one account, making it a much simpler process. In fact, you can simply add up the value of all of your accounts and do just one calculation.

There's an exception, however, for 401(k)s and most other types of employer-sponsored retirement accounts. If you have more than one, you have to calculate and take a withdrawal from each individual account.

Consider consolidating: If you have just one retirement account with one financial institution, taking your yearly RMD can be a pretty simple process. But if you have several accounts at various banks or brokerages, you might want to consolidate everything in one place. You could also consider rolling any 401(k)s still at a former employer into an IRA. This would make it easier to calculate your total RMD as well as to determine which account to tap for the distribution.

Your strategy should be to sell the lowest-rated securities in your overweighted asset classes. If your RMD satisfies your income needs, you won't have to tap into your taxable accounts. Nonetheless, **your decision on what to sell should be made in the context of all of your accounts.** In other words, before you decide what to sell from your IRA, look to where you're under- or overweighted in your entire portfolio.

➡ **SMART MOVE:** Schwab Equity Ratings, which range from a letter grade of A to F, are one way to quickly evaluate stocks. This can be a great starting point for your deeper research.

Example: Let's say that your RMD is $25,000, which covers all the additional income you need. After reviewing the breakdown of *all* of your accounts, you see that you are overweighted in large-cap domestic stocks and international stocks and underweighted in bonds. By selling your lowest-rated large-cap and international stocks from your IRA, you get your entire portfolio back to your target allocation.

See "Withdrawing Income and Rebalancing Your Portfolio" on pages 203–204 for an example of how the numbers can work in your overall portfolio.

SMART MOVE: Just because you have to withdraw an RMD doesn't mean that you have to spend it. If you don't need the money now, you can deposit it into your brokerage or savings account for future use.

3. Sell Overweighted and Lower-Rated Investments from Your Taxable Accounts

If you need to withdraw more than your RMD, look to your taxable accounts next. Withdrawals from taxable accounts are taxed as capital gains rather than as ordinary income, with a preferential rate for gains on investments you've owned for more than a year. Of course, if you've lost confidence in any of your other investments, they are also good sell candidates.

SMART MOVE: Try to postpone selling appreciated investments that you've owned for less than a year. You need to have owned the security for one year and one day to get the long-term capital gains tax rate.

If you have to sell high-rated securities, you can minimize your tax bill by starting with those that will generate a loss, before you sell those that will generate a gain. Also, whenever you're considering selling an investment in a taxable account, think about matching gains to losses as a way to control your taxes. See **Question 25**, pages 220–221, for more about this process, known as *tax-loss harvesting*.

WITHDRAWING INCOME AND REBALANCING YOUR PORTFOLIO, ALL IN ONE

It's smart to plan your withdrawals at the same time that you rebalance your portfolio. Once you've decided which asset class or classes need trimming, look at your lowest-rated holdings for potential sales.

As a simplified example, let's say that you're a new retiree with the following moderate portfolio. You intend to withdraw 4 percent, or $40,000, at the end of the year.

Investment	Taxable Account	IRA	Total Portfolio	Allocation
Large-cap stocks	$350,000	0	$350,000	35%
Mid/small-cap stocks	$100,000	0	$100,000	10%
International stocks	$150,000	0	$150,000	15%
Taxable bonds	0	$350,000	$350,000	35%
Money market funds	$50,000	0	$50,000	5%
Total	$650,000	$350,000	$1,000,000	100%

At the end of the year, your portfolio looks like this:

Investment	Taxable Account	IRA	Total Portfolio	Allocation
Large-cap stocks	$410,000	0	$410,000	37.3%
Mid/small-cap stocks	$120,000	0	$120,000	10.9%
International stocks	$178,000	0	$178,000	16.2%
Taxable bonds	0	$340,000	$340,000	30.9%
Money market funds	$52,000	0	$52,000	4.7%
Total	$760,000	$340,000	$1,100,000	100%

As you can see, your domestic and international stocks had a good year, but your bonds were down. By selling some stocks and adding to your bonds, you can rebalance (getting back to your target allocation) and generate your $40,000 at the same time.

Investment	Taxable Account	IRA	Cash Out (or In)	Total Portfolio	Allocation
Large-cap stocks	$410,000	0	$39,000	$371,000	35%
Mid/small-cap stocks	$120,000	0	$14,000	$106,000	10%
International stocks	$178,000	0	$19,000	$159,000	15%
Taxable bonds	0	$340,000	($31,000)	$371,000	35%
Money market funds	$52,000	0	($1,000)	$53,000	5%
Total	$760,000	$340,000	$40,000	$1,060,000	100%

For more on rebalancing, see **Question 5**, pages 71–73.

☎ **TALK TO AN EXPERT:** You may become quite adept at rebalancing your portfolio once you've been through it a few times. As a new retiree, however, it can make sense to enlist the help of a trusted advisor.

4. Sell Overweighted and Lower-Rated Assets from Your Tax-Deferred Accounts

Generally, your tax-deferred accounts will be your last place to look for income, starting with outsized asset classes and lower-rated securities. If you're 70½ or older, you know that at a minimum you have to withdraw your RMD. But you can take more if you need it. Or, if you're younger than 70½, you may still want to tap your tax-deferred account despite the fact that you will be paying taxes at your ordinary income tax rate.

It's often smart to tap into your Roth IRA last. Not only can it continue to grow without taxes, but you'll be able to withdraw that money tax-free at a later date. Roth IRAs are also a great way to pass on money tax-free to your heirs. In fact, some retirees may want to convert all or a portion of their IRA to a Roth IRA.

DOES A ROTH CONVERSION MAKE SENSE?

Converting your traditional IRA to a Roth IRA means coughing up taxes now in order to avoid taxes later. Usually we think of this as a strategy better suited for younger investors, but it may make sense for you as well.

Recapping a few basics (for more details, see **Question 4,** page 32):

- Money put into a traditional IRA is generally tax-deductible, but you pay ordinary income tax rates on withdrawals.

- Money put into a Roth IRA is not tax-deductible, but you can withdraw earnings tax-free if you're at least 59½ and have held the account for at least five years. You don't have to take an RMD.

As a result:

- Roth IRAs generally make the most sense for those with a long time horizon who believe that they will be in a **higher** tax bracket when they withdraw funds.

- Traditional IRAs generally make the most sense for those with a shorter time horizon who believe that they will be in a **lower** tax bracket when they withdraw funds.

As a retiree, you have less time for tax-deferred growth and probably a lower likelihood for a higher tax bracket in the future. Still, a conversion may make sense. Let's take a closer look at some potential pros and the one big con.

PROS

- If you're planning to leave your IRA assets to your heirs, it's a real plus for them. In effect, you'd be prepaying the income taxes on their behalf without it being a taxable gift. Your heirs can then take income-tax-free withdrawals during their lifetimes.

- The tax you pay up front on the conversion reduces your gross taxable estate, especially when you pay from assets other than your IRA.

- There is no RMD for a Roth IRA. If your current RMD is more than you need or want, converting to a Roth will allow you to take less— preserving more for your heirs.

- If you pay the tax now, you can make future withdrawals tax-free.

CON

The biggest deterrent to converting to a Roth is that you have to pay income taxes up front. Note in particular:

- The assets you convert are added to your gross income in the year you make the conversion, so you could be bumped into a higher tax bracket.

- Ideally you should have the cash on hand to pay the income tax. If you have to sell appreciated assets to pay the tax, you'll also have to pay capital gains tax. If you have to pay the tax from your IRA, you lose the potential benefit of tax-free growth on the amount.

Also realize that a Roth conversion isn't an all-or-nothing proposition. You can choose to convert just a portion of your IRA, and you can also convert portions over a number of years.

⚠ **CAUTION:** If you decide to convert to a Roth, be sure to take your RMD for the year before completing the conversion. RMDs are calculated based on your traditional IRA balance at the end of the previous year and cannot be part of a Roth conversion.

Next Steps

- To read more about income taxes in retirement, see **Question 25.**
- To refresh your memory on the rules for different retirement accounts, see **Question 4.**
- To refresh your memory on investing fundamentals, see **Question 5.**
- Concerned about running out of predictable income? Read **Question 20** on annuities.

Important Disclosure

Schwab Equity Ratings and the general buy/hold/sell guidance are not personal recommendations for any particular investor or client and do not take into account the financial, investment, or other objectives or needs of, and may not be suitable for, any particular investor or client. Investors and clients should consider Schwab Equity Ratings as only a single factor in making their investment decision while taking into account the current market environment.

Q24.

I was forced to retire early for health reasons. How can I make up for the unexpected shortfall in savings?

The best-laid plans to postpone retirement—or to never fully retire— can unfortunately be derailed by certain realities. I've mentioned the Retirement Confidence Survey conducted by the Employee Benefit Research Institute several times in this book, and once again, the statistics it cites are relevant. For instance, in 2013, while 36 percent of workers stated they didn't plan to retire until past age 65 (and 7 percent don't plan to retire at all), close to half of retirees reported that they actually had to retire sooner than they expected, primarily because of health or a disability. Whatever the reason, they found themselves facing a future with less money than they had hoped.

It's a tough situation and makes a case for private disability insurance, as I discuss in **Question 17.** But if you don't have your own disability insurance, you're not left out in the cold. There are several practical steps you can take—from being extra vigilant about how you spend and protect the money you have to possibly tapping into available government and private foundation resources.

While I can't promise this will be easy, it is in your power to make the most of what you've already managed to save. And the sooner you get started, the better you'll feel about the future.

Take Stock of What You Have

The first thing I'd do is look at the big picture. Start with your personal net worth. In **My Top Ten Recommendations,** on pages 1–2, I give an easy step-by-step way to create a personal net worth statement. Essentially, you add up what you own and subtract what you owe. Hopefully you'll end up in the plus, because this will be the money you'll have to manage carefully going forward.

Now get more specific and figure out your annual cash flow—what you have coming in and what's going out. As I outline in **Question 2**, list your yearly expenses (both nondiscretionary and discretionary) and put real figures by each. Do the same with your annual sources of income. Now add up each list and subtract your expenses from your income. With these figures in front of you, it's time to get practical. That may mean a change in lifestyle, downsizing your home, or rethinking your future goals—but at least you'll know where you stand and can make decisions based on your true financial situation.

Micromanage Spending

With a shortfall in retirement savings, chances are you're going to have to curb your spending. You may think you're already living frugally, but take another look, focusing specifically on your discretionary expenses. Are all those "nice-to-haves" really necessary? Create a detailed monthly budget (see **Question 2**), and then track your spending for thirty days to see where your money is actually going. Look for creative ways to cut back wherever possible (see **Question 21**). If you need help staying on top of your budget, try an online monthly budget planner like the one on schwabmoneywise.com.

> ➤ **SMART MOVE:** Check with your local water, garbage, sanitary, and cable companies to see if they offer discounts to seniors, the disabled, or those with low incomes. The Federal Communications Commission's Lifeline program is an example. And don't forget to ask for senior discounts wherever you shop—*before* you settle the bill!

File for Social Security

Delaying taking Social Security benefits until at least your full retirement age is great if you can afford it. But if you can't make ends meet, you may need this money sooner. Your monthly check will be permanently reduced by about 25 percent if you start benefits at age 62, but you may ultimately break even. **Question 31** goes into more detail on how to determine what your benefit will be; **Question 30** discusses strategies for maximizing your benefits.

Protect Your Savings

Money management in retirement can be tricky for anyone, but if your assets are limited, you need to take extra care. Ideally, you'd keep cash for a year's expenses in a safe, liquid account such as a short-term CD or a money market fund. On top of that, put another two to three years' living expenses in longer-term CDs or high-quality bond funds. This way you won't be forced to sell assets to cover expenses when the market is low.

And while I usually recommend keeping at least a portion of your assets in stocks to hedge against inflation, you probably should gravitate to the more conservative side. When you have limited resources, it's especially tough to weather a personal crisis (for example, a health problem) or a market downturn. **Question 22** talks about how to keep a balanced portfolio in retirement.

⚠ **CAUTION:** Never put money you know you'll need in the next two or three years in the stock market. Always protect yourself with a cash cushion!

Don't Let Your Health Insurance Lapse

As you probably already know, health insurance is a must. So even as you cut back, be sure you have adequate coverage. If you're not yet on Medicare, maintain at least a high-deductible policy. You can comparison shop on your state's or the federal health insurance exchange website and also look into COBRA.

At the same time, don't spend precious dollars on insurance you don't need. Check out **Question 27** for an overview of which types of insurance make sense—and which don't.

Check Into Government Programs

Both federal and state governments offer a variety of assistance programs for people with disabilities and those over age 65. However, in general the income and asset limitations to qualify are very low. Even if you no longer have earned income, your retirement assets may put you beyond those limits. But it doesn't hurt to explore the possibilities. There are a wide variety of other government-sponsored programs to help seniors with basic costs from health care, to utilities, to nutrition. Benefits .gov is a good place to begin a search for benefits you might be eligible to receive.

AT A GLANCE: GOVERNMENT ASSISTANCE PROGRAMS

Supplemental Security Income (SSI)	SSI pays monthly benefits to people with extremely limited income and disabilities. These payments are not tied to your work history. For 2013, the asset threshold to qualify is $2,000 for an individual or $3,000 for a couple (generally excluding the value of your home and one vehicle). Income limits are $710 per month for an individual or $1,066 for a couple; however, not all income is counted. The maximum monthly payment is the same as the monthly income limit. Most states offer supplements to the federal SSI payment. Best to check ssa .gov/ssi for details.
Social Security Disability Insurance (SSDI)	Unlike SSI, SSDI is dependent on how many Social Security work credits you've earned. However, as I discuss in **Question 33**, qualifying for SSDI is particularly difficult. In a nutshell, your disability must prevent you from working and be expected to last twelve months or until death. The average monthly payment is about $1,100. There are no asset limitations to qualify for SSDI, but if you earn over a certain amount, you'll no longer be considered disabled. Also, if you have sizable unearned income, say from interest or investments, or your spouse makes a certain amount, a portion of your SSDI benefits will be taxed. Once again, you can get more information at ssa.gov.
Medicare	While you're generally not eligible for Medicare until age 65, you may qualify for early benefits if you have end-stage renal disease. You also will get Medicare coverage automatically after you've received SSDI benefits for two years.
Medicaid	Similar to SSI, qualifying for Medicaid is subject to strict income and asset limitations. In many states, if you qualify for SSI, you are also automatically eligible for Medicaid.
State disability insurance	As I mention in **Question 17**, California, Hawaii, New Jersey, New York, Rhode Island, and Puerto Rico offer short-term disability insurance for six months to a year.

Search for Private Foundations That Help Seniors

There are a number of foundations, such as the AARP Foundation, that provide grants, loans, and direct assistance to seniors. You may not need this type of help now, but it's good to know it exists. There are plenty of websites, such as LoveToKnowSeniors, that list the tremendous variety of foundations across the country offering services particularly to seniors.

DO YOU QUALIFY FOR AFFORDABLE HOUSING?

Affordable housing means different things to different people. At its most basic, it means housing that someone with a median income in a specific community could afford. Often, affordable housing means rent-subsidized housing available to someone who makes below the median income and is therefore considered low income. But what's considered low income varies greatly from state to state and county to county and is modified yearly. Here's a sampling for 2013.

LOW INCOME FOR A FAMILY OF FOUR:

- Marin County, California—**$84,400**
- Lenawee County, Michigan—**$51,080**
- Abilene, Texas—**$43,900**

That's quite a range! If you're looking to save money on housing, check out the parameters for your own county at hud.gov, then do a local search. A quick survey of one northern California county came up with twenty-two options for low-income and senior housing.

Next Steps

- If you own your home, downsizing may be a good way to save on expenses and cash in on equity. **Question 18** talks about the tax consequences.

- A reverse mortgage is another way to potentially boost your retirement income—but be cautious. See **Question 26** for the pros and cons.
- Review your portfolio. **Question 22** provides guidelines for investing during retirement.
- Create a cash flow. **Question 23** offers ideas on which accounts to draw from first.

Important Disclosures

Keep in mind that, unlike CDs, money market funds are neither insured nor guaranteed by the Federal Deposit Insurance Corporation or any other government agency. Although a fund seeks to preserve the value of your investment at $1.00 per share, it is possible to lose money by investing in the fund.

Bond fund investment return and principal value are subject to fluctuation with changes in market conditions, such that shares may be worth more or less than the original cost when redeemed.

Q25.

Can I lower my income tax bill now that I'm retired?

By the time you've been paying taxes for decades, you get it. The tax code is absurdly complicated and enough to make any of us (myself included) want to run for cover. On the other hand, like me, you probably want to be a good citizen and pay your fair share but not a penny more.

Unfortunately, these two realities don't fit together. Just completing your tax return every year can be a monumental task. And figuring out how to manage your tax bill takes even more work. It takes long-term planning, short-term decisions, and a solid understanding of tax concepts. I'll go over some basics here, but I also highly recommend that you enlist the ongoing help of a great CPA, particularly as you first move into retirement.

When it comes to taxes, there are both advantages and disadvantages to being a retiree. On the plus side, you may have more control over your income, and therefore more strategies for controlling your taxes. On the minus side, you may well have more at stake, and certainly more to think about.

➲ **SMART MOVE:** Looking for a CPA? The American Institute of Certified Public Accountants website has a search feature that will help you find an accountant in your area who is also a personal finance expert. You can also look for a tax accountant on the National Association of Enrolled Agents site (note, however, that an IRS-enrolled agent is a tax specialist, not a CPA). However, I always think that it's best to ask trusted friends, family members, and colleagues for a recommendation. When you interview a prospective accountant, be sure to ask about their areas of expertise and also make sure that you understand their fee structure.

Understand How Different Types of Income Are Taxed

Before I get into strategies, it's important to understand how the IRS categorizes (and taxes) different types of income. In the eyes of the IRS, there are three major categories of income, which are taxed as follows:

- **Ordinary income:** From wages, self-employment, interest, dividends, etc.
  - **Taxation:** In 2013, ordinary income is taxed at a *marginal* rate ranging from 10 percent to 39.6 percent, with the highest earners paying the most. Note, though, that some interest income is tax-exempt (for example, interest from state and local municipal bonds), and some dividends are considered *qualified* and therefore receive special long-term capital gains tax treatment.

FACT: According to a 2011 Charles Schwab Retirement Income Survey, nearly half (47 percent) of investors have not anticipated what impact taxes will have on their retirement income, and a quarter have not thought about tax expenses at all.

SMART MOVE: If you own company stock when you retire, you may be able to save on taxes by taking advantage of what is known as *net unrealized appreciation*. See **Question 14**, pages 138–140.

MARGINAL VS. EFFECTIVE (OR AVERAGE) TAX RATE

Because taxes are progressive, meaning that we pay a proportionately larger amount of taxes on higher levels of income, there are two tax rates that you need to be aware of: your *marginal* rate and your *effective* rate.

Your **marginal tax rate** is the amount of tax you pay on your *last dollar of income*. For example, in 2013 if you're married filing jointly and in the 25% tax bracket, you will pay $25 in taxes for every $100 of taxable income above $72,500 and up to $146,400. This is important, so that you will know, for example, how a bonus or other extra income is taxed.

Your **effective tax rate** is the average tax rate you pay when you take all of your income into account. This is important, for example, if you're figuring out the tax impact of an investment. Your effective rate (also known as the *average* rate) is most likely lower than your marginal rate.

- **Capital income:** From the sale of property. Capital gains and losses can either be *short-term* (held for one year or less) or *long-term* (held for more than one year). There are also special categories for things such as collectibles.
  - **Taxation:** Short-term capital gains are taxed as ordinary income. In 2013, long-term capital gains and qualified dividends are not taxable for taxpayers in the 15 percent ordinary bracket or lower. For those in the 25 percent bracket or higher, long-term capital gains and dividends are taxed at 15 percent. For single filers with taxable income over $400,000 (or $450,000 for married filing jointly), long-term capital gain and qualified dividend income over that amount is taxed at 20 percent. Long-term capital gains on collectibles are taxed at 28 percent.
- **Passive income:** From investments in real estate, limited partnerships, or business activities where participation is "immaterial."
  - **Taxation:** Ordinary income tax rate. Passive losses can usually only offset other passive income, not ordinary income.

AT A GLANCE: HOW YOUR RETIREMENT INCOME IS TAXED

Social Security benefits	Up to 85% of benefits taxed at your ordinary income rate. In 2013: **Singles**—income less than $25,000, benefits not taxed; income $25,000–$34,000, 50% of benefits taxed; income over $34,000, 85% taxed **Married filing jointly**—income less than $32,000, benefits not taxed; income $32,000–$44,000, 50% of benefits taxed; over $44,000, 85% taxed
Pension income	Fully or partially taxed as ordinary income, depending on whether contributions were tax-deferred
Annuity income	Fully or partially taxed as ordinary income, depending on whether contributions were tax-deferred
Traditional 401(k) distributions	Fully taxable as ordinary income
Traditional deductible IRA distributions	Fully taxable as ordinary income
Traditional nondeductible IRA distributions	Distributions of contributions tax-free, earnings taxable as ordinary income
Roth IRA and Roth 401(k) distributions	Tax-free provided you are 59½ and the funds have been in the account for at least five years
Taxable account withdrawals	Taxed as short- or long-term capital gains. Interest from municipal bonds is exempt from federal income tax, but gets added back for computing taxability of Social Security benefits (however, interest from "private activity" bonds could be included when computing the alternative minimum tax). Income from Treasury bills and bonds is exempt from state (but not federal) income tax.

Note: As a result of the Affordable Care Act, there is a 3.8% surcharge on net investment income for taxpayers with an adjusted gross income over $200,000 (for single filers) or $250,000 (for married filing jointly).

➲ **SMART MOVE:** If you believe that you will be in a higher tax bracket at a later date (for example, if you're currently delaying Social Security or if you're expecting an inheritance), you can consider converting all or part of your IRA to a Roth IRA. Not only will your eventual withdrawals be tax-free; there also will be no RMDs. Plus, converting your account to a Roth can be a boon to your heirs. See **Question 23,** pages 205–206 for more.

Be Smart About Where You Place Your Investments

I've said it repeatedly: As an investor, your first priority is your asset allocation. Next comes diversification and your individual security selection. But paying attention to your taxes is important, too. To minimize taxes, and therefore maximize what you actually get to keep, put your most tax-efficient investments (those that lose less of their return to taxes) in your taxable accounts and your least tax-efficient investments (those that lose more of their return to taxes) in your tax-deferred accounts—as shown in the following chart.

AT A GLANCE: TAX-SMART PLACEMENT FOR YOUR INVESTMENTS

Taxable accounts are the best place for:	Tax-deferred accounts such as traditional IRAs and 401(k)s are the best place for:	Roth IRAs or Roth 401(k)s are the best place for:
• Individual stocks you plan to hold more than one year • Tax-managed stock funds, index funds, exchange-traded funds (ETFs), low-turnover stock funds • Stocks or mutual funds that pay qualified dividends • Municipal bonds/I Bonds	• Individual stocks you plan to hold one year or less • Actively managed funds that may generate significant short-term capital gains • Taxable bond funds, zero-coupon bonds, inflation-protected bonds, or high-yield bond funds • Real estate investment trusts (REITs)	• Assets that you believe have the greatest chance for the largest return

Be Tax-Wise as You Withdraw Your Income

To the extent that you rely on income from your portfolio, it's important to consider taxes as you sell investments and withdraw funds. **Question 23** provides a detailed step-by-step framework for withdrawing your money in a way that will minimize taxes. In a nutshell, though, it's generally best to:

1. Sell from your taxable accounts before tapping your tax-deferred accounts

2. Sell securities from overweighted asset classes

3. Sell lower-rated securities before higher-rated securities. If you need to sell high-rated securities from your taxable accounts, sell those that will generate a loss before those that will generate a gain.

> ➲ **SMART MOVE:** When it comes to taxes, it's essential to think long-term. But you can have an impact by thinking year-to-year as well. For example, if you've made a large charitable contribution or have paid extraordinary medical bills, you might be able to take a larger distribution without increasing your taxes. Conversely, you might want to reduce your distributions in a year with unusual income.

Harvest Your Losses from Your Taxable Accounts

No one wants their investments to lose money. But **tax-loss harvesting** can turn a loss into a plus, if not an out-and-out win. Here's how the process works:

When you sell your investments in a taxable account, you can erase your taxable capital gain with a capital loss. Both capital gains and capital losses are categorized as either short-term (for an investment that you've owned for one year or less) or long-term (for an investment that you've owned for more than a year), which means that almost every sale will create one of the following four results:

- long-term capital gain (LTCG)
- long-term capital loss (LTCL)
- short-term capital gain (STCG)
- short-term capital loss (STCL)

You net these out with the following three steps:

1. Net your LTCGs against your LTCLs

2. Net your STCGs against your STCLs

3. Net your long-term result against your short-term result to arrive at a single taxable figure

Example: In one year, Sam sold several investments in his taxable accounts, resulting in:
> LTCG: $11,000
> LTCL: $6,000
> STCG: $5,000
> STCL: $6,000

He nets them out as follows:
> 1. LTCG $11,000 and LTCL $6,000 → LTCG $5,000
> 2. STCG $5,000 and STCL $6,000 → STCL ($1,000)
> 3. LTCG $4,000

This long-term gain then receives the preferential long-term capital gain rate. However, if the netting process resulted in a capital loss, **up to $3,000 can be deducted against ordinary income. Any amount over $3,000 can be carried over as a deduction in future years.**

⚠ **CAUTION:** If you decide to sell a stock or mutual fund to take a tax loss, but you know that you want to buy it back at a future date, watch out for the *wash-sale rule.* If you sell a security at a loss and buy the same or a "substantially identical" security within thirty days, the loss is generally disallowed for tax purposes.

➲ **SMART MOVE:** If you make a partial sale, your broker is required to report the cost basis for stocks purchased after January 1, 2011. The default method is FIFO, or "first in, first out." Instead, you may be able to minimize taxes by specifying shares with a higher cost basis.

Plan Your Charitable Gifts with Taxes in Mind

As you plan charitable contributions, there's no harm in lowering your tax bill at the same time. For example, think about the following:

- You can deduct up to 50 percent of your adjusted gross income for contributions to qualified charitable organizations. To see how various types of donations are valued by the IRS, see **Question 10**.
- Give appreciated stock instead of cash. If you donate appreciated stock that you've owned for more than a year, this can be a win-win for you and the recipient. If you sell appreciated stock, you will owe capital gains tax. But you can gift the stock tax-free to a qualified charity *plus* receive a charitable tax deduction equal to its full market value. Caution, though: If you've owned the stock for one year or less, it's considered a short-term holding and you'll be able to deduct only the purchase price, not the full market value.
- Conversely, it's better to sell depreciated stock before you donate the proceeds. This way you can realize a capital loss, which you can either use on your current year's taxes or bank for future years. Plus, you can still claim the value of the gift as a charitable deduction.
- If you're 70½ or older, you can make a direct contribution to a charitable organization from your IRA without paying any tax. The downside is that you can't also claim a charitable deduction for this donation. However, it can count toward your RMD.

Next Steps
- To read about estate tax considerations, see **Question 39**.
- To bone up on RMDs, see **Question 23**.
- Not sure when to file for Social Security? See **Question 30** for some thoughts.

Q26.

Does a reverse mortgage make sense?

I have to be honest with you. I hesitated about even including reverse mortgages in this book because I don't want anyone to think that I'm a proponent. Of course, financial institutions that offer reverse mortgages make them sound like a solid idea. In his role as pitchman, actor and former senator Fred Thompson makes them sound like an absolutely splendid idea. But before you jump on board, realize that reverse mortgages have several potential serious pitfalls that could end up costing you (and your heirs) plenty.

The advantage of reverse mortgages is that they allow homeowners to turn the equity in their homes into cash. The bank, in effect, makes a mortgage payment to you that you never have to pay back until you sell your house. This can be a welcome boost to retirement income—and in some cases may be essential to help people stay in their homes and avoid poverty.

However, I strongly urge you to get all the facts and figures—and consider all your alternatives—before taking this step.

Start with the Basics

A **reverse mortgage** is a loan that uses your home as collateral, but instead of making payments to a lender, the lender pays you. As long as you live in the house, you're not obligated to pay it back. You (and your spouse if your spouse cosigns) must be 62 or older and have equity in your home. No credit check or income verification is required.

The amount you can borrow depends on a number of factors, including your age, the amount of your home equity, and current interest rates. Once you have the loan, you can take the cash in a lump sum, monthly payments, a standby line of credit, or a combination of all three—and use the money however you wish.

However, your equity in your home will decrease over time as your loan amount and interest expenses grow. You continue to hold the title to your home, but the bank owns a little more of it every day. When you die or move, you (or your estate) must pay back the loan, with interest, within six months. However, your obligation is limited to the value of the home at the time you repay, even if you had borrowed more.

Also realize that as long as you own your home, you're responsible for property taxes, homeowner's insurance, and upkeep. If there comes a time when you can't make these payments or keep your property in good condition, it could be considered a default and the loan will come due. If you can't pay off the balance, you'll be at risk of losing your home.

AT A GLANCE: PROS AND CONS OF A REVERSE MORTGAGE

Pros	Cons
More money in your pocket with no required credit check or income verification	Potential high fees: loan origination, appraisal, mortgage insurance
Not obligated to pay back the loan as long as you live in the house	Your equity goes down; the bank owns more of your home each day
Never have to pay back more than the value of the house at the time of sale, regardless of balance of reverse mortgage	Debt is rising—with interest
Can take the money as a lump sum, monthly payments, or line of credit	Risk losing the house if you don't pay taxes and insurance and keep your property in good shape
Can use the money however you wish	Heirs will have to sell the house if they can't repay the loan

Get into the Details

If you're seriously contemplating a reverse mortgage, there are several important factors to consider:

- **Program:** Most reverse mortgages are insured by the FHA through its **Home Equity Conversion Mortgage (HECM) program.** The insurance protects the lender in case the value of the home declines. Borrowers can choose to borrow a larger percentage of their home's value with a standard HECM loan that charges relatively high fees or borrow less with an HECM Saver loan with lower fees. In addition, there are some privately funded reverse mortgages, although those are becoming increasingly rare.

- **Lump sum, monthly payment, or line of credit:** As a borrower, you can choose to take the cash as a lump sum, a monthly payment, a standby line of credit, or a combination of the three. A lump sum comes with a fixed interest rate, and the others an adjustable rate.

⚠ **CAUTION:** Although fixed-rate standard mortgages are safer than adjustable mortgages, the opposite is often true with reverse mortgages. If you borrow more than you absolutely need, you will still be paying interest on the entire amount.

- **Your age:** The younger you are, the less you can borrow against your home equity—which is a good thing. Although you're eligible for a reverse mortgage as early as age 62, it's best to postpone if you can. Otherwise, you could easily find yourself without any financial resources as you age.

⚠ **CAUTION:** If you're relatively young and are thinking about taking out a reverse mortgage to pay off a traditional mortgage, or to invest the proceeds elsewhere, stop. The federal Consumer Financial Protection Bureau (CFPB) has identified both of these practices as particularly risky.

- **Your spouse:** Some couples make the mistake of putting only one spouse's name on a reverse mortgage. They may do this because only one spouse is 62, or because they can borrow a larger amount under the older spouse's name. Or other times a couple may marry after the mortgage is in place. The risk is that if the borrowing spouse dies or is forced to move (for example, to a nursing home), and the other spouse can't repay the loan, he or she could be forced out of the home. Ditto for any other family members who live with the borrowing spouse.

➲ **SMART MOVE:** If you are married, make sure that your spouse's name is on both the title and the reverse mortgage. Otherwise, he or she may be prematurely forced out of the home.

- **Your heirs:** A reverse mortgage comes due when the last surviving borrower dies or no longer lives in the home for twelve continuous months. This includes living in a nursing home. Your heirs must pay off the loan if they want to keep the home. If your heirs can't afford to pay it off, they will have to sell the house to pay the loan.

THE CONSUMER FINANCIAL PROTECTION BUREAU (CFPB) ON REVERSE MORTGAGES

The regulation for all mortgages, including reverse mortgages, was transferred to the Consumer Financial Protection Bureau under the Dodd-Frank reform law. In its first report on the subject, the CFPB concludes that reverse mortgages are risky business. In particular, the bureau points out concerns over:

- A general lack of understanding of product features

- Younger borrowers

- Lump sum payments

- Deceptive marketing and sales practices

- The need for consumer counseling

You can find the full report at consumerfinance.gov.

Take Advantage of Required Counseling

There's a lot to consider. Fortunately, if you're applying for a HUD loan, you're required to speak with an approved counselor. If you're considering a reverse mortgage, don't just think of this as an inconvenience. Take complete advantage of this opportunity by asking lots of questions. Don't sign until you are sure that you understand all of the issues and potential scenarios, and how they will impact your financial future.

⚠ **CAUTION:** Reverse mortgage counseling sessions, although required, are generally not free. Make sure you know the cost and that you are paying for trustworthy advice.

Consider Your Alternatives

If you're 62 or older and in need of cash, there may be a more appropriate alternative. For example, if your home is your largest asset, you can consider a home equity loan or a **home equity line of credit**. Although both of these require monthly payments and are dependent on your income and credit, the up-front costs and ongoing interest charges are much lower than those for a reverse mortgage.

Another option is downsizing to a smaller, less expensive home and pocketing the difference. Or if you're really in a bind, you may qualify for a state or local program that will allow you to defer property taxes or save on other bills.

On the surface, a reverse mortgage can sound like a great deal. And for some folks it may just make sense. Realize, though, that there are plenty of risks. Proceed with caution.

Next Steps
- Consider the money you might make—and save—by downsizing. **Question 18** has some insights.
- To get ideas on how to make up for lost time in saving for retirement, see **Question 2**.
- If you were forced to retire early and are short on savings, see more ideas in **Questions 21** and **24**.

Q27.

What insurance do I need at this point in my life?

Insurance is a big part of our lives—and our budgets. But it's generally not something we like to dwell on. In fact, once we've waded through the intricacies of various policies, it's tempting to just keep paying the premiums and assume we're covered.

But as costs go up for all kinds of insurance (especially as we get older), there are two good reasons to reevaluate your coverage. You want to make sure that 1) you have enough of the right kind of insurance and 2) you're not paying for insurance you *don't* need. To me, certain types of insurance are essential at every stage of your life—and others are just a waste of your hard-earned money.

Start with the Must-Haves ·

HEALTH INSURANCE

I rarely deal in absolutes, but I make an exception with health insurance. Long before the Affordable Care Act mandated it, I believed that health insurance is an absolute necessity. Now that health insurance is required by law, all the better. If you're still working at least part-time and have adequate coverage through your employer, that's great. However, if you lose your group coverage before you're eligible for Medicare, you'll need to fill that gap with an alternate policy.

COBRA is one way to do that. This basically continues the coverage you had through your employer for up to eighteen months, but on your dime. You'll be responsible for paying the entire premium, which will most likely be significantly higher than what you were paying as an employee. However, depending on the policy and the cost, this could be your best choice. While you're still working, check with your employer to make sure you're eligible for COBRA. If so, request the necessary paperwork from your employer. You have sixty days from the time you receive the paperwork to decide if you want to enroll.

FACT: More than half of all workers intend to work longer than they would like to keep their health insurance at work, according to research conducted in 2013 by the nonpartisan Employee Benefit Research Institute (EBRI). But, in reality, fewer than 1 in 5 retirees say they actually were able to work longer to continue receiving health insurance through their jobs. EBRI research also found a growing proportion of older American workers who would retire earlier if they were assured of health coverage: In 2003, 15 percent of workers reported that they would retire earlier than planned if they were guaranteed access to health insurance; by 2012, that percentage had nearly doubled (27 percent).

SMART MOVE: If you're eligible for COBRA, your spouse or other dependents who have been on your policy are eligible as well.

If you don't have access to coverage through an employer, you can shop for a policy through your state's or the federal health insurance exchange. Premium and cost-sharing programs are available to low-income individuals.

You might also want to consider a high-deductible policy. This may allow you to open a Health Savings Account (HSA), which carries with it some tax benefits. Annual contributions to an HSA are tax-deductible, similar to a traditional IRA. And you won't pay taxes on withdrawals as long as the money is used for qualified medical expenses. In 2013, the maximum annual contribution for an individual is $3,250. For families, it's $6,450. If you're 55 or older, you can add another $1,000 as a catch-up.

⬗ SMART MOVE: Contribute the maximum to your HSA if you can. It's not "use it or lose it," like a flexible spending account. It's more like an IRA for health care. You can even make withdrawals for any reason at age 65 without penalty, although you will pay ordinary income taxes if it's not for a qualified medical expense.

SHOULD YOU SIGN UP FOR MEDICARE IF YOU'RE STILL WORKING?

If you're already taking Social Security, you're automatically enrolled in Medicare at age 65. But if not, it's a good idea to enroll in at least Part A as soon as you're eligible, even if you're still working and have health insurance through your employer. Part A is free for most people and covers hospitalization. You can delay enrolling in Part B (for which there's a premium) without penalty as long as you have adequate coverage through your work.

However, whether or not delaying Part B is a good idea depends on the size of your company. If it has more than twenty employees, no problem. But if it has fewer than twenty employees, Medicare would act as your primary insurance and your company's coverage would be secondary. In fact, in this case, your employer's insurance can refuse to cover anything that Medicare would have covered, so it could be well worth the premium to sign up for Part B as well. I suggest that you talk to your employer's human resources department before making your decision.

Once you leave your job, you'll have an eight-month window in which to enroll in Part B. Medicare enrollment deadlines are quite strict, so you don't want to miss the deadline. See **Question 35** for details.

Once you're on Medicare, you should look into supplemental policies such as Medigap or Medicare Advantage. **Question 36** talks about your choices.

CAR INSURANCE

Most states require you to carry at least basic liability insurance to cover damage you may do to others, including both bodily injury and property damage. Liability insurance also pays for potential legal bills. This insurance is a must-have to protect yourself from a financial crisis in the event of an accident.

Whether or not you want to carry expanded coverage for collision, vandalism, fire, or theft depends on your car and your other resources. If you no longer have a loan on your car, you're not required to carry collision. Dropping it can lower your premium significantly. You can also lower your premium by increasing the deductible.

> **◗ SMART MOVE:** If you're between 50 and 70, check with your auto insurance company to see if they have discounts for mature drivers. Even if you're past 70, you might be able to lower your premium by successfully completing a senior driver refresher training program.

Reexamine Your Need for Certain Types of Protection

Your need for insurance always depends on your personal circumstances, and will evolve with time. For instance, as I discuss in **Question 16**, once your kids are grown, you may no longer need life insurance. Likewise, in **Question 17**, I talk about how disability insurance can be important during your peak earning years—but once you're retired, it no longer makes sense. If you currently have either of these, now would be a good time to reevaluate.

On the other hand, there are a couple of other types of insurance that I strongly recommend you consider to protect your possessions—and yourself.

HOMEOWNER'S INSURANCE

If you have a mortgage, you're required to have homeowner's insurance. But once your mortgage is paid off, it's still important to have adequate coverage to protect both your dwelling and your possessions. That's why it's wise to periodically review your policy. Make certain your policy offers guaranteed replacement value—not fair market or cash value. It's also possible that your property has appreciated beyond your coverage, so double-check to make sure you have enough to cover current replacement costs in the event your property is damaged or destroyed.

A homeowner's policy generally covers possessions up to a specific dollar amount. If you've collected a lot of valuables over the years, such as jewelry or art, you may want to look into extra coverage up to the appraised value of the items.

And depending on where you live, check on disaster insurance that would cover you in case of events such as an earthquake or flood. Unfortunately, these natural disasters are typically excluded from general homeowner's policies. Premiums for disaster policies are usually quite high, and it may be hard to shell out that extra money, but it's a cost/value proposition you should consider.

⊙ **SMART MOVE:** Many insurance companies offer discounts for homeowners who are 55+ or retired. Ask your company about a "mature insured credit."

RENTER'S INSURANCE

If you rent, you probably already have renter's insurance. It's important to have your own policy because your landlord's policy will cover only damage to the dwelling, not to your possessions. A renter's policy usually covers events such as fire, theft, and vandalism and may protect you from damage due to things like faulty wiring, water, or weather. Make sure you have enough insurance to cover your current possessions. Renter's policies are extremely inexpensive compared to what it would cost to replace everything.

⊙ **SMART MOVE:** Periodically take an inventory of your possessions. Photograph or video them, and then make a list and check on replacement costs. This can be really helpful if you ever need to make a claim. And many insurers have online tools to help you.

UMBRELLA LIABILITY POLICY

For extra protection, you might also consider an **umbrella liability policy.** This provides coverage above and beyond your car or homeowner's insurance in the event that you might be sued for an injury caused by you or your property. What's the likelihood? Think of a neighbor taking a nasty fall because of uneven pavement on your front walkway, or a car accident for which you're responsible.

A typical homeowner's policy might cover only up to $300,000 of personal liability. Auto insurance liability minimums vary by state, anywhere from under $50,000 to over $100,000. If you have significant assets—and even if you don't—a substantial judgment could easily put your finances at risk.

Fortunately, umbrella policies are pretty reasonable. You can buy them in increments of $1 million of coverage. A million dollars in coverage might cost only a couple of hundred dollars a year. A nice "bonus" is that most umbrella policies provide additional coverage for things like libel or slander, including paying for legal representation. Brokers like to tell you that an umbrella policy premium may be less than the cost of a single meeting with an attorney in the event of a lawsuit—and they may be right!

> ⮞ **SMART MOVE:** If you have your car and homeowner's insurance with the same company, ask about their umbrella policies. You might get a better rate.

WHEN AN UMBRELLA POLICY ISN'T ENOUGH

An umbrella policy is an extra ounce of prevention. But there are times when you need even more. That's because umbrella policies have exclusions. For instance, most of them don't cover aircraft or boats. More important, they don't cover business pursuits (even if you work from your home) or professional services liability, or workers' compensation. Here are some additional types of insurance to be aware of:

- **Professional liability insurance**—If you have business or professional liability, you may already have this. And it's a good idea to keep it, even if you decide to work part-time. You might also look into what's called *tail insurance*, which would protect you for a certain period of time after your policy expires. It's an extra safety measure that will cover recent projects after you retire.

- **E&O insurance**—Most people are familiar with malpractice insurance for doctors, but many other professionals need insurance against "errors and omissions" that might cause financial harm to a client or customer. Lawyers, stockbrokers, financial advisors, real estate brokers, and accountants, for example, need E&O insurance to protect their assets against a costly lawsuit. Premiums vary widely depending on the kind of work you do, but if you're in a business or profession that could result in financial harm to someone, it could be worth it.

- **Workers' compensation insurance**—If you have employees, you may need workers' compensation insurance, depending on the state you live in and the number of employees you have. Even workers' compensation for domestic workers may be required, depending on the number of hours worked and amount of money earned. Guidelines vary by state, so check with your state's department of labor.

LONG-TERM CARE INSURANCE

You may have already read this in **Question 7**, but it bears repeating. The U.S. Department of Health and Human Services estimates that about 70 percent of people over 65 will require some type of long-term care services at some point. Long-term care insurance isn't cheap and premiums and benefits vary widely. But whether you're concerned for yourself or for aging family members, you should think about how the cost of care versus insurance would affect your overall financial health.

Don't Be Taken In

As I said earlier, some insurance can be a waste of money. For instance, don't pay for private mortgage insurance (PMI) if you're not required to. Once the equity in your home is above 20 percent, send a written request to your lender to drop PMI. This could save you quite a bit.

And the list of questionable insurance goes on and on, including:

- Life insurance for kids—Remember, life insurance is for those who have dependents.
- Car rental insurance—This is usually covered by your own auto insurance and by some credit cards. Check on the coverage you already have *before* you get to the car rental counter, so you don't feel pressured.
- Pet insurance—I know pets are precious and vet bills are high. But so are premiums. Carefully consider any policy, including exclusions for preexisting conditions, deductibles, etc.
- Flight insurance—If you have adequate life insurance, you don't need this. However, trip cancellation insurance can be appropriate for nonrefundable tickets.
- Wedding insurance, disease insurance, mortgage life insurance— all should be taken with a large grain of salt.

Next Steps

- Go to the Insurance Information Institute at iii.org for a more in-depth discussion of different types of insurance.
- Carefully consider your need for long-term care insurance. See **Question 7** for help in weighing the pros and cons.
- For the latest on the impact of the Affordable Care Act, go to healthcare.gov.
- Reevaluate your need for life and disability insurance. **Questions 16** and **17** can help you put things in perspective.

Q28.

If I go back to work (even part-time), what do I need to know? Can I still collect Social Security? Contribute to my 401(k)?

How times have changed! In our parents' day, retirement was kind of like the end of the rainbow. It was the rare retiree who even thought about going back to work. But now—whether for personal or financial reasons—more and more retirees are choosing to get back on the job track, at least part-time. And it can be a great decision. It keeps you engaged, both mentally and socially, and it helps make those retirement savings go even further.

However, every plus has a potential minus. While going back to work earns you more, it can potentially cost you more. It can also affect your Social Security benefits, taxes, and possibly health insurance. It's smart to weigh all these factors in advance, so there won't be any surprises after you're already back in business.

Add In the Costs of Doing Business

Whether you go back into the office or work from home, your everyday expenses are likely to go up. If you take a job, costs for transportation, clothes, and possibly caregivers if you have dependents—all the expenses you happily got rid of when you retired—will have to be added back into your monthly budget. If you work from home, you may have to pay for office equipment, supplies, and additional computer and Internet needs. It's a good idea to crunch the numbers and create a new budget. Ideally, the income you expect to make will cover the new expenses and then some.

> ⊃ **SMART MOVE:** Use an online monthly budget planner like the one on schwabmoneywise.com to play with the numbers before you make your back-to-work decision.

Subtract Any Reduction in Social Security Benefits

If you're already collecting Social Security, Uncle Sam will continue to pay your benefits—but possibly at a slightly reduced rate. It all depends on your age and how much money you make.

If you've already reached what the IRS defines as **full retirement age (FRA),** no problem. (For people born in 1943 or later, FRA is between 66 and 67.) You can make as much money as you want and your monthly benefit will remain the same. But if you start your benefits early and then go back to work before you reach your FRA, $1 of benefits will be deducted for every $2 you make above the annual limit. For 2013, the limit is $15,120. The numbers get better in the calendar year in which you reach your FRA. Then the limit goes up to $40,080 (for 2013) and $1 of benefits is deducted for every $3 you earn above that limit. Plus, only money you make before your birthday that year is counted. As soon as you hit your FRA, your benefits are no longer reduced no matter how high your income goes.

Actually, you shouldn't let this color your decision too much. The reduction is kind of like withholding. You'll get it back in the form of an increased benefit once you reach your FRA. But in the meantime, you need to factor it into your monthly budget.

> **⮕ SMART MOVE:** Estimate how much your benefits may be reduced based on your estimated earnings. Go to the SSA's Retirement Earnings Test calculator on ssa.gov.

Consider How Your Social Security Benefits May Be Taxed

Earning more money can mean paying more income taxes, including taxes on your Social Security benefits. Once again, it all depends on how much money you make. If your modified adjusted gross income (MAGI) increases above a certain threshold (from earning a paycheck, for instance), a greater percentage of your benefits will be subject to income tax up to a maximum of 85 percent. The exact amount varies from person to person, but basically if half your Social Security benefit plus all of your other income (salary, dividends, interest, retirement accounts, etc.) is more than $25,000 for an individual or $32,000 for a couple, your benefits may be taxable.

SOCIAL SECURITY BENEFITS: WHAT IF YOU CHANGE YOUR MIND?

Taking Social Security benefits can seem like a good idea at the time, but when you're considering going back to work, you may be rethinking your choice. Is there anything you can do? Actually, the SSA does give you a second chance.

If you took benefits early: If you previously elected to receive early Social Security benefits at a reduced rate, you have the *option* of paying back to the government what you've already received and restarting benefits at a later date to take advantage of a higher payout. The option to pay back Social Security is limited to one year's worth of benefits and is available to you only in your first year of retirement.

Example: Let's say you decided to take early benefits at age 62. You're now 63 and thinking of going back to work. You could stop receiving Social Security, pay back the year's worth of benefits you received, return to work, and then wait until later to restart your benefit checks at a higher level. You don't have to pay any interest on the benefits you've already received and there are no fees. The catch is that you have to come up with the repayment money.

It's not an easy decision. On top of your having to repay a potentially large sum, whether this option makes sense for you depends on your tax situation, your age, and your life expectancy.

If you've already reached your full retirement age (FRA): You have another option. You could ask the SSA to temporarily suspend your benefits. You won't owe the government anything and your benefit will increase until you reach 70. You'll find more details at ssa.gov. Also see **Questions 30** and **31**.

☎ **TALK TO AN EXPERT:** Changing your Social Security election should be done with caution. There are a number of details to consider. It's probably best to talk to your tax or financial advisor as well as to the SSA before you make your decision.

Review the Rules Regarding Retirement Accounts

Your retirement accounts aren't impacted by your decision to go back to work, but there are a couple of things you should be aware of:

1. **Traditional IRAs**—Working or not, you can't make contributions to a traditional IRA past age 70½. And you must still take a required minimum distribution (RMD) once you reach that magic age.

2. **Roth IRAs**—There are no age restrictions for contributions to a Roth IRA. As long as you have earned income, you can continue to contribute. And there are no RMDs for a Roth IRA.

3. **Employer plans**—You should be able to contribute to your employer's plan as long as you're still working, regardless of your age. And if you continue to work past age 70½, and don't own more than 5 percent of the business you work for, you should be able to postpone RMDs from your current employer's plan up until April 1 of the year after you retire. But be sure to check with your plan administrator.

⚠️ **CAUTION:** Some pension plans require that benefits be suspended if you retire and then start working again for the same company. Check with your plan administrator. If you work for a different company, your pension benefits shouldn't be affected.

ALREADY ON MEDICARE? CONSIDER YOUR OPTIONS

Moving in and out of the workforce can change your insurance needs. So what happens if you retire, enroll in Medicare, and then find yourself back at work with employer coverage once again? In this situation, you can drop Part B while working and reenroll at any time while you have group coverage or during the eight months after your employment or group health coverage ends without risk of penalty or higher premiums. (While Medicare gives you a special eight-month reenrollment window, make sure you do it early enough so that you're always covered!)

Whether or not dropping Part B is a good decision depends on the size of the company you work for. If your company has twenty or more employees, your group health plan is still the primary payer of your medical bills, making your Medicare benefits of limited value. However, if your company has fewer than twenty employees, Medicare would be the primary payer and your company plan would be the secondary payer. In either case, it's best to talk to your employee benefits administrator as well as to Medicare before you make any decisions.

Next Steps

- Even if you go back to work, you need to manage your retirement money carefully. See **Question 22** for tips.

- If you're trying to stretch your retirement income—and are uncertain about going back to work—take a look at **Question 21** for ideas on how to cut back on expenses.
- If you're approaching 65 and not yet taking Social Security, make sure you sign up for Medicare. **Question 35** talks about dates and deadlines.
- If you're considering going into business for yourself, see **Question 15**.

I handle all of the family finances. How can I create a turnkey system for my spouse in case something happens to me?

Every couple handles their finances differently. Some share everything; others keep certain things separate. Often one person will take the financial lead. But to me, no matter what approach works best for you and your spouse, the most important thing is that each of you is aware of how your finances work. That doesn't mean that you both have to be equally on top of the details, just that you share the important decisions and know where everything is.

That's the ideal, but the reality can be very different. Sometimes one spouse or the other doesn't want to be involved. Or absolutely refuses to be involved. I always suggest talking about financial matters. But what do you do when the other person won't listen?

I have a friend whose wife was like that. She didn't want to talk about finances; she didn't want to listen. She just wanted her husband to take care of everything forever. Maybe she couldn't accept that there might come a time when her husband wouldn't be around to handle everything.

My friend, who is also a financial planner, responded by writing his wife a personal guide to their finances, complete with insights and information about the basics of investing. It was a loving gesture that, while a bit more than most people need to do, underscored the fact that having knowledge about family finances and access to financial information is crucial for the well-being of both spouses.

I heartily agree with my friend's instincts. You don't need to write a book, but if your spouse or partner relies on you for all financial matters, you have one more important responsibility: to make sure that if anything happens to you, he or she knows where to turn for information and help.

Gather All Your Financial Information in One Place

It can be as simple as a physical binder or it can be an online filing system, but whatever the method, you need to gather all of your financial information in one easy-to-access place to make sure your loved ones can take over when you're no longer able to run things. Create separate sections and clearly mark them. Here's a suggestion on what to include:

- **The big picture**—Start with statements of your **net worth** (what you own and what you owe) and your current **cash flow.** For a simple way to create a net worth statement, see **My Top Ten Recommendations**, pages 1–2. **Question 2,** page 18, discusses how to easily document cash flow—what comes in when and where, and what goes out on a regular basis (mortgage payments, insurance premiums, property taxes, as well as monthlies such as utilities, transportation, and groceries). Combined, these statements provide a great overview of your finances.
- **Your advisors**—Next make a list of all your advisors: financial advisor, tax accountant, attorney, insurance agent—anyone your spouse could turn to for advice. Give phone numbers, addresses, and emails. It might be good to give a brief description of how each has worked with you in the past.

➲ **SMART MOVE:** If your spouse hasn't yet met these advisors, perhaps you could set up an introductory meeting.

- **Bank, brokerage, and retirement accounts**—List all your taxable investment and bank accounts, with account numbers, location, and how much is in each. Do the same for your retirement accounts—IRAs, 401(k)s, pensions. Be sure to include the beneficiaries for the accounts.

- **Liabilities**—Do you have a mortgage or an equity line of credit? Where are they held and what are the balances? Be sure to include information on when payments are due. If you have a car loan, include the balance and payment schedule. Don't forget to list all your credit cards.

- **Insurance policies**—Outline the policies you have: life insurance, car insurance, health insurance, homeowner's insurance, umbrella policy, etc. Give specifics on where the policies are held, the amount of coverage, and premiums. Be sure to include information on where the physical policies are located.

- **Tax documents**—Indicate the location of past tax returns and important documents such as property tax notices, receipts for charitable contributions, etc.

- **Estate planning documents**—Provide an overview of the estate planning documents you have: wills, trusts, and powers of attorney. Don't forget to include health-care directives. Be sure to state where the physical documents are located.

➲ **SMART MOVE:** If you keep your important documents in a safe-deposit box, be sure you include the location, box number, and where to find the key.

- **Benefits overview**—Your spouse may be entitled to certain benefits, such as Social Security, life insurance, employer insurance, or veteran's benefits. If so, list the contact information for each and a brief description of the steps needed to get the benefits.

⊃ SMART MOVE: Your finances are never static. Update this information periodically to make sure it remains accurate. I'd suggest a yearly review (maybe even with your spouse).

Simplify Where You Can

Now would be a good time to look at how you might simplify your finances, for both the present and the future. If you have multiple bank and brokerage accounts, consider consolidating them for easier management. Old 401(k)s held at a previous employer could be moved to a rollover IRA at the financial institution that holds your other accounts. See **Question 14** for the best way to do this.

Put as much as you can on auto-pay—mortgage, insurance premiums, monthly utilities, even savings. It will make it easier on you as well as on your spouse.

Create a One-Page Summary

No matter how organized you are, all this information may be overwhelming to your spouse. You might want to create a simple step-by-step guide. For example, your guide might read: "1) contact your attorney, 2) check in with financial advisors, 3) make sure certain bills are paid, 4) notify insurance companies." Just knowing whom to turn to first may give your spouse greater confidence.

THINGS TO DO FIRST WHEN A LOVED ONE DIES

None of us really wants to think about losing a loved one, but we all need to face the reality of what should be done in that eventuality. Having this list as part of your financial organization system will make it easier on your loved ones—and give you greater peace of mind.

- Notify family and friends
- Make funeral arrangements

- Contact an estate planning attorney to review the will and/or trust, and to handle the legal and tax implications

- Notify employer, insurance companies, government offices, and financial providers

- If your own financial picture may change, assess what this means

- Contact a financial planner or investment advisor to review your assets and determine a financial plan to meet your current and future needs

See **Question 47** for more on dealing with the death of a spouse.

Give Your Spouse a Heads-Up

Now make sure your spouse knows what you've done and where to find the information he or she needs. While you may get resistance when it comes to handling the details, knowing that you've set up a system to carry your spouse forward financially when you no longer can should make you both feel a lot better.

For good measure, alert your attorney and, if appropriate, another family member as to the whereabouts of this financial overview. If you can provide them with copies, so much the better.

☎ **TALK TO AN EXPERT:** If you have a lot of assets or your finances are complex, consult with your attorney or financial advisor about what to include in your financial system. Your tax advisor could also provide some important guidelines.

Next Steps
- Need to get more organized? See **Question 11** for tips on how to better manage your paperwork.
- If you spouse is completely reluctant to get involved in your finances, **Question 46** has ideas on how to pique his or her interest.

PART IV

Maximizing Social Security and Medicare

S ocial Security and Medicare provide essential financial and medical support for millions of seniors and disabled Americans. The sustainability of both programs has been the subject of much debate, but to me, the more immediate concern is that many citizens don't fully understand or maximize their benefits. This section provides the basic workings of Social Security and Medicare, as well as some strategies to help you take full advantage of both.

When it comes to Social Security, it is essential to take some time to consider your options *before you file*. Otherwise, you may be losing out on thousands of dollars over your lifetime. **Questions 30–34** review benefits for the primary beneficiary as well as for family members.

Medicare comes with its own set of decisions. **Questions 35–37** address your choices and the costs for Medicare and supplemental programs, and also discuss ways to plan for out-of-pocket health-care expenses.

Q30.

When should I file for
Social Security benefits?

Oh, how I wish I had a magic wand, because this straightforward question is among the hardest to answer. In fact, the entire Social Security system, which is intended to be fair and accessible, is mind-numbingly complex. The unfortunate result is that many retirees lose out on valuable benefits, generally because they choose to start to collect too early. So listen up.

The Basics

Most people are eligible to start collecting Social Security benefits at age 62. But if you wait until what the Social Security Administration calls your **full retirement age (FRA)**, which is 66 for those born between 1943 and 1954, you'll get a larger monthly benefit, known as your **primary insurance amount (PIA)**.

> ➲ **SMART MOVE:** If you were born before 1943 or after 1954, find your FRA on the **Social Security Administration's website, socialsecurity.gov.**

After you reach your FRA, your monthly benefit will **continue to increase until you reach age 70**—at which time you max out. The rationale is clear: You can get a smaller payment for a longer amount of time or a larger payment for a shorter amount of time. In theory these two balance out over time, at least when looking at data for millions of people. But when you're thinking about what's best for one person or one couple, the averages don't apply. Once you understand how the system works, you are in a position to make the best decision for your own situation.

⚠️ **CAUTION:** The term *full retirement age* can be misleading. In general, your benefits will continue to increase until age 70.

WHAT THE NUMBERS TELL US

A comprehensive study by economists John Shoven of Stanford University and Sita Slavov of Occidental College identifies the conditions when it is most advantageous to delay Social Security benefits. They conclude that gains from delaying are greatest:

- When interest rates are low

- For married couples relative to singles

- For single women relative to single men

- For two-earner couples relative to one-earner couples

- For a married couple, deferring the primary earner's benefit as compared to deferring the secondary earner's benefit.

⚠️ **CAUTION:** Unless you've already filed for Social Security, you need to enroll in Medicare when you turn 65 (there's a seven-month window, starting three months before your 65th birthday). Otherwise your medical and prescription drug coverage could be delayed, and you could face a penalty in the form of higher premiums. See **Question 35** for details.

Think About Your Life Expectancy

According to the Social Security Administration, the typical 65-year-old today will live to age 83, one in four will live to age 90, and one in ten will live to 95. Women have a slightly higher life expectancy than men, and the odds are even better that one person in a married couple will outlive the averages.

Then consider that for a person born between 1943 and 1954, delaying the start date from age 62 to age 66 increases benefits by 33 percent. Delaying to age 70 results in an increase of 76 percent.

A break-even analysis shows you how long you have to live to increase your overall benefit. For example, let's say that you're entitled to a $1,000 monthly benefit at age 66. If you start collecting benefits at age 62, your monthly draw will be reduced to $750. If you hold off until age 70, your monthly benefit will increase to $1,320. Take a look at the following chart.

LIFETIME SOCIAL SECURITY BENEFIT

	Begin Age 62 Monthly Benefit $750	Begin Age 66 Monthly Benefit $1,000	Begin Age 70 Monthly Benefit $1,320
Live to age 70	$72,000	$48,000	0
Live to age 75	$117,000	$108,000	$79,200
Live to 78	**$144,000**	**$144,000**	$126,720
Live to age 80	$162,000	$168,000	$158,400
Live to 83	**$189,000**	**$204,000**	**$205,920**
Live to age 85	$207,000	$228,000	$237,600
Live to age 90	$252,000	$288,000	$316,800
Live to age 95	$297,000	$348,000	$396,100

As these numbers show, if our 62-year-old lives *beyond* age 78, she will collect more by postponing the start of benefits to age 66. If she lives to age 83, which is the national average, she will collect the most by postponing her start to age 70.

Of course you can't predict how long you will live. But if you're healthy and longevity runs in your family, most likely you'll increase your lifetime benefit by postponing your start date.

➲ LOOK BEFORE YOU LEAP! According to the Social Security Administration, almost three-quarters of eligible workers file for benefits before their FRA. Before you file for Social Security benefits, be sure to calculate your benefits over your anticipated life span. Otherwise you could be losing out, big-time!

Think About the Current Interest Rate Environment

Every year that you delay collecting Social Security between the ages of 62 and 70, your monthly benefit will increase between 6⅔ and 8⅓ percent. If you were born between 1943 and 1954, and your FRA is 66, the numbers look like this:

Delay	Benefit Increase
Age 62–63	6.66%
Age 63–64	8.38%
Age 64–65	7.6%
Age 65–66	7.2%
Age 66–67	8%
Age 67–68	8%
Age 68–69	8%
Age 69–70	8%
Beyond age 70	None

Now compare these rates against the return you could get from a risk-free investment like U.S. Treasuries or an insured savings account. Clearly, the lower the prevailing interest rates, the more you stand to benefit over the long run by delaying Social Security. This is particularly true when you think about what economists call "real" interest rates, or the rate you earn after inflation.

As an example, let's say you're 64 and trying to decide whether to tap into your 401(k) savings or collect Social Security. If part of your 401(k) is invested in Treasuries, in 2013 you're effectively earning no interest after inflation. You'll get a better return by withdrawing those funds and allowing your Social Security benefit to grow.

Or let's say that you're considering buying a commercial annuity that will pay you for life. By instead choosing to delay Social Security, you are in effect buying an inflation-adjusted annuity from the U.S. government. The primary difference is that you most likely get a better rate. The lower the prevailing interest rates, the better the deal.

However, when the economy recovers and interest rates rise, this may not be the case. Shoven and Slavov conclude that delaying Social Security is most advantageous when real interest rates are 3.5 percent or lower.

Think About Your Income from Other Sources

If you don't have enough savings and are dependent on Social Security income to pay for necessities, you may have no choice but to collect Social Security as soon as you can. But if you have savings or income from other sources, and can afford to postpone your start date, you will likely benefit by delaying.

Also realize that if you file for Social Security benefits before your FRA but you continue to work, and your earnings exceed certain limits, part of your benefit will be *temporarily* withheld. In 2013, if you file for benefits at age 62, $1 in benefits will be withheld for every $2 you earn above $15,120. In the year you reach your FRA, $1 is deducted for every $3 you earn above a higher limit, currently $40,080. Once you reach your FRA there is no earnings deduction, and you will get the money previously withheld in the form of a higher benefit.

AT A GLANCE: SOCIAL SECURITY RETIREMENT BENEFITS

Recipient	Amount
Worker at least 62 but under FRA	Reduced primary insurance amount (PIA), the amount you would receive at your FRA
Worker at FRA	100% of PIA
Worker older than FRA	Increased beyond PIA
Spouse, under age 62	No benefit
Spouse, age 62 to FRA	50% of PIA, reduced

Recipient	Amount
Spouse, at FRA	50% of PIA
Spouse, at any age, caring for a child who is under age 16 or disabled	50% of PIA
Unmarried child under age 18 or any age if disabled before age 22	50% of PIA, subject to family maximum

If You're Married, Compute Your Combined Benefit

This is where Social Security gets really tricky. As an individual, you try to maximize your lifetime benefit. But as a couple, your goal is to maximize your combined benefit over both of your lifetimes as well as survivor benefits. This involves analyzing your personal benefits as well as the potential to take advantage of spousal benefits.

Basic Rules for Spouses

- As a spouse, at age 62 you can choose to take a benefit based on your own earnings or a spousal benefit based on your spouse's earnings. The only caveat is that to receive the spousal benefit, your spouse must have already filed.
- The spousal benefit is up to 50 percent of the earner's benefit. The actual percentage depends on when you both file; if you both wait until FRA or later, you collect a higher benefit. For example, if a husband files early at age 62, his benefit would be reduced by 25 percent. If his wife waited until FRA to file for a spousal benefit, she would collect 50 percent of his **reduced** benefit. However, if the wife decided to take spousal benefits at age 62, her benefit would be **reduced even more** to 35 percent of his reduced benefit.

➲ **SMART MOVE:** A husband or wife maxes out their spousal benefit (50 percent of spouse's benefit) at FRA. There is no benefit to waiting longer.

- The impact on survivor benefits is similar. At FRA a widow or widower can collect up to 100 percent of their spouse's benefit (or a reduced benefit starting at age 60). When someone opts to collect benefits early, his or her surviving spouse will also collect a reduced benefit. Conversely, when a person decides to delay benefits, he or she is providing their survivor with a larger benefit. See **Question 34** for more details on Social Security benefits for surviving spouses.

If you are divorced but were married for at least ten years and are currently unmarried, you can still collect a benefit based on your ex's record. See **Question 32** for more details.

Unfortunately, unmarried couples don't have spousal rights under Social Security. See **Question 9** for more.

SOCIAL SECURITY STRATEGIES FOR SPOUSES

Working as a team, spouses have some choices that can significantly boost their combined benefit.

A warning, though: These types of strategies can get very complex, and their effectiveness depends on a number of variables, including the difference in ages and earnings records between the two spouses.

With the first strategy, sometimes called the "62/70 split," the lower-earning spouse takes Social Security as early as age 62 and the higher-earning spouse postpones filing until age 70 to maximize his or her benefit. With this scenario, the higher earner has the option of receiving a spousal benefit as a bonus during the years that he or she is waiting to claim on his or her own record.

Alternatively, the higher earner could file for benefits at FRA and immediately suspend them. This strategy, known as "file and suspend," allows the lower earner to collect a spousal benefit based on the higher earner's record, potentially getting more than they receive on their own, while the higher earner's benefits continue to grow. The higher earner then collects once their benefit has maxed out. A few notes on file and suspend:

1. You must be at least at your FRA to file and suspend.
2. Either spouse can file and suspend, but not both.
3. By suspending, you are not eligible to collect a spousal benefit.

The only way to determine if either of these strategies will work for your family is by crunching the numbers. Unless you are extremely facile with Excel spreadsheets and financial modeling, it is best to work with a financial advisor as you make your determination.

☎ **TALK TO AN EXPERT:** If you're married and want to maximize your joint Social Security benefits, I highly recommend that you consult with a financial advisor who has in-depth knowledge of the Social Security system.

Think About Your Tax Situation

What Uncle Sam gives, he also takes away in the form of taxes. Regardless of when you retire, up to 50–85 percent of your Social Security income may be taxable if your modified adjusted gross income (MAGI) reaches certain levels. There is nothing to be done about this; simply be aware that your Social Security benefit may bump you up to a higher income tax bracket. (This could be another reason to delay.) See **Question 25** for more about taxes in retirement.

Bottom line? The most common error people make when it comes to Social Security is starting to collect their benefit too early. Yes, it's tempting to take the money and run. But before you do, carefully weigh your options. On further scrutiny, you are likely to find that you will get the best return on your money by postponing and allowing your monthly draw to increase.

Consider taking benefits early if:	Consider taking benefits later if:
You're not working and can't make ends meet.	You're still working and make enough to impact the taxability of your benefits.
You are in poor health.	You are in good health and longevity runs in your family.
You are the lower-earning spouse and your spouse can wait to file for a higher benefit.	You are the higher-earning spouse and want to be sure that your surviving spouse receives the highest possible benefit.

Next Steps

- To get a good sense of what you will collect in Social Security benefits, see **Question 31.**
- Learn about divorcee Social Security benefits in **Question 32.**
- Learn about Social Security disability benefits in **Question 33.**
- Learn about Social Security survivor benefits in **Question 34.**
- To get a sense of your retirement income tax situation, see **Question 25.**

Q31.

How much will I collect from Social Security?

Almost 90 percent of Americans age 65 and older receive income from Social Security. And to a certain extent, you have control over the amount you receive. As I discuss in **Question 30,** your monthly benefit will increase pretty dramatically the longer you postpone your start date (generally topping out at age 70). And if you're married, you can coordinate timing with your spouse to boost your combined benefit.

For context, let's back up a little. Your Social Security benefits are based on the earnings on which you paid Social Security payroll taxes. The more you earned over the years, up to a maximum amount ($113,700 in 2013), the higher your benefit. However, because the system is progressive, those with lower-than-average earnings receive a proportionately higher benefit (in terms of the benefits-received to taxes-paid ratio, not in terms of dollars).

In April 2013, the average Social Security retirement benefit was about $1,220 a month, or about $14,640 a year, which equals about 40 percent of the average earnings for someone who worked for his or her entire adult life and retired at age 65. In 2013, the highest monthly benefit for a 65-year-old was $2,533, or $30,400 a year. At age 70, the maximum was $3,350 a month, or $40,200 a year.

Not enough for a life of luxury, for sure. But Social Security provides an important, solid foundation of income for most Americans. And the sobering reality is that Social Security is the primary source of income for nearly two-thirds of beneficiaries. For one-third, Social Security is their *only* source of income. These percentages increase with age, as recipients become less likely to work and more likely to have depleted their savings.

Q FACT: Fifty-two percent of U.S. respondents in a Bank of Montreal Retirement Institute survey (2012) were uninformed about strategies to maximize Social Security benefits. Eighty percent said the Social Security Administration website would be their primary source of information, and only 25 percent mentioned a financial advisor. Sixty-one percent have not discussed their Social Security decision with anyone.

Following are ways to zero in on your own benefit.

Check Your Annual Statement

Every year the Social Security Administration mails a paper statement to all workers who are 60 or older and not yet receiving benefits. Here you'll see an estimate of your retirement and disability benefits, as well as benefits for your survivors. You will also see a confirmation of your qualification for Medicare.

This statement includes your complete earning records. Your eventual benefit is based on these figures, so it's important to make sure they're accurate. If you worked for more than one employer in any year, or if you also had self-employment income, those earnings are combined.

If you find an error, contact Social Security at 800-772-1213 or visit your local office. To correct the error, you will need a copy of your W-2 for any year in question.

➡ SMART MOVE: If you're married (or divorced) and don't have enough credits to qualify for coverage based on your own working record, you may qualify for a benefit based on your spouse's work record. See **Questions 30** and **32** for more.

HOW SOCIAL SECURITY BENEFITS ARE CALCULATED

In general, Social Security benefits are paid only to those who are "fully insured," which requires 40 quarterly credits. The required amount of earnings is very low and subject to an adjustment every year: In 2013 you earn one credit for every $1,160 of earnings in a calendar year, maxing out at 4 credits per year. Therefore, it takes a minimum of ten years of employment covered by Social Security to become fully insured.

If you qualify, your benefit is based on your average indexed monthly earnings (AIME) in your thirty-five highest-earning years after age 21. These figures are tallied at age 62 and then indexed for inflation (so that your past earnings are converted to current dollars). If you worked fewer than thirty-five years, the missing years are counted as 0, therefore bringing your average down. Earnings over a certain amount ($113,700 in 2013) are not subject to FICA taxes and do not count toward your benefit.

Finally, your AIME is translated into your basic benefit—known as your **primary insurance amount (PIA).** This is the amount that you will receive at your full retirement age (FRA), which ranges from 65 to 67, depending on the year you were born. Any variation in your actual benefit uses your PIA as the starting point.

SMART MOVE: If you want to receive the highest possible benefit, work for a minimum of thirty-five years. Otherwise, your average earnings will be reduced.

FACT: From a 2012 Bank of Montreal Retirement Institute survey of U.S. retirees:

49%:   not at all or not very knowledgeable about spousal benefits
56%:   not at all or not very knowledgeable about widow benefits
39%:   not aware they can receive up to 50% of spouse's benefit
47%:   not aware a widow gets 100% of spouse's benefit

Go Online

The Social Security Administration's website, socialsecurity.gov, has tons of helpful information and some great tools that are worth checking out. For example, you can:

- Sign up for a personal My Social Security account. Then you can see an online copy of your annual Social Security statement, which includes your earnings record as well as estimates of your future benefits.
- Use a number of online calculators to try out different retirement dates and situations.
- See how continuing to earn an income will temporarily impact your benefits.
- Check benefits for your spouse or other beneficiaries under different scenarios.
- Understand the potential impact of the Windfall Elimination Provision and the Government Pension Offset (see page 263) on your benefits.

➡ **SMART MOVE:** In most cases your benefits will continue to increase until you reach age 70. Before you file, understand the potential impact of timing on your lifetime benefit. See **Question 30** for details.

AT A GLANCE: SOCIAL SECURITY RETIREMENT BENEFITS

Recipient	Amount
Worker at least 62 but under FRA	Reduced primary insurance amount (PIA), the amount you will receive at your FRA
Worker at FRA	100% of PIA
Worker older than FRA	Increased beyond PIA
Spouse, under age 62	No benefit
Spouse, age 62 to FRA	50% of PIA, reduced
Spouse, at FRA	50% of PIA
Spouse, at any age, caring for a child who is under age 16 or disabled	50% of PIA
Unmarried child under age 18 or any age if disabled before age 22	50% of PIA, subject to family maximum

Factor in Reductions or Increases

Your annual statement provides a good estimate of your eventual benefit starting at different ages, but it's just that: an *estimate*. In reality, your benefit can be impacted by a number of variables:

- **Temporary withholding for working:** If you file for benefits before you reach your FRA and continue working, a portion of your benefit may be temporarily withheld. In 2013, if you file for benefits at age 62, $1 in benefits will be withheld for every $2 you earn above $15,120. In the year you reach your FRA, $1 is deducted for every $3 you earn above a higher limit, currently $40,080. Once you reach your FRA there is no earnings deduction, and you will get the money previously withheld in the form of a higher benefit.
- **Medicare:** Your Medicare premiums will be automatically deducted from your monthly Social Security check. See **Question 35** for information on Medicare premiums.
- **Cost of living:** In order to keep pace with inflation, every year Social Security determines if there will be a cost-of-living adjustment (COLA) based on the Consumer Price Index.
- **Increased or decreased future earnings:** If your income changes dramatically, or if you are out of work for a period of years, your average earnings (used to calculate your benefit) will be impacted.
- **Windfall Elimination Provision (WEP):** If you receive a pension based on work for which you didn't pay Social Security taxes, your benefit may be reduced. See page 263 for details.
- **Government Pension Offset (GPO):** If you receive a pension based on work for which you didn't pay Social Security taxes **and you otherwise qualify for spousal, widow, or widower benefits,** your benefit will likely be reduced. See page 263 for details.

WINDFALL ELIMINATION PROVISION AND GOVERNMENT PENSION OFFSET

The Windfall Elimination Provision (WEP) and the Government Pension Offset (GPO) impact those who qualify for Social Security benefits but also receive a government pension.

The WEP reduces Social Security benefits for people like firefighters, police officers, and public school teachers who receive a government pension. The size of the reduction depends on a number of factors, including the year the individual reaches age 62, how long he or she worked in the private sector, and how much he or she earned. For instance, the reduction for someone who paid Social Security taxes for more than twenty years and had what the SSA determines to be "substantial earnings" would be less than the reduction for someone who paid taxes for fewer years and earned less. In any case, the reduction in Social Security benefits can't be more than one-half of the pension from public employment. Anyone who paid Social Security taxes for more than thirty years has no reduction at all.

The GPO applies to those who collect a public pension and are also eligible for Social Security spousal, widow's, or widower's benefits. Essentially, it reduces their benefit by two-thirds of the government pension. For example, if an individual's pension was $900 a month, two-thirds of that amount, or $600, would be deducted from his or her spousal, widow's, or widower's benefit. So if this person was eligible for an $800 spousal benefit, he or she would collect only $200 from Social Security ($800 minus $600).

This may seem like a big reduction, but it was designed to sync up with the general Social Security rules governing benefits to spouses, widows, or widowers, which don't allow individuals to collect both their own benefits and benefits based on a husband's or wife's work record. However, there are many exceptions, so it's best to contact the SSA regarding a specific situation.

Next Steps

- To read more about how your start date will impact your benefit, see **Question 30**.

- Wondering how you and your spouse can best coordinate your benefits? See **Question 30.**
- For information on how your Social Security benefits will be taxed, see **Question 25.**
- To learn about Social Security disability benefits, see **Question 33;** for survivor benefits, see **Question 34.**

Q32.

I'm divorced. Am I entitled to a Social Security benefit from my ex?

You've hit on what is probably one of the best-kept secrets about Social Security. Most of us know that most husbands and wives are eligible for a Social Security benefit based on their spouse's work record. But what's not so widely recognized is that if you're divorced, it's still possible to collect benefits on your ex-spouse's record. However, the operative word here is *possible,* because there are qualifications you must meet. The basic rules are pretty straightforward, but there are a few permutations you'll need to consider.

The Basics

The first requirement is the length of your marriage. You're entitled to collect on your ex's Social Security record **if you were married for at least ten years.** Interestingly, it doesn't matter if he or she has remarried—you're still in the picture benefits-wise.

For you, however, remarriage is an issue. In order to collect a divorced-spouse benefit, **you must be unmarried.** If you did remarry, that marriage must have ended (by divorce, death, or annulment).

(You could then choose to collect on either spouse, whichever benefit is higher—but you can't collect on both.) Finally, **you must be at least 62 years old.**

It's also interesting to note that collecting on an ex-spouse's record has no effect on what the ex or his or her current spouse can collect. In fact, Social Security is happy to pay benefits to as many ex-spouses as one might have (provided each qualifies).

That may all sound simple enough. But there's still more to consider.

Think About Your Timing

If you meet the basic qualifications *and* the Social Security benefits you'd receive on your own earnings are less than the spousal benefit, you can file based on your ex's record. Even if your ex hasn't yet applied for Social Security but is eligible for it, you can still take benefits **as long as you've been divorced for at least two years.**

➡ **SMART MOVE:** If your ex is younger than you and isn't yet eligible for Social Security, you can collect your own benefit first and then switch to your ex's benefit when he or she reaches 62.

However, in determining the best time for you to take this benefit, there are a couple of things to consider. A spousal benefit—whether you're married or divorced—is only 50 percent of the spouse's full benefit.

➡ **SMART MOVE:** Never postpone a spousal benefit beyond your FRA. It tops out at that point. See **Question 30,** page 254, for more.

If you decide to take your benefit at age 62 rather than waiting until your full retirement age (66 for those born between 1943 and 1954), your 50 percent benefit will be permanently reduced by another 25 percent. Depending on your current financial situation, it can make more sense to wait.

There's yet another reason to consider waiting. At your full retirement age, if you're eligible for benefits on your own record, as well as that of your ex, you can choose to initially take only the divorced-spouse benefit and delay taking your own benefit until a later date. Because benefits go up by about 8 percent a year between the ages of 66 and 70, waiting to collect your own benefits could mean a significantly higher payout down the road. Just for the record, the spousal benefit doesn't go up in the same way, so there's no advantage to waiting to collect it past your full retirement age. See **Question 30** for more details on when to start collecting Social Security.

⚠ **CAUTION:** If you file early (before your FRA) for an ex-spouse benefit, you can't then switch over to your own benefit when you reach your FRA.

Understand Survivor Benefits

Your benefit could be even higher if your ex-spouse passes away. If you're 60 years old (or 50 and disabled) and you were married for ten years or longer, and you're not entitled to a higher benefit on your own, you can receive the same benefit as a widow or widower (a reduced payment starting as early as age 60, and a full benefit at your FRA). And, once again, the fact that you collect benefits won't impact what anyone else can collect. See **Question 34** for more on survivor benefits.

The rules regarding marital status are different in this case: You can be married and still collect survivor benefits as long as you didn't remarry until age 60 (or age 50 if you are disabled).

If you've been married more than once, you have even more choice, as the following example shows.

Example: Marie and Frank were divorced after thirty years of marriage when Marie was 61. Both remarried, but Marie's second husband died a couple of years later. Marie wasn't eligible for Social Security benefits on her own, but when she reached her FRA, she collected survivor benefits based on her deceased husband's record. When Frank died a few years later, Marie was able to choose to collect survivor benefits on either husband's record. She switched over to Frank's benefits because his were higher. Frank's widow was also able to collect a 100 percent survivor benefit.

AN EXCEPTION IF YOU'RE CARING FOR A CHILD

If you're caring for a child who is under age 16 (or disabled) and who is getting benefits based on the record of your former spouse, you don't have to meet the length-of-marriage rule as long as the child is your ex-spouse's natural or legally adopted child.

However, in this situation, the benefit you receive will have an impact on the amount of benefits others might collect. If this is your situation, it's best to contact the Social Security Administration.

What's Right for You?

If you're divorced, being able to boost your income with a spousal benefit can be a real plus. But no matter what your marital status, it pays to do some serious thinking about your options before you file. Your health, family longevity, and overall retirement plan are all factors to consider.

Next Steps

- Learn when to start collecting Social Security benefits in **Question 30.**
- For more details on survivor benefits, see **Question 34.**
- For information on Medicare, see **Question 35.**

Q33.

What Social Security benefit can I expect if I become disabled?

Social Security is best known for retirement benefits, but it also provides disability benefits to millions of American workers (and their families) of all ages—to the tune of about $130 billion a year. Despite the magnitude of these numbers, though, it's actually very tough to qualify for disability benefits. Not only is the definition of *disability* very strict ("a medical condition that renders one incapable of working and that is expected to last at least one year or result in death"), but the application and screening process is generally arduous and slow. Most applications are denied.

Q FACT: Out of 2.8 million SSDI applications in 2012, only about 980,000 were approved, according to the Social Security Administration.

Before we go into details, I want to point out that Social Security provides benefits to people with severe disabilities through two distinct (and separately funded) programs: **Social Security Disability Insurance (SSDI)** and **Supplemental Security Income (SSI)**. The names are similar, and the programs are often confused—but they are very different.

In this question I discuss SSDI, which compensates qualified individuals who are under their full retirement age (FRA), regardless of their income. **Once you reach your FRA, you are automatically switched to your Social Security retirement benefit (you don't receive both).** SSI, which covers only low-income individuals with extremely limited assets (and who are disabled, blind, or over age 65), is briefly covered in **Question 24**, page 212.

▶ **SMART MOVE:** If you haven't done so already, look into purchasing a long-term disability policy. See **Question 17**.

Qualifications Are Strict

In order to qualify for SSDI benefits, you have to meet several qualifications:

- You must *not* have reached your full retirement age (FRA). See **Question 30**.
- You need to have accrued enough Social Security work credits to pass two earnings tests: the "recent-work test" and the "duration-of-work" test. The credit requirement is a sliding scale, based on your age (fewer years the younger you are). At age 60 you must have had Social Security–covered employment for five out of the last ten years. You also must have worked at Social Security–covered employment for a total of at least 9½ years.
- Your medical condition must be so severe that you are incapable of working and it will last for at least one year or until death.
- You can't earn more than a minimal amount of money ($1,040 per month in 2013). If you are blind, this minimum is a bit higher; you can have a net profit of $1,740 per month.

▶ **SMART MOVE:** The SSA maintains a list of conditions so severe that they automatically define you as disabled and your application will be fast-tracked. It's worth checking to see if you qualify.

Benefits for You and Your Family

If you qualify, your benefit is based on your average lifetime earnings. Generally you'll receive the same amount that you would receive from Social Security at your full retirement age. There is no such thing as a partial SSDI benefit.

> **Q FACT:** In 2013, the maximum SSDI monthly benefit was $2,533. The average was $1,132.

Once you qualify, other family members may also be able to collect benefits based on your disability. These include:

- Your spouse, age 62 or older, provided you have been married for at least one year
- Your ex-spouse age 62 or older, if you were married at least ten years
- Your spouse or ex-spouse of any age, if he or she is caring for your child who is age 16 or disabled
- Your children under age 18, if unmarried
- Your children under age 19, if full-time students (through high school) or disabled
- Your children older than age 18, if severely disabled

Each family member may qualify for a monthly benefit equal to as much as 50 percent of your basic benefit. These family benefits are in addition to your individual benefit. However, there is a "family maximum," which is generally between 150 and 180 percent of your benefit. Once your family exceeds this amount, benefits will be reduced proportionately. You can find your family maximum on your annual statement.

If you receive other state or federal benefits (for example, workers' compensation), your SSDI check may be reduced. Your benefit may also be reduced if you're collecting benefits from a prior job in which you didn't pay Social Security taxes. See **Question 31**, page 263, for an explanation of the Windfall Elimination Provision and the Government Pension Offset. Your benefits will *not* be reduced if you're receiving benefits from the U.S. Department of Veterans Affairs or from a private disability policy.

⚠ **CAUTION:** Benefits from a private disability policy won't reduce your SSDI benefits, but you might get caught on the other side: Your benefit from a private policy may be reduced if you collect SSDI benefits. Be sure to check your policy.

In addition, you will be automatically covered by Medicare after you have received SSDI benefits for two years, regardless of your age.

▶ **SMART MOVE:** If you're approved, ask the SSA if you qualify for a "disability freeze" on your earnings. This will prevent the years of reduced earnings due to a disability from being included in your average indexed monthly earnings (AIME) calculation, thereby boosting your Social Security benefit. See **Question 31** for more on AIME.

AT A GLANCE: SOCIAL SECURITY DISABILITY BENEFITS

Recipient	Amount
Worker under FRA	100% of your primary insurance amount (PIA)
Worker at FRA	Disability benefit ends; retirement benefits begin
Spouse, age 60 or 61	No benefit
Spouse, age 62 to FRA	50% of PIA, reduced
Spouse, at FRA	50% of PIA
Spouse, at any age, caring for a child who is under age 16 or disabled	50% of PIA
Unmarried child under age 18 or any age if disabled before age 22	50% of PIA (subject to family maximum)

Apply as Soon as Possible

If you become disabled, and believe that your disability will last for at least a year, don't delay. In the words of the Social Security Administration: **"It can take a long time to process an application for disability benefits (three to five months)."** You will have to compile a library of information about yourself, your work history, and your medical condition, and to complete numerous forms. But the more thorough and accurate you are from the start, the more likely you are to speed up the process.

If You're Approved

If your claim is approved, your first check will cover the sixth full month after your disability began. If you were disabled on January 15, your first benefit would cover the month of July. However, benefits are paid for the month prior, so you wouldn't receive your July payment until August.

If You're Not Approved

If your claim isn't approved (and most claims aren't), you can appeal the decision—but you have to do so within sixty days. The only bit of good news here is that you have a better chance of being approved on appeal than you had on the first go-round.

Next Steps
- Check your Social Security benefits online at ssa.gov. Also see **Questions 30, 31, 32,** and **34** for more.
- To learn about private disability policies (and why most workers should seriously consider having one), see **Question 17.**
- To read about other insurance that you do (or don't) need in retirement, see **Question 27.**
- To read about Medicare and health-care costs in retirement, see **Questions 35–37.**

Q34.

How much will my spouse receive from Social Security if I die?

None of us enjoys thinking about our demise, but there may be some comfort in knowing that our loved ones are likely to receive some financial support from Social Security, regardless of whether they have contributed to the system themselves. In 2013, the SSA paid benefits to 6.3 million survivors of deceased workers. This number includes about 4 million widows and widowers, and 2 million children, as well as divorced spouses, dependent parents, and other family members.

Survivor benefits are different from spousal benefits. Your surviving spouse (or ex-spouse) can receive up to 100 percent of your benefit upon your death, whereas your spouse (or ex-spouse) is limited to 50 percent of your benefit while you are alive. Other family members may be able to collect up to 75 percent of your benefit.

As is generally the case with Social Security benefits, the rules and conditions get pretty complicated. Because your family member's benefit will be affected by a number of factors, including your age when you file, their age when they file, and whether you had filed for benefits prior to your death, it's worth unraveling the details. Read on.

The Basics

Your family's benefits are based on what the SSA refers to as your **primary insurance amount (PIA)**. This is the amount that you would collect at your **full retirement age (FRA)**. In order for family members to qualify, you must have been "fully insured" at the time of your death, which generally requires forty Social Security work credits (reduced for young workers). The size of their benefit will depend on your lifetime earnings; the more you paid into Social Security over the years, the more they'll get—up to a maximum that is adjusted each year for inflation.

If your surviving spouse is entitled to Social Security benefits on his or her own work record, he or she is entitled to whichever benefit is higher, but not to both.

⚠ **CAUTION:** If a survivor files early, benefits will generally be reduced for each month prior to his or her FRA. Be careful, because this reduction can cost a lot over the years.

Who Can Receive Benefits?

If you have enough credits, survivor benefits may be paid to:

- Your spouse age 60 or older (age 50 or older if disabled), provided you were married for at least nine months
- Your spouse at any age if disabled or caring for your child who is under age 16
- Your ex-spouse age 60 or older (age 50 or older if disabled) who was married to you for at least ten years, provided he or she didn't remarry before age 60
- Your ex-spouse of any age if disabled or caring for your child who is under age 16
- Your unmarried children under age 18, or older if disabled
- Your unmarried children under age 19 if attending elementary or secondary school full-time

- Your dependent parents age 62 or older (you must have been supplying at least one-half of their support)

Understand How Benefits Are Calculated

Your family's benefit is based on your earnings record. This may seem simple enough on the surface, but there are many permutations.

- If you die *before* starting benefits, your surviving spouse is entitled to a benefit equal to 100 percent of your PIA at full retirement age (FRA). If he or she files between the age of 60 and FRA, the benefit will be reduced.
- If you die *after* starting benefits, your surviving spouse's benefit cannot exceed the amount that you were being paid. Therefore, if you were receiving reduced benefits, your spouse will as well. If he or she hasn't yet reached FRA on filing, the benefit will be further reduced. However, if you delayed filing until age 70, your spouse's benefit will be based on this increased amount.
- Your spouse who is caring for a child is eligible to collect benefits even if you don't have the required number of work credits, **provided that you had 1½ years of covered work in the three years prior to your death.**
- If your spouse remarries after age 60 (or age 50 if disabled), he or she is still eligible to collect a survivor benefit based on your work record.
- A qualified ex-spouse is entitled to the same benefit as a widow or widower.
- A dependent child is entitled to a benefit equal to 75 percent of your PIA. This will generally terminate at age 18 or marriage.
- A dependent parent is eligible for up to 82.5 percent of your benefit. If you have two living dependent parents, each is entitled to up to 75 percent.
- The combined benefit for every family is subject to a "family maximum." In general, this varies between 150 and 180 percent of your

full benefit. If the sum of the benefits exceeds this amount, the benefits will be reduced proportionately. An ex-spouse's benefit is not counted in this calculation.

In addition, your spouse or children will receive a one-time payment of $255 (yes, you read that right) upon your death.

AT A GLANCE: SOCIAL SECURITY SURVIVOR BENEFITS

Recipient	Amount
Spouse, age 60 or 61	100% of your primary insurance amount (PIA), reduced
Spouse, age 62 to FRA	100% of PIA, reduced
Spouse, at FRA	100% of PIA
Spouse, at any age, caring for a child who is under age 16 or disabled	75% of PIA
Unmarried child under age 18 or any age if disabled before age 22	75% of PIA
Dependent parent	Up to 82.5% of PIA, or 75% if a couple

SMART MOVE: Consider postponing benefits until age 70, especially if you are the higher earner in your marriage. That way, your surviving spouse will collect the highest possible benefit.

IF YOU'RE A SURVIVOR WITH YOUR OWN SOCIAL SECURITY BENEFITS

Survivors with their own work record have some choices.

- **If you haven't started to collect your own benefit,** you can take a survivor benefit while you allow your own benefit to increase in value. Then, when you're 70, you can switch to your own benefit if it is higher. **Unlike with spousal benefits, you don't have to wait until you reach your FRA to take advantage of this strategy. You can take a (reduced) benefit as early as age 60, and then switch.**

- **If you're already collecting Social Security benefits based on your own work record,** and the survivor benefit would be greater, you can switch over. If you're under your FRA and want to wait until your survivor benefit grows, you can do that, too.

⚠ **CAUTION:** If you receive a pension based on work for which you didn't pay Social Security taxes *and you otherwise qualify for survivor benefits,* your benefit will likely be reduced. See more about the Government Pension Offset in **Question 31,** page 263.

Next Steps

- It's best to think about Social Security survivor benefits in the context of the rest of your estate plan. See **Question 38** for estate planning basics.
- To understand how much you can expect to collect from your Social Security benefits, see **Question 31.** For timing considerations, see **Question 30.**
- To read about the need for life insurance at this time in your life, see **Question 16.**

Q35.

When and how do I
apply for Medicare?

For many folks, reaching age 65 is kind of a milestone, in part because you're eligible for Medicare. At long last, you think, you won't have to worry so much about high health insurance premiums, what's covered and what's not, and the myriad details that seem to go hand in hand with health insurance. But hold on a second. Medicare, while an excellent government program in many ways, isn't quite that simple. And a number of people are unaware of some important Medicare facts and figures.

For instance, I recently had dinner with an old friend whom I hadn't seen for a while. She had turned 65 in the past year and said to me rather indignantly, "You know, Medicare isn't free." I think she felt like this was some type of a betrayal. Now, this friend is a professional in her field, well versed in a lot of things. But having to pay a premium for Medicare took her completely by surprise.

With this story in mind, I believe it's important to review some Medicare basics well before your 65th birthday. It's best to know what to do, when to do it, and how Medicare will fit into your monthly budget.

The Basics

There are four parts to Medicare. Part A, hospital insurance, covers hospitalization and is free for those who qualify. Part B, medical insurance—for which you pay a monthly premium—covers doctors' visits and outpatient care. Part C, Medicare Advantage, combines original Medicare with extended services and prescription drug coverage through a private provider for an additional premium. Part D, prescription drug coverage, also comes with a premium. Combined, these premiums may be less than what you've been paying, especially for private insurance, but as you can see, Medicare is hardly free.

MEDICARE AT A GLANCE

	What It Is	What It Costs
Part A	**Hospital insurance**—Helps pay for inpatient care in a hospital or skilled nursing facility (following a hospital stay), some home health care and hospice care.	Free if you or your spouse is eligible for Social Security benefits, railroad retirement benefits, or has worked long enough in a government job where Medicare taxes were paid. Otherwise available for a monthly premium ($441 per month in 2013).
Part B	**Medical insurance**—Helps pay for doctors' services and many other medical services and supplies that are not covered by hospital insurance.	For 2013, $104.90 basic monthly premium with $147 deductible. Higher for single filers with incomes over $85,000 ($170,000 for married filing jointly). There may also be copayments for certain services.
Part C	**Medicare Advantage**—Offered by a private provider to people eligible for Medicare Parts A and B. This is an alternative way to receive Medicare benefits. It covers all that original Medicare covers (hospital and medical insurance) and more. Also generally includes Medicare Part D prescription drug coverage.	Cost varies by plan.
Part D	**Prescription drug coverage**—Helps pay for medications doctors prescribe for treatment. Coverage varies by plan.	Cost varies by plan. Additional premium for higher wage earners.

➲ **SMART MOVE:** Medicare doesn't cover everything. If you're going with original Medicare Parts A and B (not a Medicare Advantage Plan), consider a Medigap policy as a supplement. See **Question 36** for how Medigap compares to Medicare Advantage and why you may want to consider it.

Who Needs to Enroll

If you're already getting Social Security benefits, you're pretty much covered. That's because anyone receiving benefits is automatically enrolled in Medicare Parts A and B. To make it even easier, premiums for Part B are deducted from your monthly benefits check. You do, however, need to enroll in Part D yourself and choose a plan to get prescription drug coverage.

It's when you're not yet collecting Social Security that you have to pay close attention. Even though you're not getting Social Security benefits, you're still eligible for full Medicare benefits at age 65. But it's up to you to contact the Social Security Administration to sign up.

WHAT IF YOU DON'T WANT PART B?

If you were automatically enrolled in Part B, but don't want it at this time, you do have the option to opt out. All you have to do is follow the instructions that come with your Medicare card and send the card back. Just be aware that unless you have coverage through your own or your spouse's employer, you may be subject to a penalty if you opt out and enroll at a later date. For more information, contact the Social Security Administration.

⚠ **CAUTION:** If you delay in signing up for Medicare Part B, your coverage will be delayed and will cost you an *additional 10 percent per month* for each twelve-month period you were eligible but didn't enroll. If you delay in signing up for Medicare Part D, you will be charged a penalty if there's a period of sixty-three days or more in a row when you didn't have Part D or other creditable prescription drug coverage. Check out medicare.gov for details. (Timing is different if you still have employer coverage. See "Deadline Exceptions If You're Covered by Your Employer's Plan" on page 283.)

When You Need to Enroll

If you need to enroll in Medicare, there are a few important enrollment deadlines to remember.

- **Initial Enrollment Period**—This is your first, and probably most important, enrollment window. It generally extends from three months *before* the month you turn 65 until three months *after* the month you turn 65—a seven-month period in total. During this time you can sign up for Medicare Parts A, B, C, and D. If you want your Medicare benefits to start right away when you turn 65, you have to sign up during the three months before your birthday. Otherwise, your benefits could be delayed by one to three months. If your birthday is on the first of the month, you get a small bonus. Your benefits can actually start a month earlier, as long as you sign up in a timely fashion.

- **General Enrollment Period for Part B**—If you miss your Initial Enrollment Period, you may have to wait until what's called the General Enrollment Period, which runs from January 1 to March 31 each year. There are a couple of drawbacks to waiting. First, your benefits won't start until July 1 of the year in which you enroll. And second, you will generally pay a penalty for late enrollment.

- **General Enrollment Periods for Parts C and D**—If you sign up for Medicare Part B during the General Enrollment Period (January 1–March 31), you must wait to sign up for a Part C Medicare Advantage Plan or Part D prescription drug coverage. The General Enrollment Period for these two parts is April 1–June 30 of each year.

⏳ **DEADLINE:** If you want to make a change in your Medicare coverage—for instance, switch to or from a Part C Medicare Advantage Plan or to a different Part D plan—you can do so each year from October 15 to December 7.

DEADLINE EXCEPTIONS IF YOU'RE COVERED BY YOUR EMPLOYER'S PLAN

If you plan to keep working and you have medical insurance through your employer, the timing is a little looser. When you're covered by a group plan—either through your own employer or through your spouse's—you can choose to enroll in Part B at any time while you're still covered by that plan. When your employment or group coverage ends, you then have eight months in which to sign up. So you could still sign up for Part A during your Initial Enrollment Period but delay signing up for Part B (and delay paying the premium).

Another alternative is to enroll in both Parts A and B at the same time and consider Medicare as your secondary insurance, which would generally pay for any services not covered by your employer's health plan. There are federal regulations that come into play, tied to the number of people employed by your company, particularly if your company has fewer than twenty employees, so it's a good idea to talk to your employer's human resources department or plan administrator before making your decision.

How to Enroll

You enroll in Medicare through the Social Security Administration. There are three easy ways to enroll, so you can choose the method that's most comfortable for you:

- **Online:** Apply online at ssa.gov.
- **In person:** Make an appointment or stop by your local Social Security office.
- **By phone:** Call Social Security at 1-800-772-1213. If you worked for a railroad, call the Railroad Retirement Board at 877-772-5772.

Next Steps

- Decide on a Medigap policy or a Medicare Advantage Plan to supplement Medicare Parts A and B. See **Question 36** for things to consider.
- Give some thought to how you'll handle out-of-pocket medical expenses. **Question 37** has ideas on how to take action now to lower health-care costs later.
- If you're not yet collecting Social Security, **Question 30** discusses the pros and cons of taking it early.

Q36.

I've heard about insurance
to supplement Medicare.
What will I need, and
how much will it cost?

While original Medicare Parts A and B cover a lot—from hospitalization to doctors' visits to necessary medical equipment—they don't cover everything. First of all, there are deductibles and copayments to consider. Then there are national and local rules and regulations that govern whether a specific medical need is covered. For instance, a treatment that is allowed by Medicare in one state or county could be denied in another.

You can always discuss these things with your doctor, and do some personal research about what's covered at medicare.gov, but the bottom line is, it's best to have supplemental medical insurance just in case. It will mean an added monthly premium, but in the long run it could save you thousands of dollars.

Look into Both Medigap and Medicare Advantage

There are two basic types of supplemental insurance to consider. You must be enrolled in Medicare Parts A and B to qualify for either.

- **A Medigap policy**—This is sold by a private insurance company and pays for things that Medicare doesn't cover, such as copayments and deductibles. Generally, Medicare pays first, up to approved amounts for covered costs. Then your Medigap policy kicks in to pay its share. Some policies also offer added coverage for services not included in Medicare, such as coverage when you travel outside the United States. These policies generally don't cover prescription drugs, or dental or vision services. And while Medigap policies are standardized and regulated by federal and state laws in terms of types of plans and coverage, there's no standardization of cost.

IMPORTANT THINGS TO KNOW ABOUT MEDIGAP POLICIES

- Medigap policies are offered by private insurance companies, but coverage is standardized and regulated.

- There are ten basic Medigap policies to choose from, each offering different benefits at varying premiums. (Massachusetts, Minnesota, and Wisconsin have different standardized plans.)

- Medigap premiums range from less than $50 to more than $300 per month, depending on the policy. This premium is in addition to your Medicare premium.

- Each individual must have his or her own Medigap policy. There are no family policies.

- You have a **six-month Medigap enrollment window** starting the month you turn 65 and are enrolled in Medicare Part B. If you sign up during this six-month window, there's no medical underwriting required and you can't be refused a policy or charged extra even if you have health problems.

- A Medigap policy is guaranteed renewable. An insurance company can't cancel your policy as long as you pay the premium. (However, premiums may go up.)

⚠ **CAUTION:** Even with a Medigap policy, you're not completely covered. Most Medigap policies don't cover things such as vision or dental care, eyeglasses, hearing aids—and definitely not long-term care. You'll still need to factor out-of-pocket health-care costs into your budget. See **Question 37.**

- **A Medicare Advantage Plan**—Also called Medicare Part C, this is actually an alternative way to receive Medicare benefits, similar to an HMO. It's offered by private insurance companies and must include all services that Medicare Parts A and B cover. Many plans also cover prescription drugs as well as extras such as vision, hearing, dental care, and health and wellness programs. Like Medigap policies, Medicare Advantage Plans vary in terms of cost and services, but premiums may generally be a bit lower than Medigap policies. However, look closely at deductibles and copayments that could drive up your out-of-pocket expenses. On the plus side, Medicare Advantage Plans are required to put an annual limit on out-of-pocket expenses.

IMPORTANT THINGS TO KNOW ABOUT MEDICARE ADVANTAGE PLANS

- Medicare Advantage Plans are a type of managed care. The most common:
  - **Health maintenance organization (HMO):** You're usually required to use a doctor or service provider that is part of the plan's network, or else pay the full cost. The HMO may require that you get approval for treatment by a specialist or a certain type of care.
  - **Preferred provider organization (PPO):** You can see doctors or service providers outside the plan's network, but at a higher cost. Referrals to specialists are not needed.

- There are a few other, less common options: Private Fee-for-Service (PFFS), Medical Savings Accounts (MSAs), and Special Needs Plans (SNPs). For a more detailed comparison, check out medicare.com, a nongovernmental website.

- Medicare Advantage Plans are approved by Medicare and must offer the same benefits as original Medicare Parts A and B.

- Additional Medicare Advantage benefits differ by plan.

- Costs for services, deductibles, and copayments can vary considerably from plan to plan and may be adjusted yearly.

- You can enroll in a Medicare Advantage Plan during your Medicare Initial Enrollment Period. (See **Question 35.**) You can change or drop a plan between November 15 and December 31 each year.

⚠️ **CAUTION:** A Medicare Advantage Plan with a low premium may carry higher deductibles and copayments. Make sure you look at the type of medical services you're likely to need and the corresponding potential out-of-pocket costs when choosing a plan.

Do Some Comparison Shopping

Premiums for Medigap policies depend on where you live and the type of policy you choose, but can range from less than $50 to over $300 a month. Cost will also vary from insurance company to insurance company. In general, Medicare Advantage Plans cost less, but out-of-pocket expense may be higher. For instance, in 2013 the average monthly premium for Medicare Advantage Plans nationwide was $60 with average out-of-pocket expenses capped annually at $4,516, according to an analysis by planprescriber.com.

But cost is only part of the equation. While Medigap benefits and services are standardized, what you get with Medicare Advantage varies by plan. So you need to do some research. You'll want to compare premiums, deductibles, benefits, and restrictions on doctors and health-care facilities, as well as what the overall cost might be to you considering your typical medical needs and prescription drug usage.

A good place to start is medicare.com, which has more information as well as a comparison tool to help identify programs and policies in your area and compare coverage and costs. Another good resource is medicare.gov, which has comprehensive brochures on basic Medicare and how it works with Medigap policies and Medicare Advantage Plans.

AT A GLANCE: MEDIGAP VS. MEDICARE ADVANTAGE

Medigap Policies	Medicare Advantage Plans
Standardized benefits and services based on policy type	Covers basic Medicare Parts A and B, but other services vary by plan
Wide network of doctors and health-care facilities	Network of doctors and health-care facilities limited by plan
Costs for services set by Medicare	Costs for services set by individual plan
Premiums range from under $50 to over $300/month, depending on the policy type and insurance company	Premiums average $60/month nationally, but deductibles and copayments for services vary widely
Does not include prescription drug coverage	Generally includes prescription drug coverage
Does not include coverage for vision, hearing, and dental	May include vision, hearing, and dental care

SMART MOVE: When shopping for a Medigap policy, find out not only the current premium, but also the history of rate increases. Also, ask if the premiums will go up as you age.

Don't Forget About a Prescription Drug Plan

As I mentioned, Medigap policies usually don't include prescription drug coverage, so you'll also have to look into a Part D prescription drug policy. These policies are offered by private insurance companies, and premiums will vary from plan to plan and state to state. For 2013, the average premium was around $30 per month, with a standard deductible of $325 (due to go down in 2014). However, individual plans may also have different deductibles, so once again it pays to comparison shop.

Most Medicare Advantage Plans include prescription drug coverage, but deductibles and copays differ. Do your homework before you sign up!

➲ **SMART MOVE:** Don't delay in getting a Part D prescription drug plan if you need it. You could be charged a penalty for late enrollment! See **Question 35** for more details.

Next Steps

- Do more research. Medicare.gov is an excellent resource. You may also want to check with your state insurance department for information on specific insurance companies or sample rates for your area.
- Review the basics of Medicare to make sure you sign up in a timely manner and avoid penalties. See **Question 35.**
- Remember that long-term care is not covered by Medicare, Medigap policies, or Medicare Advantage Plans. **Question 7** provides some food for thought.

Q37.

Once I'm on Medicare, will I have other out-of-pocket health-care costs? What can I do now to lower my health-care expenses later?

Health-care costs are a huge issue, especially for anyone close to retirement. According to a 2012 poll by Harris Interactive, 71 percent of U.S. adults—both retired and still working—worry about being able to afford unexpected health-care costs. That's not surprising, considering that the 2012 Health Confidence Survey conducted by the Employee Benefit Research Institute (EBRI) predicts that a 65-year-old couple today with median drug expenses could need well over $283,000 just to cover medical costs during the rest of their lives. While it sounds like a whopping sum, when you consider that it represents only $11,320 a year for 25 years, it's realistic—and may even be low.

Granted, there are many unknowns when it comes to predicting your own costs, such as how much health care you'll need and for how long. But it's pretty well accepted that health-care inflation will continue to outstrip the Consumer Price Index, so costs are going to go up—even for a healthy person. With Medicare covering only about 60 percent of health-care costs, there's no doubt that you'll have out-of-pocket expenses, probably more than you might think. The bottom line is that you need to factor health care into your long-range retirement plans. And the more you plan for it in advance, the better off you'll be.

Take a Realistic Look at Basic Post-retirement Health-Care Costs

If you've been fairly healthy most of your life (and you've had good insurance through your employer), it may be difficult to imagine needing so much money each year for out-of-pocket health-care costs. But remember that out-of-pocket expenses also include what you pay for premiums, for both Medicare and supplemental insurance. Let's look at a typical scenario:

Example: Susan and David are healthy 65-year-olds who have recently enrolled in Medicare. They have each also enrolled in a Medigap policy to cover the costs that Medicare doesn't (see **Question 36**) as well as a Part D prescription drug plan. They've decided to cover the costs of things like dental and vision care themselves. Here's how their annual expenses add up:

Medicare Part B premium: $104.90/month per person	$2,517.60
Medigap policy: $121/month per person	$2,904
Prescription drug plan: $30/month per person	$720
Dental average projected costs: $500/person	$1,000
Vision average projected costs: $500/person	$1,000
Copays and deductibles: $929/person	$1,858

Their baseline out-of-pocket annual expenses, including copays and deductibles, amount to around $10,000—and this is for a healthy couple!

If either person has any sort of significant illness, the costs could easily exceed $10,000 a year—especially as time goes on—and meet or exceed the EBRI projections I mentioned earlier.

BEHIND THE SCENES: SAVING FOR FUTURE HEALTH-CARE COSTS

We've discussed how out-of-pocket costs can add up quickly, but now let's take a closer look. For those of you who are mathematically inclined, we're calculating the present value of a growing annuity.

- First-year costs = $10,000

- Health-care inflation rate = 8% (roughly triple the projected Consumer Price Index)

- Rate of return on lump sum = 5%

- Time horizon = 30 years

$$\$10{,}000 \times \left[\frac{1 - \left(\frac{1.08}{1.05}\right)^{30}}{-0.03}\right] \times 1.05 + \$464{,}895.16$$

In other words, our healthy couple, who is spending only $10,000 in the first year of retirement, would need a lump sum of $465,000 just to cover inflation-adjusted health-care costs over thirty years! The reason this number is so huge is that we're assuming health-care costs will grow faster than anyone could reasonably earn in a portfolio.

This is just a rough estimate, but hopefully this exercise will show you just how much of your savings might go to health care.

FACT: According to the Employee Benefit Research Institute, Medicare generally covers only about 60 percent of the cost of health-care services (not including long-term care) for Medicare beneficiaries age 65 and older. Out-of-pocket spending accounts for 13 percent.

Make Health Care an Essential Part of Your Retirement Budget—and Your Savings Plan

In **Question 2** I talk about budgeting and dividing your expenses into essential and discretionary categories. Insurance premiums should always be considered essential. But as you approach retirement you need to look beyond the premiums and factor in the extras as well. There are a host of services that aren't covered by Medicare—and may or may not be covered by supplemental insurance. These can include dentists, vision tests, eyeglasses, hearing aids, and, most definitely, long-term care. It would be wise to make health-care extras a line item in your budget and set aside a certain amount each month to cover them. It's like creating your own Health Savings Account.

⚠ **CAUTION:** Medicare, like any enormous organization, makes mistakes. If you ever get a bill that you don't understand, pick up the phone! It happens more than we'd like to think.

And speaking of Health Savings Accounts (HSAs), if you have a high-deductible insurance policy and can open an HSA, so much the better. In 2013 an individual who is 50 or older could contribute up to $4,250 annually. It's a great way to save for future health-care expenses—and get a tax benefit at the same time. Once you're on Medicare, you can no longer contribute to an HSA, so it's smart to build it up prior to retirement.

➲ **SMART MOVE:** If you qualify for a Roth IRA (see **Question 4**), consider using that as a way to save for future health-care costs. Your money can grow tax-free, and withdrawals are tax-free once the account has been opened for five years. Plus there's no age limit for contributing to a Roth as long as you have earned income.

Consider Long-Term Care Insurance

Medicare doesn't cover long-term care insurance (LTCI). Nor do Medicare supplement policies. And as I discuss in **Question 7**, the cost of long-term care can be astronomical. While LTCI isn't inexpensive, and there's a chance you may not need it, I believe it's just part of smart financial planning to weigh the cost of a policy against your other options for paying for care should you have a chronic illness or disability.

Take Care of Yourself

As Benjamin Franklin said, "An ounce of prevention is worth a pound of cure," and that certainly is true when it comes to our health. More and more studies are encouraging us to eat well, exercise more, maintain strong social ties—all the things that make us not only feel better right now, but also live longer, fuller, healthier lives. However, according to a recent study in *JAMA Internal Medicine,* while we boomers may be living longer, we're not necessarily healthier than the previous generation, which is translating into higher health-care costs. To me that's a real call to action. Because no matter how we plan and save and take care of our finances, they can go only so far unless we also take better care of ourselves.

Next Steps
- Go to heathcare.gov to see how the Affordable Care Act may help reduce health-care costs for seniors.
- Make sure you have either a Medigap policy or a Medicare Advantage Plan to supplement Medicare. **Question 36** gives you an overview of each.
- Seriously consider long-term care insurance. See **Question 7.**

PART V

Estate Planning

When it comes to families and money, emotions run high. We have different perspectives, different values, and strong feelings about what is right or wrong. Add in the possibility of death, and anxiety skyrockets. It's really no surprise that estate planning falls right off the bottom of our to-do list.

A better perspective, I think, is to think about planning your estate as planning your legacy. It's your opportunity to make your mark on the world—to help and protect the people you care about most. It is your opportunity to give back to your community, or university, or cause. As you create your plan, don't let that vision fade.

In this section I cover some of the most common questions I hear about estate planning—from creating a basic plan to creating trusts for special circumstances. I delve a little into estate taxes, as well as the gift tax and generation-skipping tax, and also address common questions regarding the best way to divide one's estate.

Unfortunately, estate planning is made more confusing by stilted language and convoluted laws. But it's essential to get past these obstacles. I'll do my best to help you down that road.

Q38.

I want to create an estate plan. What do I need?

Like most people, I didn't think about estate planning when I was young. In fact, it wasn't until I was a mother that my husband and I started to think about it. And then it clicked in. I had kids, I had responsibilities, and I could provide for my family and my favorite charities in a way that I feel good about. And the strange thing is, once I started the process, I actually enjoyed it—not only because it gave me a sense of control, but because it gave me a sense of comfort knowing that I was caring for my family.

An estate planner friend once told me that it isn't necessarily the wealthy who have complicated estates; it's people with complicated *families* who have complicated estates. So if you're single, or if you and your spouse don't have children, your estate plan could be very simple. Add a marriage, children, an ex, or stepchildren, and you've got more to plan for.

But regardless, I encourage you to look on estate planning as an opportunity. By the time you reach 50 or so, you have had decades of building relationships and building assets. Now is the time to honor that history and document your wishes.

Work with an Attorney

Yes, there are tons of do-it-yourself estate planning books and software programs that promise to make it easy. But there are just too many ways you can make a big, ugly mistake. So regardless of your wealth, work with the best estate planning attorney you can find. This is not the time to pinch pennies.

To find an estate planning attorney, get recommendations from your friends, co-workers, and financial advisors. Make sure he or she is open to answering all of your questions in plain English. Estate planning documents are complex and loaded with legalese. Your attorney's job is to help you focus on the issues, and not get caught up in the technicalities. Empathy is also important—after all, your attorney will likely be dealing with your family at a very difficult time.

Start with a Will

Every year the majority of Americans die without a will. For practical purposes, this means that their state will dictate what happens to their assets and property. Unfortunately, all too often assets wind up in the hands of an estranged spouse or out-of-favor relative simply because there wasn't a will.

A will is especially important for every parent with a minor child, even if the parent doesn't have many assets, because this is where a guardian is designated. Once you're past the age of 50 you're likely beyond this stage, but if you have grandchildren, you might check in with your son or daughter to make sure they've taken care of this. An estate planning attorney can be a good sounding board if there is a difference of opinion between parents.

In addition, if you are in a committed nonmarital relationship, you must have a will (and possibly a trust) if you want to provide for your partner. See **Question 9** for more.

⊃ **SMART MOVE:** Even if you have a living trust, you need a "pour-over" will. That way any property that is not titled in the name of the trust will be transferred into the trust at death.

Create an Advance Health-Care Directive and Durable Power of Attorney

We all need an advance health-care directive to let our doctors, family, and friends know our wishes about emergency and end-of-life care. Very tough stuff, for sure. But unless you want someone else to decide for you, take this step. Similarly, a durable power of attorney will give a trusted person authority to act on your behalf and handle your finances if you are incapacitated.

YOUR ADVANCE HEALTH-CARE DIRECTIVE

No question, this has to be one of the toughest documents to complete. Also sometimes referred to as a *living will,* an advance health-care directive is intended to let your doctors and loved ones know what medical steps you do—and don't—want in a medical crisis.

This is one time that you don't need an attorney. But you need to do careful soul searching, perhaps in consultation with your personal physician, and have a series of conversations with your spouse or other family members. When I did my own, I kind of balked at the legal language that said in effect to "pull the plug after two days." Hmm, I thought, can't I have at least a few more days?

As you begin the process, understand that the medical system is designed to treat—not to withhold treatment. If you can't speak for yourself, and if you haven't prepared a health-care directive, your doctors will likely consult with your closest family member—who may or may not represent your wishes. The default will likely be to sustain your life regardless of your condition or prospects.

Every state has its own form that will walk you through the basic decisions about your care and appointing an agent to represent your wishes.

SMART MOVE: Periodically review your choices for guardian, trustee, or power of attorney for health and finances. Things—and people— change.

And You May Need More

A will is a good beginning—but there are a couple of big issues it won't touch: probate and taxes.

Probate is required when assets are registered only in the name of the person who has died. So whether it's your house or your bank account or your car—your property will have to go through this lengthy, costly, and public process unless you have made other arrangements.

The most common ways to avoid probate are **trusts** (revocable living trusts often being the most appropriate), designating beneficiaries on retirement accounts and insurance polices, setting up pay-on-death accounts for bank accounts and certain government securities, and titling property as joint tenancy or community property. Your attorney will guide you through the appropriate choices.

⚠️ **CAUTION:** If you have an IRA, a 401(k), or a life insurance policy, make sure that your beneficiary designations are up-to-date. These assets pass directly to your heirs without going through probate. It's common to name your spouse as the primary beneficiary and your children as secondary beneficiaries—although many parents, especially those in a second marriage, will pass their accounts to their adult children either directly or through a trust.

A common misperception is that if you avoid probate, you also avoid estate taxes. Not so. If taxes are an issue for you, your attorney may recommend a combination of trusts that will help you direct more of your estate to your intended beneficiaries. See **Question 39** for more on estate taxes.

➡️ **SMART MOVE:** If you have children from a previous marriage, you can create a *qualified terminable interest property (QTIP) trust*, which will provide for your surviving spouse and then pass assets to your children— and also qualify for the unlimited marital deduction. See **Question 42** for more.

Gifting Now

Many people derive the most satisfaction by giving a portion of their assets to their family, friends, or charities while they are still alive. In 2013 you can gift up to $14,000 a year (or $28,000 for a married couple splitting gifts) to as many individuals as you like gift-tax-free. (Instant gratification *plus* you can reduce your taxable estate. See **Question 41** for more on gifting.)

⚠ **CAUTION:** If you make a gift of more than $14,000 to any one person during the course of the year, you have to report it to the IRS as a taxable gift on Form 709. The amount over $14,000 (or $28,000 for a married couple splitting gifts) will count toward your lifetime exemption of $5.25 million. See **Question 41** for more.

Think About Life Insurance

Estates are often cash-poor. If you believe that your heirs may have to pay substantial estate taxes, and particularly if a good portion of your assets are illiquid, consider purchasing a life insurance policy. Realize, though, that if you are the owner of a policy on your own life, the proceeds will be included in your taxable estate. One good solution can be to establish an **irrevocable life insurance trust (ILIT),** which will hold the policy and pay the premiums. When you die, the trust will hold the proceeds and can provide benefits to your surviving spouse or other beneficiaries.

Discuss Your Choices

Once you have created your plan, talk to your family and other beneficiaries about your choices. By doing so, you can protect them from surprises later on. This is especially important if your decisions differ from what they might expect. And perhaps even more important, it will allow you to share your vision for the legacy you want to leave behind.

➲ **SMART MOVE:** If you're confident that you want to pass on assets to an heir, you can consider converting all or part of a traditional IRA to a Roth IRA. You have to pay the income taxes at the time of conversion, but you won't have required minimum distributions—potentially allowing the account to grow even more. A Roth IRA is a wonderful inheritance for your heir, who will be able to take withdrawals free of income tax.

Do Your Best, for Now

Don't worry about not being able to predict the future. Tax laws will continue to change. Marriage, divorce, or the loss of a spouse may impact your decisions. Make the best decisions for the present, and then plan to revisit your choices every few years.

Keep Documents Accessible

Once you've completed your estate plan, keep your documents in a safe place in your home, along with property deeds, insurance policies, a list of your accounts, and contact information for your attorney and advisors. A safe-deposit box isn't the best place because it could take a court order for someone to access it if it's in your name only. Make sure your family knows where you have stored these documents. You can also have your attorney keep copies.

Next Steps
- To read about estate taxes, see **Question 39.**
- For information about gifting, see **Question 41.**
- To organize your family finances, see **Question 29.**
- Do you have children from a previous marriage? **Question 42** discusses ways to provide for them in your estate plan.

Q39.

When I take into account the value of my home and all my investments, my estate is sizable. What do I need to know about estate taxes?

Most of us have come to fear estate taxes. But at least for now, thanks to recent legislation, federal estate taxes are an issue for the ultra-wealthy only—or for those with an estate valued at more than $5.25 million (or $10.5 million for a married couple) in 2013. But before you crack open the champagne, a couple of caveats: First, we can never say never when it comes to Congress. Even though the changes are described as "permanent," anything can happen in the future. Second, even though you may not have to pay federal estate taxes, you may be on the hook for state taxes.

That said, the best you can do is plan with the information you have. Below I cover basics as well as strategies for anyone whose estate may still be impacted. But you should be aware that estate taxation—or just about anything having to do with estate planning—is complex. It's always best to work with an experienced estate planning attorney.

Q FACT: According to the Tax Policy Center of the Urban Institute and the Brookings Institution, in 2013 only 3,800 estates (or about 1 in 700) will owe federal estate tax.

THE FEDERAL ESTATE TAX SYSTEM: BASIC STRUCTURE

The federal estate tax is actually part of a larger system of taxation called the *federal transfer tax system*, made up of:

1. The **estate tax,** which covers transfers of property at death

2. The **gift tax,** which covers transfers of property during a person's lifetime

3. The **generation-skipping transfer (GST) tax,** which covers transfers of property to people who are one or more generations younger

The estate and gift tax work hand in hand. Without the gift tax, individuals could give away all of their assets during their lifetime and avoid taxation. Without the estate tax, individuals could give away all of their assets at death without taxation. Therefore, estate and gift taxes are joined together into what is sometimes referred to as the *federal unified transfer tax system.* Both create an identical tax liability.

Estate and gift taxes share other characteristics as well:

1. They use the same tax rate schedule.
2. They share a credit (the *applicable [or unified] credit amount*) that reduces or eliminates a person's tax liability. This credit allows for an *applicable exclusion,* a dollar amount that will not be taxed.
3. Computation of both the estate and the gift tax is cumulative over one's lifetime. A gift tax credit used in one year reduces the amount of gift tax credit that can be used in future years. The total gift tax credit used during one's life reduces the credit available to use against his or her estate taxes.
4. Both have marital and charitable deductions to reduce tax liability.

The GST tax, which has a flat rate, is separate from the unified tax system and is imposed *in addition to* estate and gift taxes. The purpose of the GST tax is to prevent families from avoiding one round of estate tax by transferring assets to grandchildren instead of to children. The government adds the GST tax to the regular estate tax (yes, this is double taxation).

In 2010, the estate, gift, and GST tax exclusions were all set at $5 million, indexed for inflation. In 2013, this equates to a $5.25-million exclusion that will continue to rise with inflation. The tax rate above that exclusion is 40 percent. The unified credit in 2013 is $2,055,800.

What's Your Estate Worth?

An estate tax calculation starts with your gross estate. The basic principle for valuing property is generally its *fair market value,* or "the price at which property would change hands between a willing buyer and a willing seller . . . both having reasonable knowledge of relevant facts." The date of valuation is either the date of death or six months later (whichever date is chosen, it applies to all property). (Note: Real estate used in a closely held business or farming operation may be valued with a "special use" method.)

Sometimes the fair market value of an asset is clear-cut, but often it is not. For example, valuing a closely held family business, an interest in a limited partnership, or even a thinly traded stock can be nuanced and may require the services of a professional appraiser.

The basic rule is that a federal estate tax return is due if the gross estate exceeds the applicable exclusion amount in the year of death ($5.25 million in 2013). Often it's obvious that a particular estate will or won't fall above this level, particularly with the exemption set so high. However, many other estates require close scrutiny.

WHAT'S INCLUDED IN AN ESTATE?

In a word, everything. Many assets are straightforward: for example, your investment accounts, bank accounts, residence, other real estate, equity in a business, cash value in an insurance policy, and personal property.

However, other assets are a bit more obscure. For example, the following are also included in your estate:

- A life insurance policy that you own on the life of another person

- A life insurance policy on your own life if you own the policy or if you have an **incident of ownership** (the ability to exercise an economic right).

- A life insurance policy on your own life if you transferred ownership within the three years preceding your death

- Property held in joint tenancy

- Any property over which you have a **power of appointment** (the ability to name who will enjoy or own the property)

- The present value of a pension, retirement benefit, or annuity if there are survivorship benefits

- Any property in which you have a retained life interest (the ability to use the property under specified terms), even if you transferred the property to someone else prior to your death

- Any property that you revocably transferred prior to your death (you had maintained the right to take it back)

To value your estate, first add up your assets and subtract your debts. Then subtract the value of any assets that will be transferred to a charity on your death. If you're married, you can also deduct the assets that will go to your spouse, provided he or she is a U.S. citizen (and therefore avoid estate tax until he or she dies).

► **SMART MOVE:** You can avoid estate taxation of life insurance proceeds by creating an *irrevocable life insurance trust (ILIT)*. The irrevocable trust is the owner and beneficiary of the policy. If there are no incidents of ownership retained by you, the proceeds are kept outside the estate. However, the trust must purchase the policy or the original owner must live at least three years after transferring an existing policy into the trust.

Married Couples Get a Break

It wasn't very long ago that married couples had to set up **bypass trusts** (also known as **AB trusts** or **credit shelter trusts**) to take advantage of each other's estate tax exclusions. This has changed because of **portability,** a relatively new provision that allows a surviving spouse to add any unused portion of a deceased spouse's exclusion to her or his own exclusion. In other words, in 2013 a married couple can pass on up to $10.5 million to their heirs free from federal estate tax without a trust or any extra planning.

The following example illustrates how portability works.

WITHOUT PORTABILITY:

Husband and wife Braverman have two equal shares of an estate valued at $10.5 million. When Mr. Braverman dies, he leaves his entire $5.25 million to Mrs. Braverman. No estate tax is due because of the unlimited marital deduction. Mrs. Braverman's estate is now worth $10.5 million. When she later dies, the first $5.25 million can pass to her heirs free of estate tax. However, her estate must pay tax on the remaining $5.25 million, at a rate of 40 percent—a tax bill of $2.1 million.

WITH PORTABILITY:

Under current law, the Bravermans can take advantage of each other's exclusion. When Mr. Braverman dies, his executor can elect to transfer his unused $5.25 million exclusion to his wife. Like before, Mrs. Braverman's estate is valued at $10.5 million, but she now also has a $10.5 million exclusion from taxes. She can pass on the entire estate free of tax.

⚠ **CAUTION:** Portability is not automatic. The executor must file an estate tax return even if no tax is due in order for the surviving spouse to take advantage of the deceased spouse's exemption.

Note, though, that in our example we do not address potential appreciation. With traditional estate planning, the amount excluded from the first-to-die's estate would be put into a bypass trust for the benefit of the surviving spouse. The assets in this trust, regardless of their value and any future appreciation, would then remain outside the surviving spouse's estate for tax purposes. The trust could appreciate to any amount and still would be free of estate tax when the surviving spouse dies. Portability doesn't allow for unlimited appreciation in this way. If you expect large growth and the potential to go over the exclusion, you might consider a bypass trust.

DIFFERENT RULES FOR A NONCITIZEN SPOUSE

The federal government doesn't want someone who isn't a U.S. citizen to inherit a large amount of money, pay no estate or gift tax, and then return to his or her native country. Therefore, if your spouse isn't a U.S. citizen, you may not be able to transfer your assets to him or her tax-free.

Nonetheless, you *can* leave assets worth up to the exclusion ($5.25 million for deaths in 2013) to anyone, including your noncitizen spouse, without owing any federal estate tax. If the noncitizen spouse dies first, assets left to the spouse who is a U.S. citizen do qualify for the unlimited marital deduction.

If your estate exceeds this limit, you can also set up a **qualified domestic trust (QDOT),** which can postpone payment of estate taxes until after your noncitizen spouse dies.

⚠️ **CAUTION:** As great as portability is for reducing or eliminating taxes, it does nothing to control how or when your heirs will receive assets. As a result, you may still want to discuss the benefits of a particular type of trust with your attorney. For example, in a second marriage a *qualified terminable interest property (QTIP) trust* can provide for the surviving spouse as well as for the children from a first marriage. See **Question 42.**

Strategies to Reduce Your Taxable Estate

Even with the higher exclusion, some estates may be subject to tax. You may want to discuss the following with your estate planner:

- **Gifting:** Lifetime gifting has many advantages, not the least of which is the pleasure you can derive by seeing your beneficiaries enjoy your gift. In 2013 you can gift up to $14,000 to an unlimited number of people in a single year ($28,000 for a married couple "splitting gifts") without triggering any tax. Not only do you remove the value of the gift from your estate, but you also transfer future appreciation to the beneficiary. I'll say more about lifetime gifting in **Question 41,** but for now I simply want to point out that it's one of the best ways to reduce your taxable estate at the same time that you help others.

⚠ **CAUTION:** The value of property gifted within the last three years of life may be included in your estate if it has "strings attached." For example, if you gifted a second home to a relative but retained the right to use it as you please, the fair market value of the property could revert to your estate.

STEP UP

Before you gift highly appreciated property, also think about the potential capital gains tax for the beneficiary. If you transfer the property while you are alive, you also transfer your **cost basis.** But if you instead bequeath the property at your death, the asset's cost basis will "step up" to the fair market value on the date of death. Let's take a look at some numbers:

Let's say you give your daughter $10,000 worth of stock that you purchased ten years ago for $2,000. If she sells the stock immediately, she will owe capital gains tax on the $8,000 profit. If your daughter instead receives the stock at your death when it is worth $10,000, she will have no tax for income tax purposes. Her tax basis would be $10,000—not $2,000.

- **Making unlimited direct payments to qualified medical and educational institutions:** Any payments that you send directly to an IRS-qualified physician, hospital, or school or college on behalf of someone else aren't counted in your annual gift tax exclusion. In other words, you can pay for your grandchild's college education *plus* give them a gift of up to $14,000 a year without reducing your lifetime exclusion.

- **Charitable giving:** Bequests to a charity are fully deductible from estate taxes. One strategy is to transfer assets from your estate to a **charitable lead trust (CLT)**. The charitable organization will receive an annuity for a set number of years, and at the end of the term your heirs will receive the remainder. You can also do the opposite with a **charitable remainder trust (CRT)**. In this case, the trust will pay income for a period of time to beneficiaries you name. At the end of the stated period, the remaining trust assets pass to your charitable organization(s) of choice. You get a deduction for the portion of the value of the trust that is for the charity. For more on charitable trusts, see **Question 43**.
- **Qualified personal residence trust (QPRT):** You can transfer your home into a trust, thereby removing a portion of its value from your taxable estate. You retain the right to live in the house for a certain number of years, and at the end of that term the home is transferred to your beneficiary. You can then arrange to stay in the home and pay fair market rent. The longer the term, the smaller the gift for tax purposes. Once your home is placed in a QPRT, future appreciation accrues outside your estate.

⚠ **CAUTION:** A QPRT will help avoid estate taxes only if you outlive its term of years. If you do not survive the QPRT term, the value of the residence is included in your estate.

Does Your State Have an Estate or an Inheritance Tax?

Most people focus on federal estate taxes. However, depending on where you live, you may also be liable for significant state taxes, which can take the form of either an estate or an inheritance tax (or in a couple of cases, both).

STATE ESTATE VS. INHERITANCE TAX

Estate taxes are based on the value of the deceased person's estate no matter who receives it.

Inheritance taxes vary depending not only on the amount being transferred but also on the relationship between the deceased and the beneficiary. In most states, the closer the relationship, the lower the rate. A spouse will pay the least, a minor child will pay more, an adult child or parent will pay more still, and a brother or sister will pay even more. Nonrelatives will pay the most.

If you live in a state with an estate or an inheritance tax, you'll need to do some extra planning. In most states the exclusion is well below the federal level of $5 million–plus. Also note that none of the states that have an independent estate tax have made the exclusion portable between spouses—so for some families a bypass trust could make sense.

A Word on the Generation-Skipping Transfer Tax

If you're fortunate enough to have a large estate, and your children are also well-off, you may want to consider making gifts to your grandchildren, great-grandchildren, or unrelated people who are more than 37½ years your junior (yes, that's the way the rules are written). Like other gifts, these will reduce your taxable estate. However, if the gifts don't qualify for the $14,000 annual gift limit ($28,000 for a couple splitting gifts), they will be charged against your lifetime GST exclusion ($5.25 million in 2013) *in addition* to your lifetime gift tax exclusion. Any amounts over that will be taxed at 40 percent.

☎ **TALK TO AN EXPERT:** No matter how you look at it, planning for an estate that is larger than the estate tax exclusion—or any complex estate—takes the expertise of an estate planning attorney. Review the basics for your own knowledge, then consult with an attorney you know and trust.

Next Steps

- To learn more about gifting, and how gift taxes relate to estate taxes, see **Question 41.**
- If you want to provide for children from a second marriage, see **Question 42.**
- To read more about building charitable contributions into your estate plan, see **Question 43.**

Q40.

I'm confused about how to divide my estate between my children, who have different needs and financial resources. Is it best to divide it into equal parts?

This question raises some significant issues about fairness and about how to handle estate planning—particularly the importance of communicating with your heirs about your wishes and intentions. When it comes to family and money, even the most generous of impulses can be misinterpreted.

For instance, I felt for a friend of mine who was left out of his mother's will. It's not that he had a bad relationship with his mother, but he was financially far better off than his two sisters. His mother's estate was small and she divided it between her daughters, who really needed the money. My friend understood this, and didn't resent his sisters, yet he was wounded. He wished that his mother had discussed her decision with him before she died, so he could have been forewarned—and reassured that she loved him.

In another case a friend's father gave her less than her sibling because she was a stay-at-home mom. He justified this by saying that she was already taken care of by her husband. But to my friend it felt like her father was making a judgment about her life choice.

Consider the Emotional Message You're Sending

The more I hear stories like these, the more I believe that it makes a lot of sense for parents to treat their children equally. While it's completely understandable to consider providing extra assistance to a child with fewer resources (and that could be the best decision, depending on the circumstances), or for a child with special needs, as I discuss in **Question 50,** it's important to proceed with care.

First, understand that your children may easily perceive their inheritance as a symbol for your love. Even when they're adults, childhood insecurities can linger. A perceived slight could trigger resentment that could last for decades.

Also, remember that things can (and do) change. One child may be earning a lot more now, but it's impossible to accurately predict the future. By the time your estate is distributed, your kids' fortunes may have altered. Just look at the financial turmoil and turnarounds of the past few years!

Talk to All Your Children About Your Decision

If you do decide to divide your estate unequally, it's generally best to explain your plan to all of your children *now*. Be up front about your concerns for all of them, both financial and emotional. Hopefully, they'll be honest in their response so that you can have a good discussion.

SMART MOVE: To even things out, you can consider an estate plan that provides more money for the kids who need it, and gives family heirlooms or other nonfinancial assets to those who don't. Or you may want to give annual gifts to those who may need more financial help now (or perhaps to their children, such as contributions to a 529 college savings plan).

Of course, it's possible that you won't be able to make everyone happy. Ultimately, it's your money and your decision. The main thing is to be fair. Think carefully before you decide to give one of the kids more money than another. After all, the last thing you want to do is to foster resentment that could live on for years after you've gone.

TALK TO AN EXPERT: No matter how big or small your estate, I recommend working with an estate planning attorney to make sure your will and other documents are in good shape. If you have substantial wealth, you may also need to think about ways to minimize estate or inheritance taxes. See **Question 39.**

SHOULD ONE OF YOUR CHILDREN BE EXECUTOR OR TRUSTEE FOR YOUR ESTATE?

Appointing a family member to manage your assets can make sense, but it can also cause problems. Before you choose one of your children, give some thought to the following questions:

- **What type of management will your estate require?** The bigger your estate, the bigger the job. An executor (for your will) or a trustee (for a trust) is responsible not only for settling your accounts and distributing assets, but also for the ongoing management of those assets for current and future beneficiaries. There are tax and legal documents to file, records to keep, and ongoing financial decisions to make. If your assets are extensive and your estate is complicated, this person may need the help of outside advisors to carry out your wishes.

- **Who is most suited professionally? Emotionally? Practically?** On top of having financial savvy, an executor or trustee must be responsible, practical, organized, and able to handle potential pressure from the beneficiaries. Who among your children best combines these traits? On a purely practical level, who actually has the time for ongoing management of your estate?

- **What's the potential for family misunderstanding?** When one person in a family is given authority or power over others, there's always the potential for problems. Your children may all get along now, but could that change when money is involved or issues of control arise? Also, selecting one child over another may be interpreted as trusting or valuing one of them more. To avoid resentments, speak directly with your family about what the job will entail and why you're considering appointing one of them.

- **Would a corporate trustee be a smart choice?** Another option is to appoint a corporate trustee, such as a bank or trust company. On the plus side, a corporate trustee can potentially provide all the investment and legal expertise under one roof. A corporate trustee can also be impartial in assessing requests and distributing assets. On the negative side, your heirs would be working with an impersonal institution and have to deal with the possibility that the staff or even the ownership of the company could change over time. Another negative is that fees for a corporate trustee are often higher than for an individual trustee.

⚠ **CAUTION:** Appointing two or more people can invite trouble. When there are only two beneficiaries—for instance, a brother and sister who get along well—it could work fine. But when there are multiple beneficiaries, it's probably best to have one person or entity making the decisions and handling the details.

- **What about compensation?** Being a trustee is a time-consuming job and a fee is certainly warranted, but a family trustee might feel awkward taking a fee, or other beneficiaries might question if it's being earned. To avoid problems, designate how trustee fees will be determined. Your estate planning attorney should be able to provide some guidance.

▶ **SMART MOVE:** Once you make a decision, talk to your children. Be open about your estate plan, what they can expect, and why you've chosen a specific person. They'll be happy to know that you trust all of them with this information—and also trust that they'll honor your wishes without dissention.

Next Steps

- Need to set up an estate plan? **Question 38** discusses the basics.
- If you're concerned about estate taxes, see **Question 39**—then talk to an estate planning attorney.
- Want to include charitable giving as part of your estate plan? **Question 43** talks about ways to do that and still provide for your family.

Q41.

I'm thinking about giving my kids part of their inheritance now, as opposed to holding on to everything until I die. What does this mean for estate and gift taxes?

When I was growing up, I always knew that my family was there for me—not just my parents, but my grandparents, too. We had—and still have—a strong tradition of one generation helping the next, especially when it comes to education, a first home, or a business venture. And it's something I support, as long as I know that my kids are also able to stand on their own two feet.

The way I view it, giving away part of your estate during your lifetime has lots of advantages, both financial and emotional. With the exclusion now set at over $5 million, estate taxes have taken a backseat for many people. However, for the very wealthy, or for those who live in a high-tax state, lifetime gifting can be a valuable way to reduce the size of a taxable estate. In addition, gifting allows you to keep assets within your family, providing valuable financial support to the people you care about most. And of course you also get the psychological benefit of witnessing the positive impact of your gifts.

The Basics

As I mention in **Question 39,** the gift tax was created to prevent people from giving away their entire estates during their lifetime and therefore avoiding estate taxes. For that reason the gifts that you make during your lifetime are taxed at the same rate as property you transfer at death.

According to the IRS, any gift is a taxable gift—but fortunately, there are exceptions. Here are the basic rules:

- In 2013 an individual can make a **present interest** gift, which is an unrestricted right to the immediate use of the property, up to $14,000 a year, to an unlimited number of people not only without tax, but without any reporting requirements. A married couple splitting gifts can gift up to twice that, or $28,000 a year, to an unlimited number of people free of tax. However, they do have to file a gift tax return (IRS Form 709) when they split a gift. These exclusions will continue to grow with inflation. An individual has to file a gift tax return if she or he gives more than $14,000 in a year to any one person, even if no tax is due.

SPLITTING GIFTS

A married couple has the option of combining their annual exclusions, provided both are in agreement. In this way, in 2013 a couple can gift up to $28,000 to an unlimited number of people without having to pay gift tax. However, gift splitting does require filing a gift tax return (IRS Form 709), which both spouses must sign. Also, once a couple decides to split one gift, they must also split all other gifts during that year.

Gift splitting can be a powerful tool. For example, it allows a married couple to gift up to $48,000 a year to a married child and his or her spouse (or to any other married couple) and stay within the annual exclusion. It can also be a great way for parents or grandparents to increase the size of their contribution to a 529 college savings account.

- In 2013 an individual can give away up to $5.25 million (annually adjusted for inflation) over the course of his or her lifetime—above and beyond the $14,000 (or $28,000 for a married couple) annual exclusion—before having to pay a gift tax.

  As I explained in **Question 39,** a unified credit applies to both gift and estate taxes. In 2013 this credit is $2,055,800, which translates to the $5.25 million exemption. Any part of this credit that is used up during your life reduces the credit that you have left over to use against the estate tax. However, spouses can use their deceased spouse's unused credit, thanks to a new provision allowing **portability.** Once you use up your lifetime credit, the gift and the estate tax rates are both 40 percent.

- Direct payments for tuition or medical expenses to IRS-qualified institutions aren't taxed or included in the annual $14,000 (or $28,000 for a couple) annual exclusions.

- An individual can make unlimited gifts to a spouse (provided the spouse is a U.S. citizen; see **Question 39,** page 310) or to a qualified nonprofit institution without gift tax.

If you give assets to your grandchildren, great-grandchildren, or a nonrelative who is more than 37½ years your junior, you may also be on the hook for the **generation-skipping transfer (GST) tax.** Your lifetime exclusion for a GST is $5.25 million in 2013; however, this tax is charged *in addition to* gift and estate taxes. The GST is not portable between spouses. Gifts over $5.25 million are taxed at 40 percent.

⚠ **CAUTION:** Generosity is a wonderful quality. But before you make sizable gifts, make sure that you're leaving yourself enough to live on comfortably. Otherwise, you may wind up depending on the same people whom you were trying to help!

. . . and Some Strategies

Like just about anything else you do in life, there are some smart ways to go about gifting and some not-so-smart ways. Before you open your checkbook, consider gifting assets other than cash, and also think carefully about which asset to give to whom. Following are some strategies that can maximize the impact of your gifts—increasing the value to the recipient, or reducing your eventual estate tax bill, or both.

- Instead of giving cash, give an asset that you believe has the highest probability of appreciating in the future (for example, a growth stock or even real estate). That way you not only reduce your estate's value by the present value of the gift, but you also eliminate future appreciation. When you have several recipients, give the property that you believe will appreciate most to the youngest person—so that it has the longest time to grow.
- Give income-producing property to someone in a low income tax bracket. This way you can reduce the value of your estate and also minimize income taxes that will be due by the recipient.
- Never gift a property when its fair market value is less than its cost basis. It is better to sell the item that has lost value and recognize the capital loss for your income taxes. Then you can gift the cash proceeds. The recipient can then purchase the item if he or she so chooses.

A CRUMMEY TRUST PROVIDES TAX ADVANTAGES WITH CONTROL

In order to qualify for the annual exclusion, a gift must be of **present interest,** or an unrestricted right to the immediate use of the property. A gift of a **future interest,** which is restricted in some way by a future date, does not qualify for the exclusion.

Gifts of cash or property where the title transfers immediately are examples of present interest. A gift held in a trust that won't be available until a future date or until certain conditions are met is a gift of future interest.

To allow a gift to qualify for the exclusion at the same time that you delay the benefit, you can establish what is known as a **Crummey trust** (named for the first family that set up this type of trust). In effect, a Crummey trust (generally set up for the benefit of a minor) limits the annual withdrawal right to the amount of the current annual exclusion. However, the trustee is not required to make a withdrawal—but simply having the right to do so converts the assets to present interest.

Example: Joanne sets up an irrevocable trust for her daughter Pearl. The trust document prohibits distributions until Pearl reaches age 30. However, the trust has a Crummey provision that allows Pearl to withdraw an amount each year that is equal to the lesser of the annual exclusion or the amount contributed to the trust in that year. In 2012, Joanne contributed $5,000 to the trust, and in 2013 she contributed $20,000. Therefore, in 2012 Pearl had the right to withdraw up to $5,000, and in 2013 she had the right to withdraw up to $14,000. In 2012, Joanne's entire $5,000 contribution qualified for the annual exclusion. In 2013 only $14,000 of Joanne's contribution qualified for the exclusion, leaving a taxable gift of $6,000.

Meanwhile, Joanne had made it clear to Pearl that she wanted to keep the money in the trust so that it could grow for Pearl's future. And Pearl, being a good girl, complied. With the help of the Crummey provision, the trust continued to grow—and Joanne limited the part of her gift that could be taxed.

➲ **SMART MOVE:** If you are considering a gift to a charity, consider giving appreciated stock. Not only can you avoid paying capital gains, but you also get the benefit of a charitable deduction for your income taxes—at the same time that you reduce the size of your estate for estate tax purposes. Also, any gift to a qualified charity is free of gift tax. See **Question 10,** page 108, for more.

- If you're considering gifting highly appreciated property, also think about the capital gains consequences for the recipient. If you gift appreciated property, the recipient also receives your cost basis. But if you transfer the property at your death, your heir will get a step-up in cost basis to the item's current fair market value. See the box in **Question 39**, page 311, for more.

Next Steps

- To brush up on basic estate planning issues and tools, see **Question 38.**
- To read about different ways to structure a charitable gift, see **Question 43.**
- For thoughts on dividing your estate between children with different needs, see **Question 40.**

Q42.

My spouse and I have
three children together,
and I also have two
children from a previous
marriage. How can we
make sure that our estate
plans treat everyone fairly?

Families with children from different marriages are becoming increasingly common—in fact, according to the U.S. Census Bureau, blended families now outnumber traditional nuclear families in the United States. But while there may be comfort in numbers, it doesn't make the estate planning decisions any easier. And chances are, not everyone will agree 100 percent on the best course of action. So it's wise to give a lot of thought to what seems fair to you, what seems fair to your spouse, and ultimately what will seem fair to all your kids.

As I mention in **Question 40,** giving each of your kids an equal share of your assets is often a worthy goal. After all, it's not just about money. It's also about the way that money often represents love. That said, estate planning is highly personal. Also, it's a lot more challenging to be "equal" when you have children of very different ages and in very different circumstances. Having a spouse who is a lot younger or older than you are can complicate things further.

With a single family, the flow of assets can be simple: They go first to the surviving spouse, then to the children. But blended families have more to consider. If you leave everything to your spouse, he or she would be responsible for making sure that the children from your first marriage get their fair share. Another common issue for blended families is a possible delay in the children receiving their inheritance, especially if the second spouse is close in age to the children from the first marriage.

Start by Looking at Different Scenarios

In any case, communication is essential. I know that talking about money can be difficult. And talking about an estate can be even tougher because you're also talking about the eventuality of death. However, that's exactly what you need to do. An attorney can help you with the necessary legal documents, but you and your spouse will have to do the serious up-front thinking, and talk through your concerns openly and honestly.

For instance, let's say you and your spouse each have separate assets that you've brought into the marriage as well as assets that you own together. Here are some scenarios to consider:

- If you should die first, how do you want to split up your assets between your spouse and all of your children? Do you want some of your separate assets to go directly to your children from your first marriage? If so, how would you even that out with your other children?
- What if your spouse dies first? Does he or she want everything to go to you, which could then be passed on to all your children? Or would he or she want some of the assets to go directly to your mutual children?

- How do you want to split things up if the two of you die together?
- Are there any other organizations or people that you want to support in addition to your family?

▶ **SMART MOVE:** If you have minor children, it is essential to appoint a legal guardian. This is a critical part of your will.

Consider Your Wishes Separately and Together

There's so much emotion around estate planning that it might be easier if you and your spouse think about your wishes separately, and then bring your ideas together. Listen to each other's concerns and fears and be open to each other's attitudes about what's fair—both for yourselves and for your children.

There should be no guilt or blame here. You're talking about your individual legacies. Ideally, you'll honor each other's decisions and come to some general agreements.

Talk to an Estate Planning Attorney

Once you've done the initial thinking, consult with an estate planning attorney. He or she can be a sounding board, helping to sort out your thoughts. And if you and your spouse have areas of disagreement, the attorney could suggest ways to find common ground.

Probably the most powerful estate planning tool for a blended family is a **qualified terminable interest property (QTIP) trust.** A QTIP trust won't help you with estate taxes, but since the exclusion is above $5 million, estate taxes aren't a concern for the vast majority of individuals. A QTIP trust's value comes in helping you to structure your estate in a way that can provide lifetime support for your spouse at the same time that it allows you to maintain an inheritance for your children or other heirs. See **Behind the Scenes** on the next page for details.

⬤ **SMART MOVE:** Don't forget about personal possessions (for example, jewelry, artwork, household items, etc.), many of which may have sentimental as well as financial value. Your wishes on how to distribute this type of property should be spelled out in a separate letter of instruction, which is in addition to a will or trust.

You might also want to consider purchasing a life insurance policy. Particularly if your spouse and first set of children are close in age, life insurance can provide an inheritance for your children during your spouse's lifetime. If estate taxes are an issue, your attorney might recommend that the life insurance be held in an **irrevocable life insurance trust (ILIT)** so that the proceeds remain outside your estate.

⚠ **CAUTION:** Make certain that the beneficiary designations for your retirement accounts, life insurance policies, etc., are in sync with your will or trust. If there's a discrepancy, the beneficiary designations will prevail.

BEHIND THE SCENES: THE QTIP TRUST

A qualified terminable interest property (QTIP) trust is a unique legal structure especially suited to the needs of a blended family. The surviving spouse is granted a life interest in trust property and is entitled to receive income from the trust. He or she can also make use of any trust assets, such as a house—but upon his or her death, the property passes to the heirs selected by the first-to-die spouse.

A QTIP trust postpones, but does not eliminate, estate taxes. At the death of the surviving spouse, the trust assets are included in his or her gross estate for estate tax purposes even though he or she does not have any control over who will inherit the property. For this reason it qualifies for the unlimited marital deduction. Also, it is a revocable trust, which means that it can be changed or altered during the grantor's lifetime. QTIP assets don't go through probate at either the grantor's or the surviving spouse's deaths.

QTIP REQUIREMENTS

- The property transferred to the trust must qualify for the unlimited marital deduction. This means that it must be in the estate of the first-to-die spouse and be transferred to the surviving spouse.

- The surviving spouse must be entitled to all of the trust income for life, and that income must be paid at least annually.

- The surviving spouse must have the authority to compel the trustee to sell non-income-producing investments and reinvest those proceeds in income-producing investments.

- During the surviving spouse's lifetime, no one can have the right to appoint the property to anyone other than the surviving spouse, even in the case of remarriage.

Also, for the trust to qualify as a QTIP, the executor must make an election on the deceased's estate tax return stating that the trust qualifies for the marital deduction. This election postpones tax until the death of the surviving spouse.

A QTIP TRUST IS APPROPRIATE ONLY FOR SOME MARRIED COUPLES

The QTIP trust is appropriate only for married couples. However, many couples, particularly those in first marriages, have no need for one. For instance, if a couple owns most or all of their property together and wants the same people—usually their children—to inherit it, then there's no reason for either spouse to control the final disposition of his or her own property.

☎ **TALK TO AN EXPERT:** The intricacies of any trust—QTIP or otherwise—require the advice of an estate planning attorney.

Set Expectations

When your kids are old enough, share your plans as well as the reasons for your decisions. Setting everyone's expectations for his or her inheritance is important to avoid family resentments. Having this conversation now may mean not only greater family accord today, but also greater family harmony in the future.

Next Steps

- Review your estate plan to make sure you have everything that's needed. **Question 38** covers the basics.
- If you're considering leaving different amounts to different children, take a look at **Question 40,** which discusses some potential concerns.
- Think about the possibility of giving your kids some of their inheritance ahead of time. See **Question 41** for information on gifting.
- Concerned about estate taxes? **Question 39** gives you insight into today's estate tax rates and regulations.

Q43.

I want to leave the bulk of my estate to my children, but also want to make meaningful contributions to a few charities. How can I incorporate this into my estate plan?

Building charitable giving into your estate planning is a wonderful way to extend your generosity and leave a meaningful legacy. Many people might think that this is something only the very wealthy can do. After all, how many folks have a big enough estate to take care of their children as well as give to charity? But the reality is that there are practical ways to do both, even if you don't have a lot of money.

Take the case of a couple I knew who had been affiliated with a certain university most of their lives. They had met there as undergrads and continued on to graduate school. Later the school became the center of both their professional and social lives, and the university granted full scholarships to each of their four children. This couple wanted to return something to this institution that had been so generous to them, even though they weren't wealthy. After careful consideration, the couple decided to transfer a portion of their assets into a trust that would provide them with income during their retirement years and ultimately pass on to the university.

Read on for more information about this and other ways to turn your generous inclinations into a workable (and potentially tax-advantageous) strategy.

Make an Outright Gift in Your Will

Certainly the simplest way to include a charitable contribution in your estate is through your will. The amount you give will reduce your estate for estate tax purposes—potentially increasing the amount you will be able to leave to your heirs.

BEQUEATHING RETIREMENT ASSETS

Donating a retirement account can be a simple and tax-effective way to support a charity. The donor simply has to designate the charity as the beneficiary. Because the charity is exempt from both income and estates taxes, it can receive 100 percent of the account's value. This also allows heirs to receive nonretirement assets that don't have the same income tax burden. In addition, the heirs may receive a step-up in cost basis of nonretirement assets, potentially further reducing their tax liability.

Make a Split Interest Gift

There are also several strategies for those who want to make a donation to a charity but also retain an interest in the assets. For example, the couple mentioned above needed retirement income but wanted the assets to transfer to their alma mater upon their death. Conversely, someone else might not need the current income but, on his or her death, would like the assets to pass to a spouse or other heir.

Gifts of split interest include a **charitable remainder trust,** a **charitable lead trust,** and a **pooled income fund.** With all three, the donor gets a charitable income tax deduction at the time of the transfer, retains some rights to the property, and reduces the value of his or her taxable estate. In addition, the donor may avoid capital gains on the assets transferred to the trust.

- **Charitable remainder trust (CRT):** A CRT provides either a fixed payment or a fixed percentage to the donor (or another beneficiary) every year. In either case, the amount must be at least 5 percent but not more than 50 percent of the property's fair market value. The trust is irrevocable and must make payouts at least annually. The term can be for the life of the donor or for a set number of years. At the end of the term, the remainder goes to the charity.

⇨ SMART MOVE: If your primary goal in setting up a CRT is to maximize the payments during your life, consider whether you think the trust assets will appreciate. If they do, you are better off receiving a *percentage* of the trust's value every year. On the other hand, if the assets decline in value, you are better off receiving a *fixed payment.*

- **Charitable lead trust (CLT):** A CLT is the reverse of a CRT. It provides income to a charity for a set number of years, after which the remainder passes to the donor's heir. This type of trust is most commonly used by high-net-worth individuals who do not need the lifetime income from a particular asset. The trust is often structured to get an income tax deduction equal to the fair market value of the property transferred, with the remainder interest valued at zero to eliminate a taxable gift. Like a CRT, a CLT is irrevocable.
- **Pooled income fund (PIF):** A PIF is a trust created and maintained by a public charity. Individual donors contribute to the fund, which works much like a CRT with the charity acting as the administrator. As with a CRT, the donor receives a flow of income

during his or her lifetime; upon the donor's death the funds are under the control of the charity. Contributions to pooled income funds qualify for charitable income, gift, and estate tax deductions. A PIF is especially appropriate for a smaller donor because it doesn't require the legal expense of creating an individual trust.

➲ **SMART MOVE:** If you are directing a sizable portion of your estate to a charitable organization, you might want to consider purchasing a life insurance policy that would provide support for your family.

Next Steps

- To read about charitable giving during your lifetime, including an overview of donor-advised funds, see **Question 10.**
- Want to brush up on estate tax basics? See **Question 39.**
- For a review of gift taxes, see **Question 41.**

PART VI

The People in My Life

For most of us, money and family are inseparable. Whether we're contemplating an immediate purchase or doing long-term planning, our spouses, children, parents, or other family members are at the core of our financial decisions.

This section addresses some of the most common family money questions. I've heard them all dozens of times. But the thing is, when it comes to a family, there's never a one-size-fits-all answer. So in each case I provide some suggestions, but primarily I try to bring up issues and trade-offs for you to think about.

A common theme in all of my responses is encouraging you to *talk* openly with your family and loved ones about money. Don't keep money in the closet, and don't hide your opinions. Include your family in the technical *and* personal aspects of your decisions: not just the how, but the why. If you don't agree at first, that's fine. Just keep the dialogue going, keep your mind open, and work toward a solution. At the end of the day, you'll all be better for it.

Q44.

My twenty-something child has decided that she wants to move back home. I like my new empty-nest lifestyle, but I want to help her out. How can I balance these?

This is becoming a common quandary as more and more parents find that their fledgling adult children aren't quite ready to fly. According to the Pew Research Center, roughly 29 percent of young adults ages 25–34 are now living with their parents. And it's not because the kids are necessarily looking for an easy ride. The economy and job market are just making it a lot harder for kids to take off on their own as early as we (or they) might wish.

Interestingly, the same study found that kids and parents both generally say that living together at this stage of life isn't necessarily a bad thing. It can actually forge a new and better relationship. And I know this from personal experience. My son, who graduated from college two years ago, recently moved back home to save some money while he pursues his professional dream. My husband and I are happy to help him reach his goal (up to a point). And it's also fun to have him around again.

There are a few important issues at play. First, you want to help your child. But at the same time you don't want to squelch his or her drive or sense of independence. And third, but extremely important, you shouldn't risk your own financial security.

That said, different families have different attitudes about kids moving back home and how much independence they want to encourage. So there's no one way to go about it. But I'd advise any parents facing this situation to think it through carefully and examine their feelings. They should then have a heart-to-heart with their young adult before he or she moves back home. That way everyone knows what to expect in advance. Here are some things to think about and discuss.

Establish Some House Rules

Living together again is a two-way street, so the first thing to discuss is how you'll share the house—and household responsibilities. For instance, most parents don't want to take care of their adult child like they did when they were younger. On the flip side, as an adult, your child shouldn't be expected to follow the same rules he or she followed as a teenager. To avoid any potential discord, be sure to talk about personal space, meals, having friends over (including boyfriends and girlfriends), curfews, and sharing chores.

You might even put some general rules on paper and agree to them up front so there's no misunderstanding. It really comes down to mutual respect for each other's lifestyles.

Don't Shy Away from Talking About Money

When a young adult decides to come back home for a while, it's often about money. Sometimes it's about looking for a new job. Sometimes it's just a necessary breather to get out of debt or build some savings. Whatever the situation, though, having your child back home raises some money issues for you, too. For instance, household expenses are going to go up. Will your child contribute? Will you charge rent? And what about personal expenses such as transportation, cellphone, and entertainment? Who's going to foot the bill for these things?

Even if your child's resources are limited, you might still expect her to pick up groceries or put gas in the car once in a while. It will make you both feel better about the arrangement.

⚠ **CAUTION:** When it comes to money, think twice about helping to pay off debt, allowing the use of your credit card, or cosigning for a major purchase. Your kids need to learn how to manage these things themselves—and you need to protect your own financial situation.

Also think about finances in the future. Presuming your child wants to live independently again, she'll need money for a rental deposit, emergency fund, etc. How will she fund this next step? Even if she's just working part-time until she finds a better job, encourage her to sock away some cash for her eventual move.

⟳ **SMART MOVE:** Encourage your kids to save. I've known families whose kids have come home and who agree to waive rent with the proviso that the money goes into a savings account instead.

Be Frank About Your Expectations for Moving Forward

Depending on the reason your young adult is living at home, you may want to set some expectations for next steps. For instance, if your child's goal is a new job, make it clear that you expect her to take concrete action to get one. Periodically check on her progress. You might help with decisions about whom to contact, updating a resume, following up on leads—but be very clear that it's her responsibility to keep up an active search.

Likewise, if getting out of debt or building savings is the goal, suggest that you get a regular financial update. You might help in setting up a payment or savings plan and offer advice on how you've handled this yourself.

> ➲ **SMART MOVE:** Consider setting a realistic move-out goal. Whether it's six months or a year or more, having a time limit will help your young adult realize that the clock is ticking and he or she will have to make a change, no matter how comfortable it is at home.

Encourage—and Help with—Financial Independence

So many families hesitate to talk about finances, but as your child shares your space as an adult, share some of your financial wisdom as well. Talk to her about how you budget, set goals, save for retirement, manage debt, and invest—all the things that help build a secure financial foundation. By doing so, you'll not only be giving her support in the present; you'll also be setting her up for future financial success.

> ⌕ **FACT:** According to a study from the Pew Research Center in 2013, about 48 percent of adults ages 40–59 provided financial support to grown children in 2012, up from 42 percent in 2005.

MAKING FINANCIAL INDEPENDENCE A LITTLE EASIER

Learning to be independent is one of the most important skills you can help your kids develop. Whether your child is leaving home for the first time, or needs a little brushup on the basics, this checklist is a good financial road map to independence.

- **Make a budget.** This is crucial to smart financial management and being on one's own. A budget should cover essentials like rent, loans, groceries, utilities, insurance, car costs, clothing, entertainment, and travel. And of course, don't forget savings! An online monthly budget planner like the one on schwabmoneywise.com makes this easy to do.

- **Set up an emergency fund.** Emphasize the importance of saving and setting aside enough cash to cover at least three months' rent and basic living expenses. It's an important cushion to have—just in case.

- **Pay off debt.** Pay student loans and credit card balances on time. Being prompt with loan payments not only helps one's credit rating; it also imposes financial discipline. When it comes to a credit card, paying the balance in full every month will actually save money that would otherwise be spent on finance charges or late fees.

- **Open key financial accounts.** If your young adult doesn't already have them, now's the time to establish checking and savings accounts, and an IRA (particularly a Roth IRA), if he or she has earned income. See **Question 4** on the types of retirement accounts.)

- **Continue—or begin—to save money.** Remember, time is a young person's biggest asset. Even saving a small amount each month adds up and helps develop a discipline that can pay big rewards in the long term.

- **Don't forget about insurance.** Shop around for affordable health, auto, and renter's insurance policies. Health and auto insurance are must-haves at any age. (On a positive note, your child can stay on your health insurance policy until he or she turns 26; you can decide if you want him or her to pay for the coverage.)

Next Steps

- To help your young adult—and yourself—get organized financially, take a look at **Question 11.**
- Now that your kids are grown, review your insurance needs. See **Questions 16** and **27.**
- Make sure you're on track for your own retirement goal. **Question 1** will help you assess where you are.

Q45.

As a retiree, I don't have a lot of extra money. I've always helped my children and other extended family members—but now it's tough. How do I sort this out?

While we're most often called baby boomers, another common designation for some people our age is the "sandwich generation." And those who find themselves financially helping kids, older parents, or other family members certainly understand what that means. According to a 2013 Pew Research study, about one in seven middle-aged adults provides support to both an aging parent and a child. That may be somewhat easier during your earning years, but once you reach retirement, it's another story. As counterintuitive as it may be, especially for a parent, it's now time to put yourself first.

That doesn't mean you have to suddenly drop out of the picture. There are lots of ways to show your family members that you still care, even if you can no longer write big checks. For instance, a friend's grandmother always sent birthday cards to the grandkids with a $5 bill and a note that said, "Just a thought." And the grandkids didn't need or expect more. The thought was enough.

However, there are plenty of other stories where unthinking grown kids have just expected their parents to keep footing certain bills, with the kids having little regard to the parents' financial strains. And whether it's your own kids or someone else whom you've been helping out, that's the kind of situation you want to avoid. To me, it's not being selfish; it's just being prudent and realistic.

Be Up Front About Your Circumstances

As you read through this book, you'll hear a common theme: It starts with a conversation. That holds true here as well. People won't know your concerns until you tell them. So whether you've been financially helping grown kids, an aging parent, or another family member who needed a boost, it's up to you to tell them you can't do it anymore.

Be honest about the fact that you're living on a fixed income. You don't need to give the details, but you might provide an overview of your resources and your obligations—and your financial limitations. By discussing your own situation, you might encourage them (especially your kids) to look a little closer at their own income and expenses to see how they could better manage without your help.

If you've been providing constant support, this may be more difficult and require you to make a gradual change. But if it's just a situation where you've always been there in a pinch, this would be a great opportunity to discuss how each person can make better financial decisions.

STARTING THE MONEY CONVERSATION

Talking about money can be difficult. But all of us are dealing with some pretty common issues. Whether you're speaking with a young adult or an aging parent, if you talk about your own daily management issues, you can help them handle theirs. Here are some things to start with:

- **Staying on top of a budget**—Do your kids or your parents have a budget in place? If not, you can help them get a clearer idea of where their money is going and how they can better manage on what they have. See **Question 2** for more on budgeting and managing cash flow.

- **Paying bills on time**—If someone is having trouble keeping up with due dates and bill paying, talk about establishing automatic payments from their bank account. That's a convenience at any age.

- **Handling credit**—Juggling credit card balances on a small or a fixed income is difficult for everyone. You can discuss how they can systematically pay down debt or consolidate to make it easier. (See **Question 13** for ideas.) You might also use this as an opportunity to discuss good versus bad debt as I do in **My Top Ten Recommendations**, page 3.

- **Basic banking**—Online banking, direct deposit, and automatic bill pay can all make banking easier for young and old alike. Make sure you're taking advantage of them to simplify your own finances—and encourage and help your kids and your parents to do the same. One caveat, though: Don't let automatic banking cause you to lose track of where your money is going. It's still important to stay on top of your monthly bank and credit card statements.

- **Automatic saving**—The easiest way to save is to make it automatic. Explain that it doesn't have to be a big amount—but by setting up a regular transfer, the account will build over time.

Look for Nonfinancial Ways to Be Supportive

Now is the time to think creatively. There are many ways to show your love and support that can be financially helpful but involve your time rather than your money.

If you have grandchildren, you can offer to babysit—for an evening, a couple of days a week, or even for an extended period so your kids can take a vacation. That represents a big savings on child care. Or how about offering to be the chauffeur if someone needs to get to a music lesson, ball game, or doctor's appointment? If you like to garden, maybe you can offer to put your skills to use for another family member. Even offering to be the chef for a night can be a fun—and less costly—way to show your family that you care.

Make Caring for Extended Family a Joint Effort

If someone in your family has special needs and you've been taking care of it yourself, it's time to share the burden. Have a family powwow to discuss what you've done in the past, the financial and time considerations, and how you can work together with the rest of the family to cover the need. It's not about shirking a responsibility, but sharing it.

➲ **SMART MOVE:** If someone in your extended family has an ongoing financial need, think about creating a rotating schedule where a different family member covers the bill every month. That way each person can put that particular obligation into his or her budget.

Protect Your Retirement Savings

I'm putting this last for emphasis, but it's really the number one point. First of all, you worked hard to accumulate your retirement savings, and you deserve to enjoy it. And second, by protecting your retirement nest egg, budgeting wisely, and not overextending for other family members, you're doing yourself—and them—a big service. If you don't take care of yourself, you could end up being a financial burden on someone else. Your children, in particular, will appreciate that your financial wisdom now may well spare them from being in a sandwich situation down the road.

Next Steps
- See **Question 23** for ideas on creating and maintaining a reliable retirement income stream.
- Worried about the stock market? **Question 22** offers suggestions on investing in retirement.
- Thinking about downsizing your home? See **Question 18**.

Q46.

My husband has no interest in our finances. How can I get him involved?

Every couple figures a way to divvy up responsibilities according to their skills and preferences. But when it comes to money, it's essential that both partners participate in some capacity—and that both are completely aware of what's going on. In my family I'm more of the day-to-day person, but my husband is involved in every decision and knows whom to call if something comes up.

To me, that's a crucial distinction—and one that you're wise to address now. That's not to say it will be easy to get your husband's attention. It may be especially difficult because it's harder to change behaviors once they've been in place for a long time. But it's something that's best to tackle sooner rather than later.

You'll also want to keep in mind that every person has a different way of doing things. A colleague of mine who is a financial expert keeps a spreadsheet for all his investments and retirement projections, but his wife won't even look at it. She sees all the numbers and long-term goals and her eyes glaze over. She, on the other hand, deals with the couple's everyday finances and easily stays on top of accounts, bills, short-term needs, etc. Ironically, my financial expert colleague professes to be clueless about these daily basics—and says he would be lost if anything happened to his wife.

The moral of the story is that even financially savvy people can have a hard time staying involved in things that don't fit their personal style. So it's important to present your finances to your husband in a way that will make sense to him and pique his curiosity.

Q **FACT:** Nearly 80 percent of women in relationships bear the responsibility of managing household finances, often with little help from their significant others, according to a 2013 survey conducted by the national nonprofit American Consumer Credit Counseling.

Be Honest About Your Concerns

To me, it has to start with an honest conversation. Tell your husband that you're concerned about what would happen should you no longer be able to handle the family finances. Be clear that you're not asking him to take charge. Rather, you're asking him for his help and advice—both for his well-being and for your peace of mind.

Talk About Life Goals

As a couple, you've probably talked a fair amount about your vision for the future. Do you want to travel? Will you relocate? Start a new business venture? Maybe you agree with each other, maybe not. But regardless, money is probably an important part of whatever lifestyle you select. At this point, talking about money may be less about numbers and more about what you want out of life. That can be exciting.

Look at the Big Picture

Before you get into the nuts and bolts of managing day-to-day finances, you might pique your husband's interest by talking about the bigger picture—what you have, what you owe, and how you're protecting yourselves. Here are some important points:

- **Net worth**—This is a look at what you own (home, investment accounts, retirement savings) and what you owe (mortgage, credit lines, car loans, credit card balances). Are you in the plus? See **My Top Ten Recommendations,** page 1, for how to create a net worth statement.
- **Cash flow**—How much money comes in each month and how much goes out? Is there a deficit or a surplus? Could you save more? See the "Cash Flow" box in **Question 2,** pages 18–19, for an easy way to set up a cash flow statement.
- **Retirement**—Have you calculated how much money you'll need each year in retirement? Are your lifestyle expectations realistic, or do you need to do some rethinking?
- **Insurance**—Review your health, life, homeowner's, and automobile insurance policies. Are you adequately covered? See **Question 27** for more on insurance you need—and don't need.
- **Estate plan**—Do your wills and trusts reflect your current wishes? Do you have the appropriate powers of attorney in place for both health and financial matters? If you need to get started on a basic estate plan, see **Question 38.**

As you look at these items together, you'll be able to spot trends. If you need to make adjustments to meet your future goals, use it as an opportunity for more thoughtful discussion on what's important to each of you and discuss changes you might want to make.

➡ **SMART MOVE:** Before you get into the details, make sure you're organized. See **Question 11** for ways to systematize and categorize financial paperwork.

Simplify the Details

This is where people's eyes usually glaze over, so it will be up to you to make the details appear straightforward and simple. I'd start with a concise list of:

- **Advisors**—Include contact information for your financial advisor, tax accountant, attorney, insurance agent—anyone your husband could turn to for advice. If he hasn't yet met these advisors, perhaps you could set up a meeting to introduce him.
- **Accounts**—List all your investment and bank accounts, with account numbers, location, and how much is in each. This could be an opportunity to consolidate accounts to make things even simpler.
- **Documents**—Make sure your husband knows where to find all important documents, that is, loan papers, wills, trusts, insurance policies.
- **Everyday bill paying**—Consider setting up automatic bill pay for most of your monthlies. This way your husband would only have to know which account the bills are paid from and how much of a monthly balance to maintain.

➲ SMART MOVE: Don't forget about passwords! In this increasingly online world, not knowing the passwords to your accounts can be a big hassle. Keep a list in a couple of secure places and make sure your spouse knows where it is.

Take It Step by Step

You're probably not going to change your husband's attitude overnight. And presenting all this information at once may serve only to convince him that he wants to stay on the sidelines. So make it a gradual thing. You might want to make a date once a month, go out for coffee or even for dinner, and plan to discuss one aspect of your financial life.

Then, once you have your husband's ear, be sure to include him in all major financial decisions. He may never get down to picking stocks or rebalancing your portfolio, but he may find that, rather than being a burden, having a say in family finances gives him a sense of accomplishment and control—and ultimately brings you closer together.

☎ **TALK TO AN EXPERT:** Next time you plan to meet with your financial advisor, encourage your husband to come with you. It might be a pleasant as well as eye-opening experience.

Next Steps

- Create a turnkey system for helping your spouse handle the finances should something happen to you. **Question 29** has some ideas.
- Look ahead to how you might want to change your investing style in retirement. See **Question 22** for things to consider.
- Develop a strategy for creating your retirement "paycheck." **Question 23** talks about which retirement accounts to draw from first.

My husband of fifty years has just died. He always handled our finances, and I'm feeling at sea. How can I manage?

The death of a husband or wife can make everything else pale in significance. My heart goes out to anyone who has to adjust to the loss of a loved one. As this question implies, there are a lot of practical and financial issues that you'll need to deal with. And those can seem especially difficult when you are facing them alone.

It's really important to reach out at this time to friends, family, and trusted advisors who perhaps can help you see things more clearly and prioritize what you need to do to protect and manage your finances. Don't be afraid to ask for help—and don't let yourself become isolated. There are lots of community services available if you know where to look for them. For my part, I can provide a few guidelines on what to do first and point you toward some resources.

Start with an Overview of What You Have

The first step in getting a handle on your finances is to look at what you own and what you owe. The easiest way to do this is to create a basic net worth statement. **My Top Ten Recommendations**, page 1, goes into a little more detail on this, but basically you need to make two lists. The first is a list of your assets—things like your home, bank and investment accounts, and retirement savings. The second is a list of your debts. For instance, do you still have a mortgage or a car loan? Do you have outstanding balances on your credit cards? Then subtract your debts from your assets. This will give you a good idea of your general financial situation, which is basically how much money you have to work with. With this information in front of you, you can now look at the specifics.

Get Organized

To make it easier on yourself—and easier to share information with someone who may be helping you—take some time to get organized. Create a simple filing system for things like bank, brokerage, and credit card statements, receipts, insurance policies—anything you may need to refer to periodically. You might also set up a system for paying bills so you don't miss any due dates. For instance, if you have a computer, using online bill pay through your bank and setting up automatic payments for regularly recurring bills is an excellent way to stay on top of things.

Update Information on Personal Accounts and Property

Next, you'll want to contact your banks and credit card companies to request the proper forms for changing joint loans, accounts, and credit cards to your name only. You should also:

- Review and update beneficiary designations on retirement accounts, annuities, and insurance policies

- Update health and life insurance records as needed
- Update titles on all property owned by the deceased

DOCUMENTS TO GATHER

Dealing with the details when you lose a loved one is never easy. But if you have the necessary documents in one place, handling them may be less stressful—and it will also help you as you look at the bigger financial picture. Here are some of the essential documents and information to gather:

- Will and/or trust documents

- Funeral and burial plans

- Social Security number

- Bank, brokerage, and retirement account statements

- Stock certificates or bonds

- Documentation of business ownership interests

- Pension plan information

- Life insurance policies and annuities

- Prior income tax and gift tax returns

- Marriage, birth, and death certificates

- Real property deeds and titles to motor vehicles

- Health insurance information

- Outstanding bills or obligations

- Inventory of personal belongings, household goods, etc.

Make Sure You're Getting the Maximum Social Security Benefits

If you haven't yet contacted the Social Security Administration, do it now. A widow or widower at full retirement age (FRA), as defined by the SSA, qualifies for **100 percent of a spouse's benefits.** (If you're younger than your FRA, benefits are reduced by age.) You may be eligible for an increase in benefits. **Question 34** goes into greater detail about survivor benefits.

You will need to contact the SSA and provide specific information to get your spouse's benefits (for example, a death certificate, your marriage certificate, and Social Security numbers for both of you). The SSA will work with you to ensure that you receive the maximum benefit you're entitled to. You can find more on how to apply for survivor benefits at ssa. gov or by calling 800-772-1213. You can also contact your local Social Security office.

Review Your Medicare Coverage and Supplemental Policies

As I discuss in **Question 35,** generally, you're eligible for Medicare if you or your husband worked for at least ten years in Medicare-covered employment, you're 65 or older, and you're a U.S. citizen or permanent resident. If you're already receiving Medicare benefits, nothing should change here. In fact, with new regulations under the Affordable Care Act, coverage for medications will be expanded over the next few years.

However, it would be a good idea to take a look at the Medigap policy or Medicare Advantage Plan you may have, which covers things Medicare doesn't (see **Question 36**), and your Part D prescription drug policy if you have one. You should at least be aware of the insurance companies that carry your policies, and have contact numbers available. It will make you feel more confident to know that your medical needs are taken care of and whom to contact if you have questions.

If you have questions about Medicare itself, there are two primary sources of information:

- For eligibility, enrolling, or applying for the Extra Help benefit available under the prescription drug program if your income is low, contact the Social Security Administration.

- For covered medical services, choosing a Medicare part D drug plan, or finding a local doctor or hospital that accepts Medicare patients, contact the Centers for Medicare and Medicaid Services (800-633-4227 or medicare.gov).

☎ **TALK TO AN EXPERT:** Handling these details can be confusing and time-consuming. If you don't have a family member or friend who can help, it would be wise to turn to a trusted attorney or CPA.

BE SURE TO FILE FOR BENEFITS

A surviving spouse may be entitled to a number of benefits, but a certain amount of paperwork is required. It's best to contact agencies by phone to find out what documents you may need to file. Once again, a family member or trusted friend may be willing to help you. Just be sure to keep records of all correspondence.

Depending on your circumstances, agencies to contact may include:

- **Social Security Administration**—You'll need a death certificate, Social Security numbers for yourself, the deceased, and dependent children, birth and marriage certificates, divorce papers if you're a surviving divorced spouse, and self-employment tax returns for the most recent year if applicable. Note that Social Security benefits may also be available for unmarried children up to age 18 (19 if in high school; 22 if disabled). For more information on survivor benefits, go to ssa.gov or call 800-772-1213.

- **Insurance companies**—Contact the insurance company's local office and obtain a death claim form. Complete the form and return it along with a certified copy of the death certificate and a copy of the policy.

- **Employer group insurance**—The employee benefits department of your spouse's employer can provide a list of the benefits you may be eligible for and how they're paid. You'll need to provide a number of certified death certificates and other documentation.

- **Veterans' benefits**—To apply for veterans' benefits, you may be required to appear in person at a local office of the U.S. Department of Veterans Affairs. Visit iris.va.gov for more information.

Stay Actively Involved in Your Finances

I know it's not easy, but it's very important to maintain an active role in your financial life. This doesn't mean that you have to do it alone; for example, you could ask a family member or trusted friend to help you with day-to-day tasks. And by all means seek out advice from a financial advisor. But it's important for you to be involved in decisions, and on top of where things stand.

**IMPORTANT THINGS YOU CAN DO TO TAKE
CONTROL OF YOUR FINANCES**

- Set short- and long-term goals. This will give you a sense of purpose.

- Develop and stick with a budget. If you know you have enough to live on, you'll be more confident you can manage on your own.

- Build a financial safety net. If you can, keep enough assets in cash to cover two to three years' expenses.

- Review and update health, disability, and life insurance policies. Make sure coverage is up-to-date and beneficiaries are properly designated.

- Reevaluate and rebalance your investment portfolio. Talk to a financial advisor to make sure you're not taking on too much risk at this point in your life.

- Review or create your estate plan. Talk to your family about your wishes.

⚠ **CAUTION:** If you've inherited a large sum of money, be cautious and careful about how you manage and invest it. Take your time; don't feel pressured to make any quick decisions. If you're not sure, feel free to get a second opinion.

Also be on your guard against people who might want to take advantage of you. To stay on top of things:

- Pay your taxes first.
- Look at this new money in light of your overall financial picture.
- Don't rush to pay off a mortgage or pay cash for a new home.
- Get professional advice from a trusted advisor.

Check Into Senior-Focused Agencies

Friends and family may be willing to help you, but there may be times when you need to reach out to other organizations. Fortunately, there are a number of agencies that are dedicated to senior issues.

- **National Association of Area Agencies on Aging**—This can be a good place to start, and chances are there's a local branch in your community. These agencies (n4a.org) are dedicated to helping seniors get assistance with health care, home care, transportation, and more. Many offer specific help with Medicare and Medicaid issues and provide volunteer counselors and community education programs.
- **Department of Health and Human Services**—To find out what's offered in your community, you might first contact your county's department of health and human services, which likely has a division on aging and adult services. They can direct you to specific programs.
- **Administration on Aging**—If you have access to a computer, there are a number of websites dedicated to senior care issues, such as the Administration on Aging (aoa.gov), that provide online tools for finding local resources and support services—as well as information on government health and disability programs, legal resources, and more.

⚠ **CAUTION:** It's always smart for anyone at any age to be on the lookout for financial scams. But seniors are particularly vulnerable. Never, ever give out your personal or financial information to someone you don't know well, and never invest without doing thorough research. When an offer seems too good to be true, it generally is. If you have been the victim of fraud, identity theft, or deceptive business practices, you can file a complaint with the Federal Trade Commission at **ftc.gov** or by calling 877-FTC-HELP (877-382-4357).

Another option is to find an attorney who specializes in senior issues and can guide you to any help you may need. This may be more costly—and you want to make sure you get an attorney who is highly recommended—but it could be worth it. The National Academy of Elder Law Attorneys has an online locator (naela.org) that can provide a starting point for finding a qualified attorney in your area.

The key is to stay active and involved, reach out, and in some ways be your own advocate. By doing so, you may find that you have more of a support system than you imagined.

➲ **SMART MOVE:** Depending on your personal preferences and financial resources, you may want to consider moving to an active adult/senior residential community. These retirement-oriented communities often offer access to a wide variety of resources, from job counseling to legal services, as well as providing a supportive social environment.

Next Steps

- Work with a financial advisor who can help you understand your financial situation. With someone to guide you, you'll feel more in control. **Question 6** talks about how to find an advisor who's right for you.

- Get organized so you can more easily stay on top of your finances. See **Question 11** for insights on what's essential to keep, and on how to categorize and create a simple filing system.
- Create a budget, looking carefully at both your essential and discretionary expenses. **Question 2** has ideas on budgeting and staying on top of your cash flow.
- Make use of books like this and websites such as schwabmoney wise.com to educate yourself on financial basics.

I'm 50 and contemplating a divorce after 25 years of marriage. My husband has always been the chief breadwinner and has been in control of our money. How can I cope?

A friend of mine was in a similar situation a couple of years ago. She came to me to ask my financial advice, but ultimately what she really needed was someone to help her think more clearly about her decision and the challenges of making it on her own. I was happy to be a sounding board, and I think it helped her take a step back and thoughtfully consider all her options.

This is important because, even in the most amicable of divorces, emotions can run high and cloud your financial judgment. Yet you may have to deal with some potentially contentious issues such as division of assets, payment of outstanding debts, and spousal and child support— all of which can seem overwhelming, especially if you're not used to handling financial matters. So my first recommendation is to find someone, either a trusted family member or friend, who can help you sort through these issues. You might also want to consult with a divorce attorney so you more clearly understand your rights and the decisions you'll have to make.

Preparation is your best protection. There are a number of things to think about, whether or not you ultimately decide to divorce. And while you may have to handle many of the details yourself, having advice right from the get-go may help you stay focused on the important issues and take things step by step.

Collect Financial Information

To me, no matter what the circumstances are, each partner in a marriage should be aware of overall household finances and have access to financial information. Gathering this information will be the first step toward feeling more secure. Records you should have on hand include:

- Property owned (that is, house, car) and how it's titled
- Outstanding mortgage or home equity loans
- Bank and investment accounts, including account numbers and balances
- Consumer debt such as credit card balances and auto loans
- Types of insurance (homeowner's, auto, life, health) and where the policies are kept
- Retirement accounts, both your own and your husband's
- Estate planning documents (wills, trusts, etc.)

It would also be wise to take an inventory of household goods and personal property. All of these things can factor into a divorce settlement.

☎ **TALK TO AN EXPERT:** Once you've clarified some of your thoughts and collected initial financial information, schedule a meeting with a divorce attorney. You'll want to understand the process and divorce requirements in your state as soon as possible. Be sure to discuss your overall financial situation, including options for dividing your assets and any concerns you may have about alimony and child support.

Establish Individual Credit

If you don't already have at least one major credit card in your name only, open one immediately and use it. This will help you establish a personal credit history, which will be essential should you decide to be on your own.

Once you have your own credit in place—and you've started divorce proceedings—it would be a good idea to close old joint credit card accounts. It's best to do it in writing, clearly stating that you're no longer responsible for new charges. Be sure to date the letters and keep copies.

Figure Out Short- and Long-Term Financial Needs

You should also do some serious thinking about what you need to support yourself and your dependent children. Things to think about include:

- Monthly living expenses, including mortgage or rent, utilities, groceries, transportation, health care, insurance, etc.
- Big-ticket items for children such as private school tuition, orthodontics, extracurricular programs, cars, computers, etc.
- College costs

I believe this is the type of planning everyone should do, regardless of marital status. If it's all new to you, start by creating a line-by-line budget. It's not difficult; it just takes a bit of thinking and organization. Take a look at **Question 2,** which walks you through budgeting and managing cash flow.

Separate Assets

It would be good for you to complete the previous steps even if you don't go through with a divorce. If nothing else, it will give you a keener sense of control and strength as a mature adult and a partner in your marriage.

If you do decide to divorce, depending on state laws, you can also begin to separate your assets even before divorce papers are served. You should check with your attorney and banker about closing any joint checking and savings accounts and putting half the money into your own account. Another option is to place assets from a closed account in an escrow account until your divorce settlement is complete.

Should you and your husband separate, you can also freeze assets in all joint brokerage accounts by immediately notifying your brokerage company in writing and asking that no transactions be made without your approval.

LONG-TERM CONSIDERATIONS TO THINK ABOUT NOW

The division of your marital assets will have a significant impact on your future financial well-being. As you negotiate your settlement and start planning your future income, be certain to:

- Include pensions, retirement plans, company stock options, and other types of deferred compensation in your settlement considerations.

- Take into consideration any business interests that may be considered joint property. You may need to employ a professional business valuator.

- Discuss with your attorney or advisor the tax implications and long-range investment consequences of how you divide your assets.

- Factor in Social Security retirement benefits. Those 62 or older who were married for at least ten years and haven't remarried may be entitled to collect benefits equal to one-half of their ex-spouse's benefits. You must be 62 or older to be eligible, and if you've been working, you can choose between your own benefits or spousal benefits, whichever is greater. Go to ssa.gov for more information. Also see **Question 32** for more on ways to maximize Social Security benefits.

⚠ **CAUTION:** The division of retirement assets can be tricky. Make sure your spouse's pension and retirement accounts are included in your settlement agreement. To divide IRA assets, you must submit a divorce decree signed by a judge, sometimes accompanied by a settlement agreement.

Consider Mediation

If you and your husband are on relatively good terms, you might want to look into mediation. Mediation is often less contentious than litigation— and can help reduce both the emotional and financial costs. There are organizations such as the Academy of Family Mediators (acrfamilysection .org) that provide online resources and referrals to qualified mediators.

Look to the Future

Regardless of whether or not you get a divorce, I encourage you to start to become more financially independent. Familiarize yourself with your current accounts, holdings, and advisors. Then set some goals, develop a budget, create an emergency fund, and begin saving for your own retirement. See **My Top Ten Recommendations**, pages 1–8.

Thinking about these things in advance should give you a bit more assurance in dealing with the financial aspects of a potential divorce. Whatever your decision, ideally you'll end up with more financial knowledge and a greater sense of personal security.

PRACTICAL DETAILS TO CONSIDER FOLLOWING A DIVORCE

Following a divorce, take these steps to make your financial transition smoother and to make sure your new life is reflected on all your financial documents.

- Take the necessary steps to make any name change official. Get a copy of your court order for use when requesting that agencies and creditors change your name in their records.

- Review and update files for all personal accounts and property.

- Update your will and estate plan.

- Update beneficiaries for your IRAs, 401(k) plan, and life insurance. This is often overlooked and assets go to the wrong person!

- Update your health and life insurance policies as needed.

- Update your name on the titles of all property you own.

- Request copies of your credit report to check for accuracy. You can request copies at annualcreditreport.com.

- Update your income tax filing choices and W-4 as needed.

SMART MOVE: A divorce might also mean a chance to explore career choices. A new job can open up new possibilities—professionally, financially, emotionally, and socially. Reach out to friends and family and explore opportunities in your community. Even part-time work can make you feel more connected and independent.

Next Steps

- Get organized. See **Question 11** for tips on setting up an accessible filing system for your financial information.
- Find a good financial advisor. "Navigating the Maze of Financial Advisors" in **Question 6** on page 78 talks about what to look for to find an advisor who's right for you.
- Think about your own retirement. **Question 1** is a good place to start, and **Question 4** gives you more information on types of retirement accounts.
- Review and revise your estate plan. **Question 38** discusses the essentials you should have in place.

Q49.

I'm a widow and about to remarry. What should I be thinking about from a financial perspective?

There's a lot of sensitivity around money and marriage at any age. And for a widow, potentially with grown children and a lifetime of acquiring assets and managing those assets, the issues can be more complex. Chances are, you're not just dealing with dollars; you're also dealing with emotions.

Of course, the success of any marriage depends on communication. So no matter what your circumstances, you and your fiancé should make a big effort to talk openly and honestly about your finances. That's the best way I know to nurture your relationship at the same time that you both protect yourselves.

Consider a Prenuptial Agreement

Joining your lives and your money when you're older—especially the second time around—can be complicated. If one or both of you are bringing substantial assets into the marriage, seriously consider working with an attorney to write a prenuptial agreement. Even if you decide against a formal legal document, openly discussing your finances and putting your decisions in some type of written format is essential.

As you go through this process, complete disclosure is essential. If you hold back on sharing information or your feelings, you're just paving the way for trouble down the road. You both also need to be sensitive to each other's point of view. Choose a time that works for both of you, find a mutually comfortable environment, and approach issues as partners. Agree to listen to each other and honor each other's feelings. Here are some of the questions you should address:

- **Will you keep assets separate?** You can consider all assets acquired before the marriage separate and those acquired after your marriage joint. Alternatively, you can continue to keep all assets separate. It's a good idea to consult an attorney so that you clearly understand the laws in your state regarding property ownership, including issues like commingling assets.
- **What will you do with your homes?** Will you sell your current homes and jointly purchase a new home? Do either of you want to keep your home so that it stays in the family? Or if one of you moves into the other's home, will you change the title to joint ownership? Once you agree, be sure to talk to an attorney about the safeguards you'll need to put in place to protect both of your interests.
- **Who will be financially responsible for what?** Be clear on the expenses you'll share and those you'll keep separate. When it comes to everyday accounts, a "yours, mine, and ours" approach works for many couples because it allows for both joint and individual spending decisions. If one of you is responsible for a child or other dependent, discuss how that will impact your day-to-day finances.
- **How will you handle debt?** While marriage doesn't make you responsible for each other's existing debts, agree now how you'll pay off any debts you bring into the marriage. Also discuss your opinions about debt as you look to the future.

- **Will you file a joint tax return?** In the vast majority of cases, married couples benefit by filing a joint return. There are exceptions, though (for example, when one person has high medical costs), so discuss this with your tax advisor.
- **What about medical and long-term care insurance?** Make sure each of you has sufficient medical coverage. If one of you becomes disabled or has significant medical expenses, decide how you'll pay for it as a couple.
- **What happens if you divorce?** Discuss your feelings about things like spousal support and retirement savings. Some states will allow you to waive spousal support. A spouse may also waive rights to retirement benefits.

Talking about these issues is sure to raise others. Once again, an attorney can help you put everything on the table and explain your choices.

See a Financial Advisor Together

Depending on the complexity of your financial situations, it would be wise to consult a financial advisor together, even before you're married. An advisor can help you organize your finances in a way that will protect all of your individual assets while forging a new, supportive financial relationship.

> ⏵ **SMART MOVE:** As a widow, you're entitled to Social Security survivor benefits even if you remarry, provided that you didn't remarry until age 60. Talk to the Social Security Administration to make sure you understand all of your options.

Revise and Refine Your Estate Plans

You and your fiancé both need to rethink your estate plans. Discuss your individual responsibility to children and grandchildren—or to any other dependents or family members—and how you want to provide for them. **Question 42** talks about different trusts to consider. Also discuss any charitable organizations that you want to support. **Question 43** looks at ways to make charitable giving a part of your estate plan. As you go through this process, don't forget about your late spouses' wishes for their heirs.

While you're at it, update beneficiaries on all pertinent accounts, such as retirement plans, pensions, or annuities, and make certain all assets are titled correctly.

⚠️ **CAUTION:** Every year millions of dollars go to unintended recipients because of out-of-date beneficiary designations. Don't let this happen to you!

Talk to the Kids

Last, but not least, it's extremely important to be up front with your kids or other close family members. For a variety of reasons, late-in-life marriages can come under a lot of scrutiny. Tell them the agreements you've come to and how you're protecting yourself. If you decide to draw up a prenuptial agreement, think about giving adult children a copy. Also talk openly about your estate plan so there are no surprises. If they know that you're taking care of yourself as well as including them in your new life, you'll all be able to approach the future with confidence.

Although talking about money can be uncomfortable at first, many couples find that open, honest discussions bring them closer together. After all, when you talk about money, you're also sharing your values and priorities. It's a great opportunity to get to know each other on a deeper level as you forge your new life.

Next Steps
- If you're thinking about purchasing long-term care insurance, see **Question 7.**

- To find a trustworthy financial advisor, see **Question 6.**
- Review your Social Security options. Read more about survivor benefits in **Question 34.**
- If you're unsure about how to accommodate your children in your estate plan, see **Questions 40** and **42.**

Q50.

I have a child with special needs. What can I do to make sure that she will always be taken care of?

While handling the day-to-day care of a special needs child can be challenging, planning for the future is equally important—and potentially complicated. While there are a number of government assistance programs, the manner in which you set up additional financial support can directly affect whether your child will qualify for public benefits. So it's not just a matter of providing a financial safety net; the methods you use are also crucial to the ongoing well-being of your child.

Here are some things you can consider doing now to help give your daughter the security she needs—and give yourself some peace of mind.

Q FACT: According to the U.S. Centers for Disease Control and Prevention, approximately 20 percent of U.S. adults have a disability. Recent CDC data also state that 1 in 88 children has been identified with an autism spectrum disorder.

Establish Yourself as Legal Guardian

Be sure to establish yourself as your daughter's guardian when she turns 18. Otherwise she will be considered an independent adult under the law, and you may not have access to her medical records or be able to make decisions on her behalf.

Apply for Government Benefits

There are two government programs that your daughter could qualify for: Medicaid, which covers most medical services; and Supplemental Security Income (SSI), which provides a monthly stipend for basic living needs. In order to maximize benefits, apply for these benefits when your daughter first becomes eligible at age 18.

Consider a Special Needs Trust

SSI and Medicaid are a good start. But if you want to make sure your daughter has more than the bare bones, there's a catch. In most states, an individual with special needs can't have more than $2,000 in assets to be eligible for assistance. This means that if your daughter owns or inherits more than the eligibility requirements allow, she'll lose government support.

Fortunately, you can get around this problem by setting up a **special needs trust** (also called a *supplemental needs trust*). With this type of trust, designed especially for individuals with a disability, the assets belong to the trust, not to the individual, so there's no issue with continuing to collect government assistance. You designate a trustee who will manage the assets and use them for your daughter's expenses above and beyond what the government programs cover. But it's important that the money isn't used for the same things the assistance covers. For example, it can't provide for basic expenses like food or housing, but it can cover essential quality-of-life expenses such as clothing, vocational training, and travel. It's also important that the funds are not paid directly to your daughter. Both could cause her to lose her benefits.

> ➲ **SMART MOVE:** Even though a special needs trust can't pay for housing, it can pay for extras such as accessibility features for your home.

It's important to note that this is a specialized trust that must be set up and managed carefully. You can fund it either while you're alive or as a part of your will. The rules vary by state and by the source of your funding, so you'll want to consult with an attorney experienced not just in estate planning but specifically in special needs trusts. Two professional groups that can provide references to lawyers experienced in special needs are the Academy of Special Needs Planners and the Special Needs Alliance.

> ➲ **SMART MOVE:** Even if you have considerable wealth it's still a good idea to set up a special needs trust for a child with special needs. That way he or she won't be excluded from government programs and assistance.

Refine Your Estate Plan

At the same time you set up the trust, update your estate plan and leave specific instructions. The basics should include:

- **A will**—Make sure to leave any assets designated for your daughter's care to the special needs trust, not directly to her. You can specify that the trust will be the beneficiary of a retirement plan or a life insurance policy.
- **Trustee**—Appoint a trusted individual or financial institution to manage the financial aspects of the trust.
- **Guardian**—Appoint one or more guardians for your daughter to manage your daughter's day-to-day care after your death. They will make decisions about medical care, personal finances, and everyday living.

- **Letter of intent**—Here you should describe your desires for your daughter's care and plans and expectations for her future. Think of it as a guide for her caregiver.

Talk to Your Family

If you have other children, explain your plans. Tell them how you're dividing your assets and how you've provided for their sister. It may lessen their worries about the future, and hopefully also alleviate any feelings of resentment.

Also, if there are relatives who may consider giving or leaving assets to your daughter, make sure they're aware of the trust and the importance of not putting money directly in her name.

Take Care of Yourself

While you're preparing for your daughter's future, don't forget about your own. If you haven't yet reached retirement, keep contributing to your 401(k) or IRA. And try not to dip into your retirement savings to cover your daughter's needs. Ideally, the two of you will have many more years together. You want to be financially secure yourself, so you can enjoy them to the fullest.

Next Steps
- To refresh your memory on basic estate planning, see **Question 38.**
- For some thoughts on how to split up your estate among children with different needs, see **Question 40.**
- To read about Social Security disability benefits, see **Question 33.**
- Paperwork a mess? See **Question 11.**

Glossary of
Financial Terms

401(k) plan. A tax-deferred defined-contribution retirement plan offered by companies. Employees contribute via payroll deductions, and employers may make matching contributions to the plan. The IRS usually limits the percentage of salary-deferral contributions.

403(b) plan. A tax-deferred defined-contribution retirement plan for employees of charitable and nonprofit organizations, including educational institutions, to which employees contribute via payroll deductions. Employers may make matching contributions to the plan, and the IRS usually limits the percentage of salary-deferral contributions.

457(b) plan. A tax-deferred defined-contribution retirement plan for government employees, including state and local workers, police officers, firefighters, and some teachers. Employers may make matching contributions to the plan, and the IRS usually limits the percentage of salary-deferral contributions.

529 plan. A state-sponsored education savings program that allows parents, relatives, and friends to invest for a child's college education. Contributions aren't tax-deductible, but earnings can grow tax-deferred. Withdrawals are tax-free if used to pay for qualified educational fees and expenses.

actively managed mutual fund. A type of mutual fund in which the fund manager attempts to outperform an index by making decisions to buy or sell individual securities. For comparison, see *index fund.*

administrator. A person named by the court to represent a deceased person's estate when there is no will, or the will does not name an executor, or the executor named in the will is unavailable or declines to serve.

advance health-care directive. A legal document that allows a person to give explicit instructions for the type of medical care she or he would (or would not) like to receive and assign an agent to make decisions on their behalf should they become terminally ill or incapacitated. Also known as a *living will*, or an *advance directive.*

after-tax rate of return. A rate of return that takes income taxes into account, a key factor since taxes can diminish investment return.

annuity. A financial product sold by a financial services company designed to provide a fixed or variable stream of income, generally for retirement.

applicable credit amount. For estate or gift tax, the amount equal to the tax on transfers that a taxpayer does *not* have to pay.

applicable exclusion amount. The dollar value of a taxable gift or a taxable estate that will not cause a gift or estate tax liability. If a decedent makes no lifetime taxable gifts, his or her estate can avoid paying estate taxes if the taxable estate is smaller than this amount.

ask price. The price a seller is willing to accept for a security at a given time.

asset. A property that has monetary value, including personal possessions such as a house, car, or jewelry, and financial properties such as savings and investments. The opposite of a *liability.*

asset allocation. The way in which a portfolio is divided into different asset classes (for example, stocks, bonds, cash, real estate, or commodities) with the goal of balancing a desired level of risk and return.

asset allocation fund. A mutual fund that includes a mix of stocks, bonds, and cash equivalents to achieve a desired level of risk and return. This type of fund helps diversify among asset classes with one investment.

asset class. A broad investment category such as stocks, bonds, real estate, or cash equivalents.

attorney-in-fact. The person legally designated to act on another person's behalf.

balanced fund. A mutual fund that buys a combination of investments (for example, stocks, bonds, and cash equivalents) to provide both income and capital appreciation, while avoiding excessive risk.

bear market. A declining market in which prices are falling for a sustained period of time.

benchmark. A standard used for comparison. For example, the performance of large-cap stock funds is often compared to the performance of the S&P 500 Index, which serves as a benchmark.

beneficiary. The person or organization designated to receive the funds or other property from a trust, insurance policy, or retirement account.

beta. A measure of the volatility, or systematic risk, of a security or a portfolio in comparison to the market as a whole. Due to macroeconomic variables, it cannot be "diversified away."

bid and ask. The buy and sell prices for securities, representing the spread in the market. The investor buys at the *ask* and sells at the *bid*. The *ask* is always higher than the *bid*.

bid price. The price a buyer is willing to pay for a security at a given time.

bond. A type of investment that is similar to an IOU from a corporation or a municipal, state, or federal government. An investor loans the borrower money, and in return, the borrower promises to repay the full amount on a specific date, and to pay the investor interest in the meantime.

bond fund. A mutual fund that invests primarily in bonds—typically corporate, municipal, or U.S. government bonds.

bond maturity. The lifetime of a bond, concluding when the final payment of that obligation is due.

broad-based index fund. An *index fund* based on an index that includes a large portion of the market.

broker (or registered representative). A professional who works for a broker-dealer (such as Charles Schwab & Co., Inc.) who is registered to buy and sell securities on behalf of an investor. Every broker must pass an exam, register with the *Financial Industry Regulatory Authority (FINRA)*, and be licensed by the state in which they conduct business. A broker may also be called a *financial advisor*, a *financial consultant*, or an *investment consultant*.

brokerage. A securities firm that sells stocks, mutual funds, and other securities.

brokerage account. An account with a brokerage firm that allows an investor to buy and sell securities.

bull market. A rising market in which prices are going up for a sustained period of time.

buy-and-hold. An investing strategy that encourages investing for the long term by buying and then "holding," meaning not selling, rather than selling based on the market's day-to-day ups and downs. Buying and then trying to sell based on the movement of the market is the opposite investment strategy and is called "market timing."

bypass trust. A trust for married couples that is intended to minimize estate taxes on the death of the surviving spouse. Also known as an *AB trust* or a *credit shelter trust*.

capital appreciation. An unrealized increase in the value of an asset.

capital gain. The profit an investor receives when she or he sells an investment for more than the purchase price. For example, if an investor purchased stock for $1,000 and sold it for $1,500, the capital gain would be $500. Capital gains are taxable income and must be reported to the IRS on your tax return.

capital gains distribution. A payment an investor receives when his or her mutual fund makes a profit by selling some of the securities in its portfolio. Capital gains distributions are usually made annually, often at the end of the calendar year.

capitalization. The total stock market value of all shares of a company's stock, calculated by multiplying the stock price by the number of shares outstanding.

capital loss. The amount of money an investor loses when he or she sells an investment for less than the amount paid. Capital losses may be deducted from your annual income and must be reported on your tax return.

capital return. The capital gain or loss realized from the market appreciation or depreciation of an investment.

certificate of deposit (CD). A savings certificate issued by a financial institution such as a bank or savings and loan. The buyer deposits a specified amount for a specific period of time, at a preset, fixed interest rate. CDs are FDIC-insured up to $250,000 per depositor per bank.

charitable lead trust (CLT). An irrevocable trust that provides income to a charity for a set number of years, after which the remainder passes to the donor's heirs.

charitable remainder trust (CRT). An irrevocable trust that provides income to the donor or other beneficiary for a set number of years. At the end of the trust's term, the remainder goes to the designated charity.

charitable trust. A trust that is set up for a qualified charity so that all or part of a person's estate can be left to a charity or nonprofit organization. The donor also receives a tax benefit for the portion of the donated gift, allowing her or him to maximize the tax advantages of their giving. Also see *charitable lead trust* and *charitable remainder trust.*

closed-end mutual fund. A mutual fund that distributes a fixed number of shares that trade much like stocks. They are usually listed on a major exchange, and they may trade in the market at a premium or discount to net asset value (NAV).

COBRA (Consolidated Omnibus Budget Reconciliation Act). The federal law passed in 1986 that provides continuation of employer-sponsored group health insurance after certain events that would otherwise end coverage; for example, after job loss (voluntary or involuntary), reduction in work hours, death, or divorce.

commission. The fee paid to a brokerage firm for executing a transaction.

common stock. Securities that represent an ownership interest in a company.

compounding. Generally speaking, the growth potential that results from investment income being reinvested. Compound growth has a snowball effect because both the original investment and the income from that investment are invested.

conservator. An individual appointed by the court to administer the affairs of an incapacitated adult.

Consumer Financial Protection Bureau (CFPB). A federal regulatory agency created in 2010 that oversees financial products and services offered to consumers.

correlation. In investing, the statistical strength of the relationship of the returns of two assets, ranging from −1 to +1. Perfect positive correlation (+1) implies that as one security moves up or down, the other will move in lockstep. Perfect negative correlation (−1) implies that if one security moves in one direction, the other will move the opposite way. With a correlation of 0, the securities have no relationship and move independently.

cost basis. What an investor paid for an investment, as opposed to its current market value. This number, which is used for tax purposes, includes any dividends that have been reinvested, and any capital gains distributions.

Coverdell Education Savings Account (ESA). An account (formerly called an "Education IRA") established to help pay the education expenses of a child, grandchild, or other designated beneficiary who is a minor. The contributions aren't deductible; however, earnings are free from federal income tax as long as the money is used for qualified expenses.

credit quality. An assessment of a security issuer's ability to repay its debts or, in the case of fixed income, to make timely interest and principal payments on its bonds. In general, the higher a bond's rating, the lower the credit risk, and potentially the lower its yield.

credit risk. The possibility that the issuer of a bond—the borrower—will default, or fail to repay the principal or interest owed on a bond, either at the agreed-upon time or at all. Also commonly called "default risk."

credit shelter trust. See *bypass trust.*

Crummey trust. A trust that takes advantage of the gift tax exclusion at the same time that it limits when the recipient can access the money.

currency risk. The possibility that the price of an investment may fluctuate as a result of changing currency exchange rates.

current yield. The amount of annual interest on a bond divided by its current market value, expressed as a percentage.

custodial account. An account set up and managed by an adult for the benefit of a minor. It is set up in the name of a child, with a parent or trustee as custodian. Assets placed in the account are considered an irrevocable gift and belong solely to the child, with the custodian being in control of the account until the child reaches the age of majority (18 or 21, depending on state law).

defined-benefit plan. An employer-sponsored retirement plan in which a retired employee receives a specific amount of money based on salary history and length of employment. Also known as a *pension plan.*

defined-contribution plan. An employer-sponsored retirement plan in which an employee, an employer, or both contribute to an employee's retirement account. Unlike defined-benefit plans, these plans allow the employee to have some say in how and where the money is invested. In some cases, the employee is responsible for all of those decisions. These plans include 401(k)s, 403(b)s, and 457(b)s.

deflation. A decrease in the cost of goods and services as measured by the Consumer Price Index.

designated-beneficiary plan (pay-on-death account, transfer-on-death account, Totten trust). A plan that allows people to choose their beneficiaries and specify what percentage of their account assets will be left to each one. Assets passed in this way will avoid the probate process.

disability insurance. Insurance that replaces all or a portion of income in the event an illness or injury prevents the insured from working.

diversification. The division of money across and within asset classes with the goal of reducing risk. Diversification cannot, however, ensure a profit or eliminate the risk of investment losses.

dividend. The distribution of a portion of a company's earnings declared by a company's board of directors and paid to shareholders. In general, dividends are paid quarterly in the form of cash, but they can also be in the form of stock or other property.

dollar-cost averaging. Investing the same dollar amount in the same securities at regular scheduled intervals over the long term.

domestic fund. A mutual fund that invests only in stocks issued by U.S. companies. These funds are classified according to size (large-cap, mid-cap, and small-cap) and style (growth and value).

donor-advised account. A charitable-giving vehicle designed to manage charitable donations.

Dow Jones Industrial Average (DJIA or "the Dow"). One of the most commonly used measurements of the performance of the U.S. stock market. It includes thirty blue chip stocks, which are primarily industrial stocks considered leaders in the market.

durable power of attorney. A power of attorney that remains in effect even if the person who has created it becomes incapacitated.

E & O insurance. Errors and omissions insurance. Professional liability insurance that protects individuals or organizations against a claim of negligent work.

earnings. A company's net income or profit, usually quoted in millions of dollars.

earnings per share (EPS). A company's total earnings for a period (its net income minus preferred dividends), divided by the number of common shares outstanding.

Education IRA. See *Coverdell Education Savings Account.*

Education Savings Account (ESA). See *Coverdell Education Savings Account.*

effective tax rate. The average tax rate you pay when you take all of your income into account.

efficient frontier. A graphical representation of a set of theoretical portfolios that provide the greatest expected return for a given amount of risk.

employee stock ownership plan, or ESOP. A plan in which an employee acquires her or his company's stock through a company retirement plan that invests in and pays benefits in the form of company stock instead of cash contributions.

employer-sponsored retirement plan. A retirement plan offered to employees and sponsored by the employer.

equity. Another name for *stock,* representing ownership of a corporation. Also, the money value of a property or of an interest in a property in excess of all claims or liens against it.

ERISA. Employee Retirement Income Security Act of 1974. The federal law that established standards and extensive rules for qualified retirement plans.

estate plan. A document that establishes who will receive a person's property and possessions after his or her death. Its most common tools are wills and trusts.

estate tax. A tax on the transfer of wealth at death.

exchange-traded fund (ETF). Generally a low-cost, tax-efficient fund that provides access to a broad range of securities in an asset class such as large U.S. stocks, small U.S. stocks, international stocks, and investment-grade bonds.

executor. The person or institution named in a will who is responsible for the management of the assets and the ultimate transfer of the property; commonly referred to as a *personal representative.*

exotic ETFs. Exchange-traded funds (ETFs) that provide access to unusual asset classes or investment styles, typically at a premium price by ETF standards. Exotic ETFs include commodities such as gold, concepts such as clean technology, or leveraged securities that move twice (or more) as much as the market or in the opposite direction to the market. They are subject to a greater degree of risk than typical ETFs.

expense ratio. For mutual funds and ETFs, the percentage of a fund's average net assets that is used to pay fund expenses. This percentage accounts for management fees, administrative fees, and any 12(b)-1 fees.

face value. The principal amount that the issuer will pay when a security (generally a bond) matures. The face value is also generally the amount on which interest is calculated. Also referred to as *par value.* Face value is not an indication of market value.

FAFSA (Free Application for Federal Student Aid). The form that must be filed to qualify for federal financial aid for higher education.

FDIC (Federal Deposit Insurance Corporation). A U.S. government agency that insures cash deposits, including certificates of deposit, that have been placed in member institutions, for up to $250,000 for each account type.

federal transfer tax system. The federal system that includes both gift and estate taxes.

fee-based management. A method of compensation in which an investor is charged for professional financial help. With fee-based management, the investor is charged a percentage of the assets in the manager's control, usually around 1 or 2 percent.

financial planner. A professional who can provide a wide range of services, including creating a comprehensive, individualized financial plan. Although financial planners do not have separate regulation (they are registered in accordance with the other services they provide, such as investment advice), a Certified Financial Planner™ professional has completed extensive training, has passed a rigorous test, and has ongoing continuing education requirements.

FINRA (Financial Industry Regulatory Authority). An organization that regulates business between brokers, dealers, and the investing public.

fixed annuity. An insurance contract under which an insurance company makes predetermined fixed payments to the annuitant. It behaves much like a pension. Provided the issuing insurance company remains solvent, a person can count on receiving payments for a set number of years, for life, or for the life of a beneficiary.

fixed-income investment. An investment such as a bond, certificate of deposit, or preferred stock that generally pays a specific interest rate on a periodic basis and promises the return of principal at maturity. The borrower, called the *issuer*, can be a government—municipal, state, or federal—a corporation, or a bank or savings and loan.

foreign fund. A mutual fund that invests only in companies outside of the United States. Additional risks not associated with domestic investments apply to foreign funds.

full retirement age (FRA). The age at which people will be eligible for unreduced Social Security benefits. However, even after people reach FRA, benefits will likely continue to increase until age 70.

fundamental index. In equity investing, an index based on fundamental criteria such as a company's profits, dividends, book value, cash flow, sales, or number of employees.

fund family. A group of mutual funds from the same organization. Investing in funds from the same fund family usually provides exchange privileges between the funds.

future interest. An interest in a property that the owner cannot immediately use. For example, a beneficiary in a will has a future interest. Also see *present interest*.

generation-skipping transfer tax. A tax imposed in addition to the estate and gift tax on transferring wealth to persons who are two or more generations younger.

gift tax. A tax imposed on a transfer of property by gift during the donor's lifetime.

Government Pension Offset (GPO). A federal law that reduces Social Security spousal benefits if the employee receives a government pension based on work not covered by the Social Security system. Also see *Windfall Elimination Provision*.

growth fund. A stock fund that seeks long-term capital appreciation. Growth funds generally buy common stocks of companies that advisors believe have long-term growth potential.

growth stock. The stock of a company that has seen rapid growth in revenue or earnings and is expected to see similar growth in the future. Generally speaking, growth stocks pay relatively low dividends and sell at relatively high prices, considering their earnings and book value.

guardian. The person who is legally responsible for the care and well-being of a minor or, in some states, of an incapacitated adult. Appointed by a court, the guardian is under court supervision.

hardship distribution. A distribution from a retirement plan prior to age 59½ based on a qualified need such as medical expenses. Hardship distributions are subject to income taxation, as well as to a 10 percent penalty.

health maintenance organization (HMO). A medical plan where a person is usually required to use a doctor or service provider that is part of a network, or else pay the full cost. The HMO may require that you get approval for treatment by a specialist or a certain type of care.

Home Equity Conversion Mortgage (HECM) program. A type of FHA-insured reverse mortgage.

home equity line of credit (HELOC). A line of credit extended to a homeowner for which the home is collateral.

hospital insurance. Insurance that helps pay for inpatient care in a hospital or skilled nursing facility (following a hospital stay), some home health care, and hospice care.

incident of ownership. A legal term indicating control over a property. Often used when valuing an estate for estate tax purposes.

income fund. A mutual fund that seeks current income over capital growth, often by investing in bonds and high-yielding stocks.

index. A statistical composite that measures changes in the economy or financial markets. Well-known market indices include the S&P 500 Index, the Dow Jones Industrial Average, and the Nasdaq Composite Index.

index ETF. An exchange-traded fund that seeks to track the performance of a specific index.

index mutual fund. A mutual fund that seeks to track the performance of a market index, such as the S&P 500 Index, by investing in the stocks or other securities that comprise that index. When an investor purchases an index fund, he or she is essentially seeking to "buy the index" and not trying to outperform it.

inflation. An increase in the cost of goods and services, which, in turn, decreases the buying power of money over time. Inflation is usually measured by the Consumer Price Index and classified according to its severity. Mild inflation occurs when the price level—an average of all prices—rises from 2 percent to 4 percent. Moderate inflation refers to an inflation rate of 5 percent to 9 percent, and severe inflation (or "double-digit inflation") refers to an inflation that threatens a country's economy, in which money loses its value and people turn to barter rather than relying on currency.

inheritance tax. A tax on the right of a beneficiary to receive or inherit a decedent's wealth. Many states impose an inheritance tax.

intangible personal property. Any property other than real property that has value because of the legal rights it confers (for example, a stock certificate).

international fund. A mutual fund that invests outside of the United States. International stock funds can include world funds, which invest in securities issued throughout the world including the United States, and foreign funds, which invest only in companies outside of the United States. Additional risks not associated with domestic investments apply to international funds.

intestate. Having made no valid will.

investment advisor (also known as a registered investment advisor or RIA). Someone who is paid for providing advice, not for buying or selling securities. Unlike the generic term *financial advisor, investment advisor* is a legal term that identifies a professional who is registered with either the Securities and Exchange Commission or a state securities regulator. Registered investment advisors are held to a fiduciary standard, which is higher than a suitability standard, which means that they are required to act in the client's best interests at all times.

IRA (Individual Retirement Account). A self-funded tax-deferred retirement plan established by an individual, not by an employer.

irrevocable life insurance trust (ILIT). A trust that is created to hold an individual's life insurance policy and pay the premiums. The trust can provide benefits to a surviving spouse and other beneficiaries. If set up and handled correctly, the proceeds are not part of a taxable estate.

issuer. The corporation, municipality, or government agency that issues a bond or security; in other words, the borrower.

Keogh plan. A tax-deferred, qualified retirement plan for self-employed persons and employees of unincorporated businesses. Contributions and earnings are deductible from gross income and grow tax-deferred until withdrawn (certain restrictions apply). Qualified plans meet the requirements of the Internal Revenue Code, making them eligible for favorable tax treatment.

ladder. A combination of fixed-income investments with maturities staggered over a series of years.

laddering. A strategy of buying fixed-income investments with staggered maturities.

large-cap fund. A mutual fund that invests primarily in stocks of "large cap" companies, or companies that have a market capitalization that exceeds $10 billion.

large-cap stock. The stock of a company with a large market capitalization, generally more than $10 billion.

letter of intent. A preliminary agreement that specifies terms of a future intention.

liability. A financial obligation; for example, a mortgage or credit card debt. The opposite of an *asset.*

life insurance. Insurance that provides a death benefit to help compensate for a financial hardship that may result when the insured passes away.

life insurance trust. An irrevocable trust that is generally established to exclude life insurance proceeds from the estate of the insured and the spouse of the insured for estate tax purposes.

limit order. An order to buy or sell a security at a specified price or better. A limit order to buy sets a maximum purchase price. A limit order to sell sets a minimum sell price.

liquid investment. An investment that can be easily converted to cash.

liquidity. The ability of an asset to quickly be converted into cash with little or no discount. Generally, the greater the number of buyers and sellers of a particular asset, the more liquid it is.

living trust. A trust that is set up while a person is alive. Also known as an *inter vivos trust,* it can be revocable or irrevocable.

living will. A document in which a person states the type of life-sustaining assistance they would like to receive in a medical crisis. More commonly referred to as an *advance health-care directive.*

load. A commission or sales fee on a mutual fund. A mutual fund that assesses this charge is called a "load fund." One without this charge is a *mutual no-load fund.*

long-term capital gain. Gain from the sale or exchange of a capital asset held for more than one year (at least one year and one day from the purchase date). Long-term capital gains are taxed at more favorable rates than short-term gains.

long-term capital loss. Loss from the sale or exchange of a capital asset held for more than one year.

long-term care insurance (LTCI). Insurance that covers some or all of the expenses of the "activities of daily living" for a person who is chronically ill or disabled. Medicare does not cover long-term care.

lump sum. An amount of money you receive (from a pension plan, divorce, or inheritance, for example) all at once, rather than in periodic payments.

management fee. The amount a fund pays its managers to oversee the fund.

marginal tax rate. The amount of tax that you pay on your last dollar of income.

market capitalization. The size of a company, measured by its stock price multiplied by the number of outstanding shares. Small-cap stocks tend to be riskier than large caps, but they also have the potential for more upside.

market order. An order to buy or sell a security at the best price available at the time the order is received.

maturity date. For a fixed-income investment, the date on which the issuer promises to repay the principal. Generally, the longer the maturity, the higher the interest paid (all else being equal), to compensate for higher risk. Longer-term bonds tend to fall more in value than do shorter-term bonds when interest rates rise.

Medicare. Federally funded health insurance available to most Americans over age 65 and to younger people with disabilities or other medical conditions.

Medicare Advantage Plan. Also called Medicare Part C, an alternative way to receive Medicare benefits, similar to an HMO. It is offered by private insurance companies and must include all services that Medicare Parts A and B cover. Many plans also cover prescription drugs as well as extras such as vision, hearing, dental care, and health and wellness programs.

Medigap. An insurance plan designed to supplement Medicare. These policies are sold by private insurance companies (not the government) and pay for things that Medicare doesn't cover, such as copayments and deductibles.

mid-cap stock. The stock of a company whose market capitalization falls between *large cap* (more than about $10 billion) and *small cap* (less than about $2 billion)

money market mutual fund. A mutual fund that invests solely in short-term securities that can easily be turned into cash, such as Treasury bills, certificates of deposit (CDs), and short-term loans. Money market funds are designed to maintain a stable $1 share value, but there is no guarantee that they will do so. They are not FDIC-insured.

municipal bonds ("munis"). Debt securities issued by state and local governments and their agencies. Munis typically pay interest at a fixed rate twice a year, and the issuer promises to return your principal at maturity. In general, interest paid on municipal bonds is exempt from federal income tax (though it may be subject to the Alternative Minimum Tax). When a muni is purchased by a resident of the state in which the bond was issued, the interest payments are also usually exempt from state tax. Capital gains from the sale of a municipal bond prior to maturity are federally taxable.

mutual fund. A type of investment that pools the money of many investors to buy various securities, including stocks, bonds, and cash equivalents. Mutual funds can offer diversification and professional management within a single investment.

NASDAQ (National Association of Securities Dealers Automated Quotation System). A computerized system for reporting current price quotations on active over-the-counter securities. The system provides price quotations and permits execution of small customer orders. Large orders are executed by separate negotiations.

net asset value (NAV). The market value of a single share of a mutual fund, calculated at the end of each business day by adding up the value of all the securities in the fund's portfolio, subtracting expenses, and dividing the sum by the number of shares outstanding. Mutual funds are traded based on their NAVs.

net profit. The profit on an investment that remains after all expenses are deducted.

net unrealized appreciation (NUA). The change in value that shares held in a tax-deferred account will experience when sold.

net worth. The value of a person's or a company's total assets minus the sum of their total liabilities.

New York Stock Exchange (NYSE). The oldest and largest stock exchange in the United States.

niche ETFs. Exchange-traded funds (ETFs) that focus on a narrow slice of a broader asset class—for example, sectors like health care, single countries like France, or narrow parts of the bond market like high-yield bonds. They tend to have somewhat higher expenses than traditional ETFs and are generally subject to a greater degree of risk.

no-load mutual fund. A mutual fund that does not carry a sales charge or commission. These funds are bought and sold at the NAV (net asset value).

open-end mutual fund. A mutual fund that continuously sells its shares to the general public. The fund company issues additional shares as new investors ask to buy them, so the number of shares outstanding changes daily as investors buy new shares or redeem old ones.

open order. A buy or sell order that has not yet been executed or canceled.

operating expense ratio (OER). A mutual fund or ETF's annual expenses (operating expenses, management fees, and 12(b)-1 fees, if any) expressed as a percentage of the fund's average net assets. These expenses are deducted before calculating the fund's NAV.

operating expenses. Costs incurred by a mutual fund or ETF in its day-to-day operations. Every fund is subject to some degree of operating expenses, which usually include management fees, annual fees, administrative costs, and maintenance fees.

ordinary income. Income from wages, self-employment, dividends, etc.

over-the-counter. A market for securities where they are traded away from a formal exchange, between interested parties via telephone or a computer network, instead of on an exchange floor.

overweighted. A description of a portfolio that holds an excess amount of a particular type of security.

pension plan. An employer-sponsored retirement plan in which a retired employee receives a specific amount of money based on salary history and length of employment. Also known as a *defined-benefit plan.*

P/E ratio (price/earning ratio). A measurement that represents the relationship between the price of a company's stock and its earnings for the past year. To get a company's P/E, divide its current stock price by its earnings per share (EPS).

pooled income fund (PIF). A type of fund that is made of gifts that are pooled together and invested. Income from the fund is distributed to the fund's participants and beneficiaries.

portability. A characteristic that allows an employee to retain certain benefits when leaving an employer. For example, some pension plans, 401(k) plans, insurance policies, or health savings accounts may have portability. For estate tax, "portability" allows the ability of a surviving spouse to add any unused portion of their deceased spouse's exclusion to their own exclusion.

portfolio. The group of stocks, bonds, cash equivalents, and other investments held by an individual investor, a fund, or a financial institution.

portfolio manager. The person in charge of managing a fund's holdings.

power of appointment. A clause in a will or a trust that gives another party the authority to transfer title to specified property to a recipient.

preferred provider organization (PPO). A medical plan that allows a patient to see doctors or service providers outside the network, but at a higher cost. Referrals to specialists are not needed.

preferred stock. A class of stock that pays dividends or interest at a specified rate and has preference over common stock in the payment of dividends and the liquidation of assets. Preferred stock ranks higher than common stock but lower than bonds in a company's capital structure. Like bonds, preferred stock may be callable and may have a maturity date. Preferred stockholders may have different voting rights than common stockholders (or, like bond holders, no voting rights). Not all companies issue preferred stock.

prenuptial agreement. A legal contract between two people who are about to marry covering asset ownership and division of assets should the marriage end in divorce.

pre-tax rate of return. The return on an investment without taking taxes into account, as opposed to an *after-tax rate of return*.

prescription drug coverage. Insurance that covers medications doctors prescribe for treatment. Coverage varies by plan.

present interest. An interest in a property that the owner can immediately use, possess, enjoy, or consume. Also see *future interest*.

primary insurance amount (PIA). The Social Security benefit a person will receive if he or she elects to begin receiving benefits at his or her full retirement age (FRA).

principal. The amount of money that is financed, borrowed, or invested.

probate. A court process that validates a person's will and oversees the distribution of assets subject to the terms of the will.

professional liability insurance. Insurance that protects professionals (lawyers, accountants, physicians) against claims of negligence. Errors and omissions policies cover claims of financial harm, and malpractice policies cover claims of physical harm.

prospectus. A legal document that describes a mutual fund, ETF, variable annuity, or other investment and offers its shares for sale. It contains information required by the SEC and state securities regulators, including the fund's investment objectives and policies, risks, investment restrictions, fees and expenses, and how shares can be bought and sold. Every mutual fund is required to publish a prospectus and provide it to investors free of charge. Always read the prospectus carefully before investing.

qualified domestic trust (QDOT). A trust established for the purpose of permitting the federal estate marital deduction for assets transferred from the decedent's estate to a surviving spouse who is not a U.S. citizen.

qualified education expense. Education-related expenses approved by the IRS. These include tuition, fees, books, and necessary equipment.

qualified personal residence trust (QPRT). An irrevocable trust that is created to pass a residence to a beneficiary at a future date and also remove the value of the residence from the donor's taxable estate.

qualified terminable interest property (QTIP) trust. A marital trust that allows a person to provide for a spouse and also control who will receive the trust assets after the surviving spouse's death.

real estate investment trust (REIT). A company that owns and often operates income-producing real estate such as apartments, shopping centers, office buildings, hotels, and warehouses.

real property. Land and its permanent improvements (for example, a house or other structure). Also see *tangible personal property* and *intangible personal property*.

rebalancing a portfolio. Changing the way in which investments are allocated among asset classes.

redemption fee. A fee charged by some mutual funds when shares are sold, usually within a short period of time.

reinvesting. Using dividends or capital gains from an investment to buy more shares of that investment.

required minimum distribution (RMD). The amount of money that investors at age 70½ are required to begin withdrawing from most of their retirement accounts—traditional, SEP, and SIMPLE IRAs, and 401(k)s. (However, an investor who is still employed at age 70½ can delay taking an RMD from a 401(k).) There is no RMD for a Roth IRA.

retirement plan distribution. A withdrawal of funds from a retirement plan.

reverse mortgage. A loan that uses a home as collateral, but instead of making payments to a lender, the lender pays the owner. The owner (and their spouse if the spouse cosigns) must be 62 or older and have equity in the home. However, the equity will decrease over time as the loan amount and interest expenses grow.

rollover IRA. An account that holds funds transferred from a qualified plan without tax. If an employee changes jobs, retires, or gets a divorce settlement that includes a distribution from a company retirement plan, he or she can "roll it over" into an IRA to preserve capital and maintain its tax-deferred status.

Roth IRA. An individual retirement plan in which contributions are not tax-deductible but withdrawals are generally tax-free after age 59½. Income limitations apply.

SEC (Securities and Exchange Commission). A federal government agency established by Congress to protect investors against fraudulent and manipulative practices in the securities markets.

section 1035 exchange. A tax-free exchange of one annuity or life insurance contract for another annuity or life insurance contract.

sector. A specific area of the economy sharing common characteristics. There are ten sectors: Consumer Discretionary, Consumer Staples, Communications, Energy, Financials, Health Care, Industrials, Materials, Technology, and Utilities.

securities. Stocks that signify ownership interest in a company, or bonds that indicate a credit relationship with a borrower, such as a company or government agency. Some other types of securities are options, warrants, mutual funds, and ETFs.

SEP-IRA (Simplified Employee Pension-Individual Retirement Account). A retirement plan for those who are self-employed or who own a small business with employees.

settlement. The close of a securities transaction, when an investor pays their brokerage firm for the securities they've purchased, or when an investor delivers securities they've sold and receives the proceeds from the sale.

settlement date. In a securities transaction, the date when payment is due either to the customer or to the broker, and/or the date when the certificates must be in the broker's possession.

share. A unit of ownership in a stock, mutual fund, or ETF.

Sharpe ratio. A ratio that indicates whether a portfolio's or a fund's returns are due to smart investment decisions or are the result of excess risk. The higher the ratio, the better the risk-adjusted returns. A negative Sharpe ratio indicates that a risk-free asset would have performed better.

short-term capital gain. A profit on the sale of an investment held for one year or less.

short-term capital loss. A loss on the sale of an investment held for one year or less.

SIMPLE IRA (Savings Incentive Match Plan for Employees IRA). A retirement plan for employees of companies that do not have a 401(k) plan and that employ fewer than 100 people.

single premium immediate fixed annuity (SPIA). A product in which a lump sum is irrevocably turned over to an insurance company in exchange for an immediate stream of guaranteed income for a set number of years or for life, depending on the annuity. In other words, one is purchasing a cash flow similar to a pension. Guarantees are based on the financial strength and claims-paying ability of the issuing insurance company.

small-cap fund. A mutual fund that invests in stocks of companies with a market capitalization generally less than $2 billion.

small-cap stock. The stock of a company with a relatively small total market value, meaning a market capitalization generally less than $2 billion. Small-cap companies tend to be more volatile than larger companies.

Social Security. The federal social insurance program that provides benefits to retirees, disabled workers, and survivors of deceased workers.

Social Security Disability Insurance (SSDI). A federal program for covered employees who become disabled before retirement age.

special needs trust (also called a *supplemental needs trust*). A trust designed to provide income to a physically or mentally disabled person without compromising that person's ability to qualify for government benefits.

spousal IRA. An IRA established for a nonworking spouse.

Standard & Poor's 500 (S&P 500) Index. A well-known capitalization-weighted index consisting of 500 of the country's most widely traded companies that are listed on the New York Stock Exchange (NYSE) or the American Stock Exchange (AMEX).

stock. A type of investment that represents a share of equity ownership in a company.

stock split. An action from a company's board of directors, with the approval of company shareholders, that increases the total number of outstanding shares. The goal is often to reduce the price per share of a high-priced stock, making it more affordable. The outstanding shares of the corporation are simply multiplied. There is no increase in capital, and the proportionate ownership of the company's equity remains the same.

stop-limit order. A combination of a limit order and a stop order used to protect a profit or to limit a loss. This is a request to buy or sell a security at a specified limit price or better, but only after the specified stop price has been reached or passed. Even if the stop price is triggered, a stop-limit order guarantees the limit price but not the execution.

stop order. An order to buy or sell a security once it reaches or trades through a set market price, called the *stop price.* Once this happens, a pending stop order becomes a market order—which guarantees execution but not price. For comparison, see *stop-limit order.*

style. When classifying a stock or a stock mutual fund, an indication of either a value or a growth orientation.

successor trustee. A trustee who takes over when the current trustee resigns, becomes incapacitated, or dies.

Supplemental Security Income (SSI). A government assistance program that pays monthly benefits to people with extremely limited income and disabilities. These payments are not tied to work history. Most states offer supplements to the federal SSI payment. See ssa.gov/ssi for details.

systematic risk. The portion of total risk that is due to macroeconomic variables (for example, a change in interest rates), also called *beta.* Adding more securities to a portfolio will not eliminate systematic risk.

tangible personal property. Any property other than real property that has value because of its physical existence (for example, an automobile or collectible). Also see *real property* and *intangible personal property.*

target fund. A diversified portfolio of stocks, bonds, and cash managed by a professional investment manager to meet a specific time frame or risk preference.

tax-deductible amount. An amount that is deductible from one's taxable income for income tax purposes.

tax deferral. The postponement of a tax obligation.

tax-loss harvesting. A process of minimizing capital gains tax by netting out gains against losses. In addition, up to $3,000 of capital losses may be deducted against ordinary income on tax returns.

testamentary trust. A trust that becomes effective at death.

ticker symbol. An abbreviation of a security's name used to identify it for trading purposes and in printed and online price quotations.

total risk. The combination of systematic and unsystematic risk, measured by standard deviation. Once unsystematic risk has been diversified away, only systematic risk remains in a portfolio.

trade date. The date when an order to buy or sell a security is executed.

Treasuries (or "Treasurys"); Treasury bill (T-bill), note, or bond. Securities issued by the U.S. government. T-bills are short-term obligations (currently issued with maturities ranging from thirty days to one year); Treasury notes are medium-term obligations (currently issued with maturities ranging between two and ten years); Treasury bonds are long-term obligations (currently issued with maturities of thirty years).

trust. A legal arrangement in which one person (the *trustor*) transfers legal title to property to a trust and names a fiduciary (the *trustee*) to manage the property for the benefit of the person or institution (the *beneficiary*).

trustee. The person or institution (corporate trustee) who manages a trust and trust property according to the instructions in the trust agreement and any applicable laws.

trustor. The person who establishes a trust; also referred to as the *settlor* or the *grantor.*

umbrella liability policy. An insurance policy designed to protect against claims that exceed the limits of a homeowner's or other personal liability insurance policies.

underweighted. A description of a portfolio that holds a reduced amount of a particular type of security.

unrealized capital gain. A gain that would be realized if securities were sold.

unsystematic risk. The diversifiable portion of total risk that is specific to an individual investment. In theory it can be eliminated by increasing the number of securities in a portfolio.

value fund. A mutual fund that invests in companies whose assets are considered undervalued, or in companies that have turnaround opportunities, with lower price-to-earnings ratios.

value stock. A stock that is considered to be a good stock at a very good price.

variable annuity. A tax-deferred investment with insurance protections and additional fees. Money is invested in a "subaccount" consisting of stocks, bonds, or other vehicles, and the return will vary depending on their performance. For that reason, payments aren't as predictable as they are with a fixed annuity. Payments are also contingent upon the financial strength and claims-paying ability of the issuing insurance company.

volatility. The magnitude and frequency of changes in securities' values.

wash-sale rule. An IRS rule that states that if an investor sells a security at a loss and buys the same or a "substantially similar" security within thirty days, the loss will be disallowed for income tax purposes.

will. A legally binding document directing the disposition of one's property, which is not operative until death and can be revoked up to the time of death, or until there is a loss of mental capacity to make a valid will.

Windfall Elimination Provision (WEP). A federal law that may reduce Social Security benefits for those who receive a government pension. Also see *Government Pension Offset.*

world fund. A mutual fund that invests in both U.S. and non-U.S. companies. By contrast, a foreign fund invests only in companies outside of the United States.

yield. A general term describing the expected annual rate of return on an investment, expressed as a percentage.

yield to maturity. The average annual return on a bond, assuming the bond is held to maturity and all interest payments are reinvested at the same rate. It includes an adjustment for any premium or discount from face value. Comparing yield to maturity is a common way to compare the value of bonds.

Source Notes

(Sources are listed in the order in which they appear in the book.)

MY TOP TEN RECOMMENDATIONS FOR EVERY AGE

U.S. Department of Health and Human Services. *How Much Care Will You Need?* http://www.medicare.gov/longtermcare/gov.

PART I. WHEN RETIREMENT IS AT LEAST TEN YEARS OUT

Question 1

Herman, Ruth, Mathew Greenwald & Associates, et al. *The 2013 Retirement Confidence Survey: Perceived Savings Needs Outpace Reality for Many.* Issue Brief No. 384, Employee Benefit Research Institute, 2013.

Question 2

Herman, Ruth, Mathew Greenwald & Associates, et al. *The 2013 Retirement Confidence Survey: Perceived Savings Needs Outpace Reality for Many.* Issue Brief No. 384, Employee Benefit Research Institute, 2013.

Question 3

Sallie Mae. *How America Pays for College 2013.* Conducted by Ipsos Public Affairs.

College Board Advocacy and Policy Center. "Trends in Student Aid 2012." http://trends.collegeboard.org/student-aid/.

Joint Economic Committee of the United States Congress. *The Causes and Consequences of Increasing Student Debt,* June 2013, Democratic staff calculations based on data from the Project on Student Debt, *Student Debt and the Class of 2011,* October 2012, and the U.S. Department of Labor, Bureau of Labor Statistics, Consumer Price Index.

U.S. Census Bureau. "New Analyses of Census Bureau Data Examine Nation's 65 and Over Labor Force, Working Students and Changes in Self-Employment."

http://www.census.gov/newsroom/releases/archives/american_community_survey_acs/cb13-15.html.

Sallie Mae. *How America Saves for College 2013.* Conducted by Ipsos Public Affairs.

Question 4

Charles Schwab in conjunction with Koski Research. *The New Rules of Engagement for 401(k) Plans, 2010.* Retirement plan investment advice is formulated and provided by GuidedChoice Asset Management, Inc. (GuidedChoice®), which is not affiliated with or an agent of Charles Schwab & Co., Inc. (CS&Co.), Schwab Retirement Plan Services, Inc. (SRPS), or any of their affiliates.

Question 5

Herman, Ruth, Mathew Greenwald & Associates, et al. *The 2013 Retirement Confidence Survey: Perceived Savings Needs Outpace Reality for Many.* Issue Brief No. 384, Employee Benefit Research Institute, 2013.

Davidow, Anthony B. "An Evolutionary Approach to Portfolio Construction." *Journal of Investment Research.* Schwab Center for Financial Research, 2013.

Question 7

Genworth Financial. "Cost of Long Term Care Across the Nation." https://www.genworth.com/corporate/about-genworth/industry-expertise/cost-of-care.html.

U.S. Department of Health and Human Services. "Who Needs Care?" http://longtermcare.gov/the-basics/who-needs-care/.

Genworth Financial, Inc. *Cost of Care Survey, 2012.*

America's Health Insurance Plans. *Guide to Long-Term Care Insurance.* Rev. ed., 2003, 2004.

Question 8

Litan, Robert, and Hal Singer. *401(k) Loan Defaults: How Big Is the Leakage and What Can Policymakers Do to Preserve Americans' Nest Eggs?* Navigant Economics, July 2012.

PART II. GETTING CLOSER: TRANSITIONING INTO RETIREMENT

Question 13

Employee Benefit Research Institute. "Debt Levels Spike for the Oldest Americans." *News from EBRI,* February 21, 2013.

Question 17

Council for Disability Awareness. "Chances of Disability, Me, Disabled?" http://www.disabilitycanhappen.org/chances_disability/disability_stats.asp.

Social Security Administration. Fact Sheet. February 2013.

American Society of Certified Life Underwriters. *Journal of the American Society of Chartered Life Underwriters.* As reported by WebMD. http://www.webmd.com/health-insurance/disability-insurance-women.

Question 20

The Charles Schwab Retirement Survey, conducted by Koski Research between January 3 and 7, 2013, using random digit dialing of listed and unlisted numbers, with 20 percent of the sample reached by cellular/mobile phones. Quotas are to ensure reliable and accurate representation of the entire U.S. population ages 18 and over. Results of any sample are subject to sampling variation. The magnitude of the variation is measurable and is affected by the number of interviews and the level of the percentages expressing the results. The study's margin of error is +/− 3.1 percent.

Question 21

Herman, Ruth, Mathew Greenwald & Associates, et al. *The 2013 Retirement Confidence Survey: Perceived Savings Needs Outpace Reality for Many.* Issue Brief No. 384, Employee Benefit Research Institute, 2013.

PART III. LIFE IN RETIREMENT

Question 24

Herman, Ruth, Mathew Greenwald & Associates, et al. *The 2013 Retirement Confidence Survey: Perceived Savings Needs Outpace Reality for Many.* Issue Brief No. 384, Employee Benefit Research Institute, 2013.

Question 25

American Institute of Certified Public Accountants. CFP/PFS Credential Holder Directory. http://apps.aicpa.org/credentialsrefweb/PFSCredentialSearchPage.aspx.

National Association of Enrolled Agents website. https://portal.naeacentral.org/webportal/buyersguide/professionalsearch.aspx.

The Retirement Income Study by Charles Schwab was an online survey of U.S. investors conducted by Koski Research in August 2011. A total of 1,010 respondents completed interviews. Survey respondents work part- or full-time, are five years or less from retirement, are 55–70 years old, and have $100,000 or more in total investable assets. Survey respondents were not asked to indicate whether they had accounts with Charles Schwab. All data are self-reported by study participants and are not verified or validated. Investors participated in the study between August 25 and August 30, 2011. Detailed findings can be found at http://www.aboutschwab.com/press/research/retirement_research/.

Question 26

Consumer Financial Protection Bureau. *Report to Congress on Reverse Mortgages.* June 28, 2012.

Question 27

Fronstin, Paul. "Views on Health Coverage and Retirement: Findings from the 2012 Health Confidence Survey." *Notes* 34, no. 1. Employee Benefit Research Institute, January 2013.

U.S. Department of Health and Human Services. "Who Needs Care?" http://longtermcare.gov/the-basics/who-needs-care/.

PART IV. MAXIMIZING SOCIAL SECURITY AND MEDICARE

Question 30

Social Security Administration. OASDI Monthly Statistics. Old-Age, Survivors, and Disability Insurance Program. http://www.ssa.gov.

———. "Monthly Statistical Snapshot, August 2013." http://www.ssa.gov/policy/docs/quickfacts/stat_snapshot/.

Shoven, John B., and Sita Nataraj Slavov. "Does It Pay to Delay Social Security?" October 2012.

Social Security Administration. *Annual Statistical Supplement, 2012.*

Question 31

Social Security Administration. Fact Sheet, June 2013.

Congressional Budget Office. "Is Social Security Progressive?" Economic and Budget Issue Brief, December 15, 2006.

Bank of Montreal (BMO) Retirement Institute Report, U.S. Edition, October 2012. "Retirees Not Maximizing Social Security Retirement Benefits."

Question 33

Social Security Administration. "Disabled Worker Beneficiary Statistics by Calendar Year, Quarter, and Month." http://ssa.gov/OACT/STATS/dibStat.html.

Question 34

Social Security Administration. "Fact Sheet on the Old-Age, Survivors, and Disability Insurance Program," June 30, 2013.

Question 37

Harris Poll. "Retirement and Health Care Costs Weighing Heavy on Americans' Minds." Harris Interactive, November 2012.

Paul Fronstin, Ph.D., Dallas Salisbury, and Jack VanDerhei, Ph.D. "Savings Needed for Health Expenses for People Eligible for Medicare: Some Rare Good News." *Notes* 33, no. 10. Employee Benefit Research Institute, October 2012.

Dana E. King, MD, MS; Eric Matheson, MD, MS; Svetlana Chirina, MPH; Anoop Shankar, MD, Ph.D., MPH; and Jordan Broman-Fulks. "The Status of Baby Boomers' Health in the United States." *JAMA Internal Medicine*, March 11, 2013.

Question 38

Weisbord, Reid Kress. "Wills for Everyone: Helping Individuals Opt Out of Intestacy." *Boston College Law Review* 53, no. 3 (May 2012).

PART V. ESTATE PLANNING

Question 39

Tax Policy Center. "Estate Tax Tables." http://www.taxpolicycenter.org/numbers/displayatab.cfm?Docid=3775&DocTypeID=7.

Urban Institute and Brookings Institution Tax Policy Center. *2013 Budget Tax Proposals.*

Question 42

U.S. Bureau of the Census. "Households, Families, Subfamilies, and Married Couples 1980–2010." http://www.census.gov/compendia/statab/2012/tables/12s0059.pdf.

PART VI. THE PEOPLE IN MY LIFE

Question 44

Parker, Kim. "The Boomerang Generation." Pew Research Social and Demographic Trends, March 15, 2012.

Question 45

Parker, Kim, and Eileen Patten. "The Sandwich Generation: Rising Financial Burdens for Middle-Aged Americans." Pew Social and Demographic Trends, 2013. http://www.pewsocialtrends.org/2013/01/30/the-sandwich-generation/.

Question 46

"American Consumer Credit Counseling Survey Finds Most Household Finances Controlled by Women." ConsumerCredit.com. http://www.consumercredit.com/about-us/in-the-news/most-household-finances-controlled-by-women.aspx.

Question 49

Ross, Robert A. "Six Biggest IRA Beneficiary Form Mistakes." *The Codicil: The Estate Planning and Community Property Law Journal*, October 9, 2010.

Question 50

"CDC Estimates 1 in 88 Children in United States Has Been Identified as Having an Autism Spectrum Disorder." U.S. Centers for Disease Control and Prevention, 2012. http://www.cdc.gov/media/releases/2012/p0329_autism_disorder.html.

"How Many People Have Disabilities? A Tip Sheet for Public Health Professionals." U.S. Centers for Disease Control and Prevention, 2009. http://www.cdc.gov/ncbddd/documents/Disability%20tip%20sheet%20_PHPa_1.pdf.

Acknowledgments

This book is a testament to the generous and collaborative spirit that envelops Schwab. Colleagues and friends both inside and outside of the company enthusiastically rallied around what started as a "little ebook" and eventually blossomed into the book you now see. Of the many talented people who provided guidance and expertise, I would especially like to thank the following:

First, big, big thanks to Joanne, who has been my partner in crime for over twelve years. Joanne shares my passion for inspiring Americans to master their finances and isn't afraid to challenge the status quo in this pursuit. Also, a big round of applause to Terry Humphrey, our trusted and gifted colleague who worked side by side with Joanne to turn complex financial language into clear and engaging prose. We would like to extend special thanks to Kristine Dixon, our marketing powerhouse and all-around morale booster; Jennifer Davis, our project manager and social-media maven; Sarah Bulgatz, Mark Fortier, and our PR team for spreading the word; Leah Lau for editorial backup; and Judith Lerma for always lending a helping hand.

This book would not have been possible without the magnanimous support of our colleagues in the Schwab Center for Financial Research, led by the unparalleled Mark Riepe. Rande Spiegelman, Jim Peterson, Tony Davidow, Brian Cronk, and Eva Xu—hats off!

Other Schwab colleagues we'd like to call out are Rick Harris and Gary Rubin for their expert reviews; Stephen Lazar and Madelene Lees for their design talent; John Scanlan for his compliance review; and Jay Allen, Mary Rosai, and Jonathan Craig for their encouragement and business support from the very beginning. Thanks also to Mike van den Akker, my financial advisor, who helps me stay calm, knowing that my portfolio is in good hands.

And, finally, this book would never have made it off the ground without the unswerving support of our super-agent, Gail Ross, and the superb team at Random House, which includes Rick Horgan, Nate Roberson, and Tara Gilbride.

Index